ALLE · ZEIT · WACH · 1842

Reinhard Budde  Karlheinz Kautz
Karin Kuhlenkamp  Heinz Züllighoven

# Prototyping

## An Approach to Evolutionary System Development

With the Cooperation of Philip Bacon

With 41 Figures

Springer-Verlag
Berlin Heidelberg New York
London Paris Tokyo
Hong Kong Barcelona
Budapest

Reinhard Budde
GMD, Institut für Systemtechnik (F2), Postfach 1240,
W-5205 Sankt Augustin 1, Fed. Rep. of Germany

Karlheinz Kautz
University of Oslo, Dept. of Informatics, PO Box 1080,
Blindern, N-0316 Oslo 6, Norway

Karin Kuhlenkamp
Alldata Service, Münsterstraße 304,
W-4000 Düsseldorf 30, Fed. Rep. of Germany

Heinz Züllighoven
GMD, Institut für Systemtechnik (F2), Postfach 1240,
W-5205 Sankt Augustin 1, Fed. Rep. of Germany

CR Classification (1991): D.2.2, D.2.m, K.6.3-4, J.1, H.1

ISBN 3-540-54352-X Springer-Verlag Berlin Heidelberg New York
ISBN 0-387-54352-X Springer-Verlag New York Berlin Heidelberg

Library of Congress Cataloging-in-Publication Data. Prototyping: an approach to evolutionary system development / Reinhard Budde ... [et al.]; with the cooperation of Philip Bacon. p. cm. Includes bibliographical references (p. ) and index. ISBN 3-540-54352-X (Springer-Verlag Berlin Heidelberg New York). – ISBN 0-387-54352-X (Springer-Verlag New York Berlin Heidelberg) 1. Computer software–Development. I. Budde, R. (Reinhard), 1951-. II. Bacon, Philip. QA76.76.D47P78 1992 005.1–dc20 91-43252



Typesetting: Camera ready by author
45/3140-5 4 3 2 1 0 – Printed on acid-free paper

# About This Book

## What kind of book is this?

This book is not about a specific development method, nor does it present a (new) language or tool. It is a book about a view of software development. What does that mean? It is not our intention to push a particular method such as SADT or JSP as *the* prototyping method, or to present a recipe for constructing prototypes. Nor are we, in this sense, selling a new or an existing language or development system or tool. What we set out to do is to provide answers to questions like the following:

- What problems constantly crop up in software projects?
- Why is it so difficult to build correct and usable software?
- How does prototyping fit in with software development today?
- What tools are available for swift prototype construction?
- What sort of practical experience do we already have with prototyping?

This book is not designed to prove the feasibility and utility of prototyping. These are, we feel, issues that have long since been settled affirmatively in the international discussion. Our aim was to create a conceptual platform for developing new constructive ideas. We therefore focus on the impact prototyping has on software development as a whole. To put it in a nutshell: the question we address is not whether prototyping is a viable concept, but what prototyping is really all about, and when and how we can use it.

## Who should read this book?

The book is addressed to all those involved in software development. This means, of course, in the first instance, software engineers who build application systems. But it is also intended for other groups that are currently, or – in the forseeable future – are likely to be, involved in the development and subsequent use of a software system: project managers, the heads of DP departments and external consultants. The reader will quite rightly ask: What about the users and user management? The book is essentially concerned with how users can be meaningfully involved in the software development process and how their working situation and their ideas can become the decisive criteria for the design of application systems. We do not, however, wish to pretend that the book is comprehensible to readers with no prior knowledge of data processing. Undoubtedly, users who work with computers every day will recognize many of the problems described here and find the proposed concepts helpful. And it is doubtless up to user management to press for implementation of these concepts in practical software development. We have, of course, throughout, discussed the problems and our own tentative solutions to them from the developers' point of view, because they are basically the ones who, in our opinion, must undergo a process of rethinking if our ideas are to be implemented.

## What is the background of the book?

Three of the co-authors – Reinhard Budde, Karin Kuhlenkamp and Heinz Züllighoven – were working together in the early 1980s at the same research and development institution, the German National Research Centre for Computer Science (GMD). It was while there that we, along with a number of other people, organized and held the first European conference on prototyping in 1983. And it is no coincidence that Christiane Floyd's introductory paper to the proceedings of this conference entitled *A Systematic Look at Prototyping* had a programmatic impact. The conference and the work on the proceedings marked the beginning of long-standing professional and personal ties with Christiane Floyd. And this was how it came about that one of Christiane's research and teaching assistants, Karlheinz Kautz, became a co-author of this book.

It is quite evident that much of our experience is rooted in the German-speaking scientific community – a fact corroborated by a glance at the numerous references to the German scientific literature at the end of this book. And yet, the book has been shaped by "European" thinking. In particular our cooperation with fellow scientists in Scandinavia has taught us to see many of the problems and their proposed solutions in a new light. Alongside this – shall we say – European tradition of prototyping is a non-European, or more specifically, U.S. tradition. The difference between us and many of the American authors, for example, is that we tend to focus on different aspects and features in our treatment of the subject. We are primarily concerned with the question: How can we use prototyping to develop high-quality software that meets the requirements and needs of its future users? and not with the question that that tends to dominate American publications: How can I develop software more quickly and more cheaply? We attach a great deal of importance to questions regarding the technical implementation and efficiency of software development, but these are subordinate to the goal of a user-oriented or"human-oriented" software development. To this extent, we see our work as a European contribution to the international discussion on the development and use of computers.

## How should the book be read?

The reader who chooses to look on this book as a textbook will no doubt want to make use of the book's systematic structure. This allows a gradual progression from the discussion of terms to concepts and, finally, to technical and practical assessments. The chapters were arranged in their present order with this in mind. The two parts of the book may also be read separately as addressing distinct conceptual and implementational aspects. However, to the reader interested mainly in the second part of the book, we recommend reading the

Chapters 2 and 4 beforehand in order to get acquainted with our terminology. There are also a number of questions we are repeatedly asked, and each of these is dealt with separately in a corresponding chapter. For example:

- What problems are associated with classical life cycle plans? (cf. Sec. 3.4)
- What is meant by prototyping? (cf. Chap. 4)
- How would you go about prototyping? (cf. Chap. 6)
- Can prototyping be fruitfully employed other than for new developments? (cf. Sec. 5.3.4)
- What sort of tools are available for prototyping? (cf. Chap. 7)
- How does prototyping work in practice? (cf. Chap. 12)
- What does conducting a prototyping project involve for me as a manager? (cf. Sec. 13.2)

Other questions, together with details of the chapters in which they are addressed, may be found in the concluding Chapter 14 or by reference to the index.

## Acknowledgements

We would like to thank all the colleagues who discussed with us the topics treated in this book, as well as the students who helped us, in the course of numerous seminars, to clarify and elaborate the issues addressed. Our special thanks go to Doris Fähndrich for the great trouble she took in producing the TEX macros, and to Phil Bacon for his considerable achievement in transforming what was at times a rather wayward German text into such eloquent English.

# Table of Contents

**Introduction** . . . . . . . . . . 1

## Part I Software Development and Prototyping 5

**1 What is Prototyping?** . . . . . . . . . . 6

1.1 Prototyping as an Approach to System Development . . . . . . . . . . 6
1.2 The Term "Prototype" . . . . . . . . . . 7
1.3 Rapid Prototyping . . . . . . . . . . 8
1.4 Summary . . . . . . . . . . 9

**2 Basic Elements of System Development** . . . . . . . . . . 10

2.1 Informal Nets as a Means of Representation . . . . . . . . . . 10
2.2 Construction and Evaluation . . . . . . . . . . 11
2.3 Software Development Concepts . . . . . . . . . . 15
2.4 Examples of Software Development Concepts . . . . . . . . . . 18

**3 Traditional Life Cycle Plans** . . . . . . . . . . 24

3.1 Life Cycle Models and Life Cycle Plans . . . . . . . . . . 24
3.2 Life Cycle Plans in Current Practice . . . . . . . . . . 24
3.3 The Origin of Life Cycle Plans . . . . . . . . . . 27
3.4 Problems Associated with Traditional Life Cycle Plans . . . . . . . . . . 28
3.5 Where Do Life Cycle Plans Work? . . . . . . . . . . 31

**4 Prototyping** . . . . . . . . . . 33

4.1 Different Aspects of Prototyping . . . . . . . . . . 34
4.1.1 The Prototype in the Software Development Process . . . . . . . . . . 34
4.2 Goals of Prototyping . . . . . . . . . . 38
4.3 Horizontal and Vertical Prototyping . . . . . . . . . . 39
4.4 The Relationship between Prototype and Application System . . . . . . . . . . 40
4.5 Examples of Prototyping . . . . . . . . . . 41
4.5.1 An Order Processing System . . . . . . . . . . 41
4.5.2 An Office System for Planning Departments . . . . . . . . . . 43
4.5.3 Software Tools for Graphic Workers . . . . . . . . . . 44
4.5.4 Assessment of the Three Examples . . . . . . . . . . 46

**5 Evolutionary System Development** . . . . . . . . . . . . . . . . . 49

5.1 Evolutionary System Development . . . . . . . . . . . . . . . . . . . . . . . 49
5.2 Evolutionary System Development in Practice . . . . . . . . . . . . . . 51
5.2.1 The $\alpha$–$\beta$ Test Procedure . . . . . . . . . . . . . . . . . . . . 52
5.2.2 Versioning . . . . . . . . . . . . . . . . . . . . . . . . . . . . . . . 54
5.3 Problems Connected with System Development . . . . . . . . . . . . 56
5.3.1 Other Ways of Tackling the Problem . . . . . . . . . . . . . . . . 57
5.3.2 Evolutionary System Development is Necessary . . . . . . . . . 59
5.3.3 Evolutionary System Development is Possible . . . . . . . . . . 60
5.3.4 Restoring Instead of Demolishing . . . . . . . . . . . . . . . . . 65

**6 Evolutionary Process Models** . . . . . . . . . . . . . . . . . . . . . 67

6.1 Technical Implementation of Software Versions . . . . . . . . . . . . . 71
6.1.1 Object–Oriented Design . . . . . . . . . . . . . . . . . . . . . . . 72
6.1.2 The Client–Supplier Model . . . . . . . . . . . . . . . . . . . . . 73
6.1.3 The Separation of Interaction and Functionality . . . . . . . . . . 74
6.1.4 The Model–View–Controller Paradigm . . . . . . . . . . . . . . . 75
6.2 Our Assessment . . . . . . . . . . . . . . . . . . . . . . . . . . . . . . 77

## Part II Technical Support of Prototyping 79

**7 The Tool Landscape** . . . . . . . . . . . . . . . . . . . . . . . . . . . 80

7.1 Screen Generators . . . . . . . . . . . . . . . . . . . . . . . . . . . . . 80
7.2 Database-Oriented Development Systems . . . . . . . . . . . . . . . . 81
7.3 Very High Level Languages . . . . . . . . . . . . . . . . . . . . . . . . 83
7.4 Programming Environments . . . . . . . . . . . . . . . . . . . . . . . . 83
7.5 Tools and Prototype Development . . . . . . . . . . . . . . . . . . . . 84

**8 Screen Generators** . . . . . . . . . . . . . . . . . . . . . . . . . . . . 87

8.1 Screen Generators and Prototyping . . . . . . . . . . . . . . . . . . . . 87
8.2 Tool Components of Screen Generators . . . . . . . . . . . . . . . . . 88
8.2.1 Requirements and Characteristics of Screen Generators . . . . 88
8.2.2 Tool Components for Building Simple Prototypes . . . . . . . . 91
8.2.3 Tool Components for Building Complex Prototypes . . . . . . . 94
8.2.4 Prototypes and Target Systems . . . . . . . . . . . . . . . . . . . 97
8.3 Our Assessment . . . . . . . . . . . . . . . . . . . . . . . . . . . . . . 98

**9 Database-Oriented Development Systems** . . . . . . . . . . . . . 102

9.1 Concept and Features . . . . . . . . . . . . . . . . . . . . . . . . . . . 102
9.1.1 The Conceptual World of Database Systems . . . . . . . . . . . 102
9.1.2 The Levels of Description in Database Systems . . . . . . . . . 104
9.1.3 The Modelling Concepts of Database Systems . . . . . . . . . . 105

9.1.4 Language Constructs of Database Systems . . . . . . . . . . . . . 106
9.1.5 Data Integrity in Database Systems . . . . . . . . . . . . . . . . . . . 107
9.1.6 Developing Database Applications . . . . . . . . . . . . . . . . . . . . 108
9.2 Components of Database-Oriented Development Systems . . . . . . . 108
9.2.1 Example of a Conceptual Schema . . . . . . . . . . . . . . . . . . . . . 109
9.2.2 Integration of the System Components . . . . . . . . . . . . . . . . 110
9.2.3 Components for Constructing Vertical Prototypes . . . . . . . . 112
9.2.4 Components for Constructing Simple Prototypes . . . . . . . . . 114
9.2.5 Screen Design With Screen Generators . . . . . . . . . . . . . . . . 116
9.2.6 Dialog Design With Menu Generators . . . . . . . . . . . . . . . . . 116
9.2.7 Components for Constructing Complex Prototypes . . . . . . . 120
9.2.8 Language Constructs for Flow of Control . . . . . . . . . . . . . . 121
9.2.9 Language Constructs for Formulating Procedures and Transactions . . . . . . . . . . . . . . . . . . . . . . . . . . . . . . . . . . . . . . . 122
9.3 Our Assessment . . . . . . . . . . . . . . . . . . . . . . . . . . . . . . . . . . . . 123
9.3.1 Use and Handling . . . . . . . . . . . . . . . . . . . . . . . . . . . . . . . . . 124
9.3.2 Programming in the Small and in the Large . . . . . . . . . . . . 125
9.3.3 Suitability for Further Use and Target Systems . . . . . . . . . . 126
9.3.4 Development Strategies and Approaches . . . . . . . . . . . . . . . 128
9.3.5 Outlook . . . . . . . . . . . . . . . . . . . . . . . . . . . . . . . . . . . . . . . . 130

**10 Very High Level Languages** . . . . . . . . . . . . . . . . . . . . . . . . . 131

10.1 Concept and Features . . . . . . . . . . . . . . . . . . . . . . . . . . . . . . 131
10.2 Benefits and Limitations . . . . . . . . . . . . . . . . . . . . . . . . . . . . 132
10.3 The Main Groups . . . . . . . . . . . . . . . . . . . . . . . . . . . . . . . . . 134
10.3.1 Logical Languages . . . . . . . . . . . . . . . . . . . . . . . . . . . . . . . 134
10.3.2 Functional Languages . . . . . . . . . . . . . . . . . . . . . . . . . . . . 135
10.3.3 Algebraic Languages . . . . . . . . . . . . . . . . . . . . . . . . . . . . . 136
10.3.4 Miscellaneous Languages . . . . . . . . . . . . . . . . . . . . . . . . . 136
10.4 Are Object-Oriented Languages VHLLs? . . . . . . . . . . . . . . . . 137
10.5 Application Areas . . . . . . . . . . . . . . . . . . . . . . . . . . . . . . . . . 138
10.5.1 Extended Compilation . . . . . . . . . . . . . . . . . . . . . . . . . . . . 140
10.5.2 Metaprogramming . . . . . . . . . . . . . . . . . . . . . . . . . . . . . . . 140
10.5.3 Program Synthesis . . . . . . . . . . . . . . . . . . . . . . . . . . . . . . 141
10.5.4 Derivation . . . . . . . . . . . . . . . . . . . . . . . . . . . . . . . . . . . . . 141
10.5.5 Summary . . . . . . . . . . . . . . . . . . . . . . . . . . . . . . . . . . . . . 142
10.6 Selecting a Very High Level Language . . . . . . . . . . . . . . . . . . 142

**11 Programming Environments** . . . . . . . . . . . . . . . . . . . . . . . . 144

11.1 Prototyping and Programming Environments . . . . . . . . . . . . . 144
11.2 Languages in a Programming Environment . . . . . . . . . . . . . . . 147
11.3 The Requirements For These Languages . . . . . . . . . . . . . . . . . 148
11.4 Building Prototypes . . . . . . . . . . . . . . . . . . . . . . . . . . . . . . . . 151
11.5 An Example of a Programming Environment . . . . . . . . . . . . . . 152

11.6 Tools in a Programming Environment . . . . . . 153
11.7 Our Assessment . . . . . . 158

**12 Prototyping in Practice** . . . . . . 160

12.1 Prototyping and Conventional Development Models . . . . . . 161
12.1.1 Specification of Requirements . . . . . . 161
12.1.2 Requirements Analysis and Project Acquisition . . . . . . 162
12.1.3 Our Assessment . . . . . . 162
12.2 Prototyping and "Surface-Down" Development . . . . . . 163
12.2.1 Our Assessment . . . . . . 164
12.3 Prototyping and Evolutionary Strategies . . . . . . 166
12.3.1 Our Assessment . . . . . . 167
12.4 Prototyping and User Development . . . . . . 168
12.4.1 Our Assessment . . . . . . 169
12.5 Prototyping and Documentation . . . . . . 170
12.5.1 Our Assessment . . . . . . 171

**13 The Groups Involved in Prototyping** . . . . . . 173

13.1 The Developers . . . . . . 173
13.1.1 Opposition from the Developers . . . . . . 174
13.1.2 New Forms of Project Work . . . . . . 174
13.1.3 New Technical Environment . . . . . . 175
13.1.4 The Users . . . . . . 176
13.2 Management . . . . . . 178
13.2.1 The Break with Conventional Methods . . . . . . 178
13.2.2 New Forms of Project Organization . . . . . . 179
13.2.3 New Technical Infrastructure . . . . . . 179
13.2.4 New Contracts . . . . . . 180
13.2.5 New Forms of Personnel Management . . . . . . 181

**14 Summary** . . . . . . 183

**References** . . . . . . 192

**Index** . . . . . . 202

# Introduction

## Scope and Contents of the Book

Software engineers are invariably confronted with the question of which development methods to use in order to produce good software. If we ask *how* exactly software development is to be organized, we come up against a wide variety of different concepts. But there is not only an abundance of concepts, there is even greater diversity in the terms used to describe them. What one software engineer chooses to call "process model" is termed by another "project strategy"; and there are "system requirements", "requirements analyses", "user needs analyses" and "software models". How we can make practical use of the proposed concepts remains a mystery. At any rate, it would seem impossible to draw any sort of comparison between them.

To enable some sort of appraisal to be made, we begin by clarifying the concepts essential to a proper understanding of the software development process and the various models relating to it. We then go on to explain what is meant by the term *life cycle plan*, a software engineering concept widely adopted in practice to make the software development process calculable.

The fact remains, though, that much of the software being produced still fails to meet user requirements. Both the amount of effort required to develop software systems and their subsequent usability remain, ultimately, incalculable factors. It is against this background that a variety of techniques, known by the general term *prototyping*, have gained practical recognition. These techniques are often at variance with the life cycle plans officially adopted, but remain crucial to the success of software projects.

After considering these general aspects, we look at the importance of prototype construction for system development. Prototyping is an approach used in evolutionary system development. We show which forms of prototyping can be employed to tackle which problems. Case studies are used to illustrate the various approaches adopted in constructing prototypes. We also take a look at the tools used in everyday software development with a view to determining their suitability for prototyping. In this way, we attempt to elucidate prototyping as a methodological concept in more concrete terms.

Following these lines, the book is divided up into two parts:

- **Part I: Software Development and Prototyping**
  In Part I we look at prototyping as an approach for constructing and evaluating models. After giving an introduction to the basic elements and concepts of system development, we go on to discuss traditional approaches and phase–oriented life cycle plans. Prototyping constitutes an effective means of offsetting and overcoming the fundamental problems associated with life cycle plans. We elucidate various strategies and notions relating to prototyping and use three case studies to show the different ways in which prototypes

can be employed to tackle different sorts of problems. To round off Part I, we present our concept of *Evolutionary System Development.* Prototyping represents the constructive element of this process of rethinking in system development.

- **Part II: Technical Support of Prototyping**
  Technical support is a central element in prototyping. Part II shows to what extent technical support of evolutionary system development is possible. We discuss various so-called tools or systems for supporting prototyping and attempt to outline their conceptual background and scope, as well as indicating prospective trends. No attempt is made to list or evaluate systems already on the market. Three aspects which constantly crop up in discussions on prototyping are dealt with separately. These are:
  - Screen Generators
  - Database-Oriented Development Systems (e.g., the 4th generation languages)
  - Very High Level Languages

Most chapters end with a summary briefly recapitulating on the central ideas presented there.

The general discussion on these tools and systems reveals a marked trend towards so-called integrated development environments. In order to give due consideration to this trend, we have included a separate section on programming environments in which we list criteria designed to help the reader choose between the various development environments currently available or likely to become available in the near future.

In the subsequent two sections, we show the variety of ways in which prototyping can be employed in the system development process. Case studies are used to illustrate how prototype construction can be integrated in software projects on both a technical and organizational level. We draw on reports we have come across in the literature, but our main source of information has been our own case studies on prototyping. We highlight typical situations and problems encountered, and then go on to outline possible approaches for tackling these problems. We also discuss what prototyping means for the groups involved.

The final section of this book summarizes the main points made and provides cross-references. It should be seen as an extension to the index.

## Genesis of the Book

For a number of years now, our research and development work has focussed on the construction of user-oriented software systems. What this work has taught us is that the problems encountered here are not going to be solved by some new "supertool". Nor is the crux of the problem "programming in the small" or the software construction techniques in use. The crucial problems have been found to lie elsewhere: in requirements engineering, design methods and project strategies. Once this fact was recognized, numerous strategies (life cycle plans), known today as "traditional" strategies, were proposed by scientists and practitioners to remedy the situation. But all practical implementations of these strategies have caused problems which the strategies themselves offer little help in eliminating. This has given rise to fundamental doubts about the suitability of "traditional" software development methods.

We owe these insights to the work of Christiane Floyd and that of fellow scientists in Scandinavia, e.g., Pentti Kerola (see [Floyd81, Kerola79, Kerola80]). Our positions have been outlined in papers presented at the *Scandinavian Research Seminars* and the Working Conference *Systems Design for, with, and by the Users* (see [BudZue82, BudZue83a, BudZue83b]). Another conference which helped shape our view of the system development process was that entitled *Comparative Review of Information Systems Design Methodologies* (see [Lunde82]). Our ideas have also been influenced by work done in Germany on participative system development (see [Kubicek80]). However, none of these sources give attention to the technical aspects we consider crucial to our construction work.

The term *prototyping* first cropped up in software engineering literature in the early eighties. We immediately saw prototyping as a chance to combine a fundamental reorientation of system development with a construction method used in engineering. An important source of inspiration here, besides some initial ideas on the subject presented e.g. by Canning (see [Canning81]), were the *Proceedings of the ACM Workshop on Prototyping* (see [SquBraZel82]).

In order to obtain an overall view of the different approaches to prototyping, we organized, in 1983, the first European conference of its kind on this subject in conjunction with an EC–funded international project (see [BudKuhlMatZue84]).

The construction of prototypes occupies a position of precedence in our view of evolutionary system development, both from a technical and methodological point of view. Since 1985, we have been engaged in the development of a programming environment for the language Prolog (see [BudKuhlSylZue88]). This work has meanwhile borne fruit both in the form of a successfully tested set of tools for prototype construction and in a book reflecting on underlying construction principles (see [BudZue90]). Since 1986, we have been co–teaching courses at the Technical University of Berlin and have presented our ideas to practitioners at numerous seminars. Recently, we conducted an inquiry into industrial prototyping projects in the context of a working group of the German Society for Informatics (GI Ak 4.3.19). The results of these various activities have been drawn upon extensively in compiling material for the present book.

# Part I

# Software Development and Prototyping

# 1
# What is Prototyping?

Software development has undergone drastic changes in recent years. New development strategies, methods and tools have become available to the practitioner, among them numerous tools supporting program specification, construction and testing. Such tools are no longer used individually, in an uncoordinated manner, but are instead embedded in an overall development strategy. Development strategies provide guidelines for constructing software systems in a project situation. They offer procedural suggestions covering all activities in the so–called software life cycle, or prescribe a particular method for use during these activities (e.g., structured programming, SADT, etc.).

As early as 1979, a widely–cited U.S. study (cf. [GOA79, Blu87]) came to the conclusion that the failure of software projects was due largely to inadequate task description on the part of the users. However, it is only in the last few years that there have been intensive discussions on task analysis activities or, more precisely, the analysis and specification of user requirements. Today, opinions differ as to how to tackle the problems associated with these activities. It is, however, generally recognized that, from the point of view of the software engineer, coming to terms with these problems is far more complicated than was anticipated.

At each end of the spectrum of ideas about how to tackle these problems, the following two extremes are currently encountered:

- *Formalization of activities* in the early phases enabling "problematic" requirements to be detected by formal means. Successfully tested techniques for "programming in the small" are being applied to new problem areas.
- *Use of experimental methods* to help gain the experience needed for constructing usable software. The techniques used here go beyond conventional software engineering methods.

We consider prototyping as belonging to the second of these.

## 1.1 Prototyping as an Approach to System Development

To give the reader an initial idea of what is meant by the term *prototyping*, the following may serve as a preliminary characterization, to be elaborated upon later:

- *Prototyping* is an *approach* based on an evolutionary *view* of software development and having an impact on the development process *as a whole*.
- *Prototyping* involves producing *early* working versions (prototypes) of the future application system and experimenting with them.

- *Prototyping* provides a *communication basis* for discussions among all the groups involved in the development process, especially between users[1] and developers.
- *Prototyping* enables us to adopt an approach to software construction based on *experiment* and *experience.*

The idea of using prototyping came about as a reaction to the problems experienced by numerous software developers and users with traditional software development strategies:

- It is frequently not until the finished system is in use that users and user organizations are able to explicitly formulate their requirements. Traditional approaches, however, call for complete specification of requirements at the beginning of system development.
- Developers would prefer to postpone completing specification until during system construction. Traditional approaches, however, do not allow construction until specification is completed.
- Mutual coordination is required between developers and users throughout the development process, with each group continuously enhancing its knowledge about the other's work. Traditional approaches, however, terminate this essential learning process once the requirements specification is completed.
- Computer departments that screen themselves off from user departments by accepting only "definitively fixed" specifications and then delivering the "finished" implementation see their position threatened by the work of numerous application–oriented computer specialists and the tendency towards decentralization of data processing. Traditional approaches, however, preserve the organizational structures upholding this unsatisfactory division of labour.

One way of tackling the problems associated with traditional software development strategies is by using an *evolutionary development process* explicitly providing for the construction of prototypes.

## 1.2 The Term "Prototype"

We feel it necessary to include a few critical remarks on our usage of the term "prototype". In discussions on the subject, attention is quite rightly drawn to the differences between software prototypes and those used in other engineering disciplines (see [JanSmi85]).

- A software prototype is not the first specimen of a large series of products, as is the case with mass production in the automobile industry, for example: reproduction of a software product is not an engineering problem.

[1] Subsequent mention of the term *user* invariably refers to the actual end user of an application system.

– The nature of a software prototype is different from that of, say, a wind tunnel or an architectural model: it actually demonstrates in practical use features of the target system, and is not merely a simulation of it.

There are, however, similarities in the way prototypes are *used*, and these would suggest that the term can be meaningfully applied to software development, too:

– Prototypes are used to clarify any relevant specification or development problems.
– Prototypes serve as a basis for discussion and as aids to decision-making.
– Prototypes are used for experimental purposes and for gaining practical experience.

## 1.3 Rapid Prototyping

Prototyping first came under discussion in the late seventies with the emergence of Very High Level Languages such as Smalltalk and Prolog and powerful interactive software development environments. This new form of technical support made it possible for small teams of developers – and even developers working on their own – to successfully construct experimental versions of large and complex systems and adapt them with little effort to changed requirements and new wishes. The lesson, learned from numerous unsuccessful projects, that "you only know once you've finished constructing the software how you could have done a better job" was now able to be put to practical use, and that at reasonable cost. The initial excitement about these new tools is reflected in the proposals made for the use of rapid prototyping.

It is above all in the U.S. literature that the term *rapid prototyping* is frequently encountered. Most authors use it to denote a concept that does not significantly differ from our own. It acquires a totally different meaning, however, in cases where, given the efficient tools currently available for software construction, thorough requirements analyses and system design processes are abandoned in favour of an unsystematic, trial–and–error approach to software development. Rapid prototyping, in this sense, means that the prototype is the only valid document in the system development process.[2]

The initial euphoria accompanying this view of rapid prototyping soon gave way to considerations of technical product quality and division of labour in the construction process. Prototyping is not a game, but a systematic technique for directly translating ideas, drafts and concepts into software, and for their simulation and utilization in the system development process. Efficient software construction allows experience and discussion to acquire a new significance in system development.

Rapid prototyping in the sense of a purely trial–and–error approach to software development can, at best, be considered justified in cases where developers

[2] Cf. [Smith82]; also touched on in [HooHsi82].

are working to satisfy their own needs, because they are then able to assess intuitively their own requirements. Otherwise, rapid prototyping is used either as a cloak for the "start–programming–and–see–what–happens" approach now rather en vogue, as a euphemism for the traditional "muddling through", or as a "theoretical model" for the unwarrantable practice of declaring already delivered versions to be prototypes, and leaving the debugging to the users.

## 1.4 Summary

*Prototyping* is an approach to software development incorporating the following features:

- Operative versions are produced at an early stage.
- Relevant problems are clarified by experimentation.
- Prototypes provide a common basis for discussion between developers, users and other groups.

*Prototyping* has grown out of the realization that

- requirements frequently do not become apparent until a system is in use;
- specifications cannot be completed until during the construction process;
- users and developers must learn from each other;
- computer specialists are being increasingly assigned to work in user departments.

Software prototypes are used in similar ways to prototypes in other engineering disciplines.

# 2
# Basic Elements of System Development

*System development* is the extension of information system development. The term *information system* is used to denote the interaction between people whose working and communication activities are considered from the point of view of the exchange and processing of information within an organization, together with the relevant organizational arrangements. Our interest focusses on information systems in which computers form the technical core, along with their relevant application software. When we speak of *software development* in the present book, we invariably mean the process of manufacturing application software for use in an information system. Developing software involves drawing up models and encoding some of them in a machine–interpretable language. Software development is embedded in system development. The introduction of new or changed software in an information system results in changes in working and communication activities.

We now go on to define some of the basic terms used in software development as a basis for more detailed discussion of various software development concepts in the following chapters. This involves describing essential system development activities and documents. The most important elements here are construction activities, coupled with evaluation activities providing feedback. Different software development concepts are obtained by refining or coarsening, or by differently weighting these construction and evaluation activities.

## 2.1 Informal Nets as a Means of Representation

We use informal nets as a means of representation, giving them the following interpretation (see Fig. 1)

- Boxes indicate activities that bring about a change in the system under consideration.
- Ellipses indicate states or documents that are used or modified by activities.
- Ellipses and boxes are connected by arrows. No two elements of the same kind are connected: an arrow always goes from a box to an ellipse or vice versa. An arrow going from an activity (box) to a state (ellipse) indicates that the activity determines, changes or brings about the state. An arrow going from an ellipse to a box means that the state is a prerequisite for the activity or at least influences it.[3]

[3] To prevent misinterpretations, we should point out that arrows are *not* to be taken as indicating a *temporal* sequence.

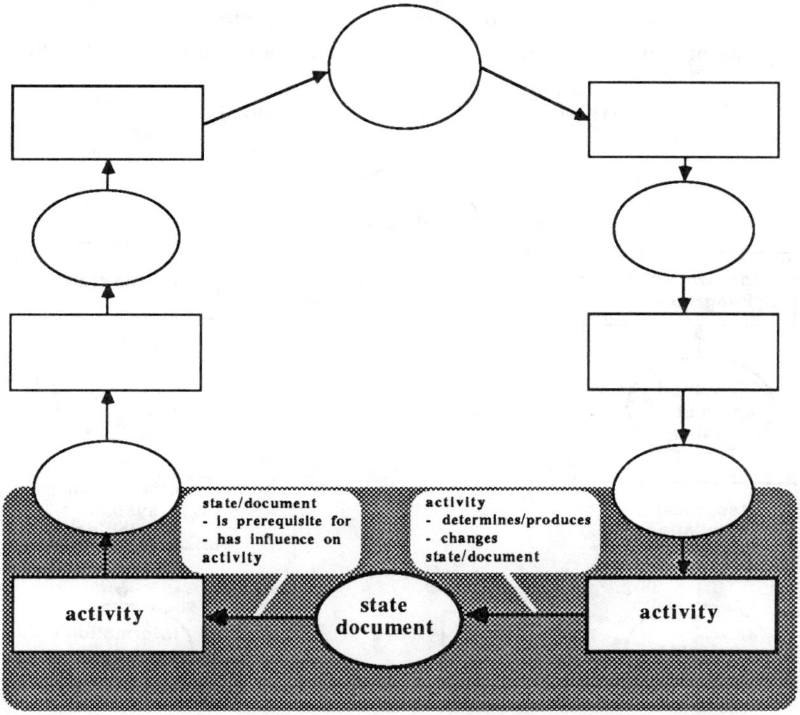


**Fig. 1.** The components of informal nets

## 2.2 Construction and Evaluation

In order to highlight the significance of prototyping as compared with traditional approaches, we begin by looking at software development in abstract terms.

A construction step is invariably based on documents and always results in new or changed documents. In software construction, an instance of such a step is the derivation of an implemented model from a specifying model.[4] Let us take, for example, the activity "information system modelling". Here, an information system model (the "implemented model") is constructed on the basis of the problem in hand (the "specifying model").

Activities with input and output states can be sequenced or refined while retaining their structure, as the following examples show:

- *Sequencing*: The result of the information system modelling influences the software design.

[4] The term "implemented model" as used here should not be confused with implementation in the sense of the "algorithm of an application system".

- *Refinement*: A system specification can be decomposed into specifications of subsystems. The subsystems can be implemented separately and their implementations recomposed to produce the system implementation.

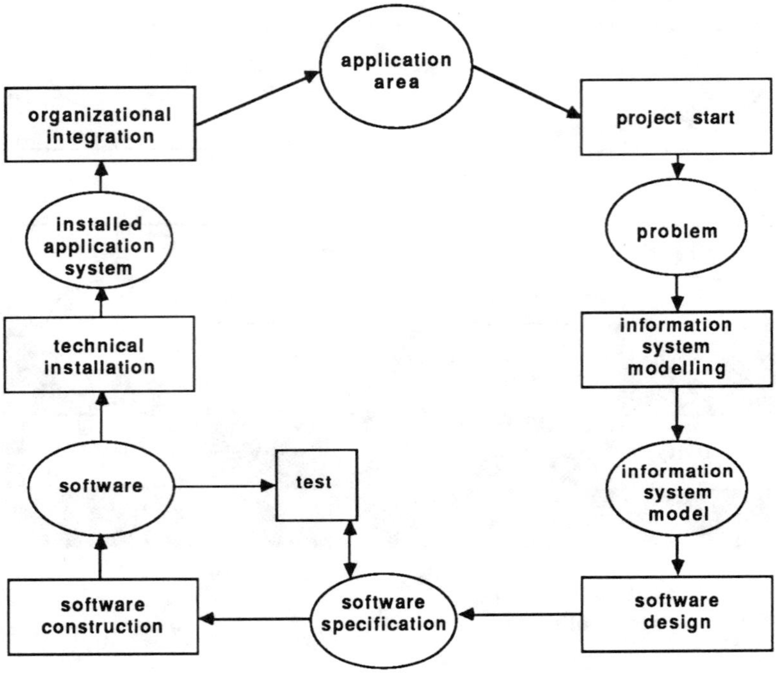


**Fig. 2.** Construction and feedback by testing

Software engineers invariably take it for granted that software construction proceeds from a specification and results in a *tested* program. If we wish to add the testing activity to our diagram, we have to represent it as *feedback* from the activity of software construction (see Fig. 2). Testing involves comparing the program with the specification, changing or adding to the specification if necessary. This gives rise to further construction activities.

If we consider the "installed application system", we find that the situation is a similar one: an application system can only be called installed if its function and performance have been tested. Such testing must be introduced as feedback from the technical installation *and* the software construction (see Fig. 3). User knowledge (application knowledge) is a necessary prerequisite for this activity.[5]

[5] It may justifiably be argued that this feedback extends as far as the information system model; the software specification is its minimum "range".

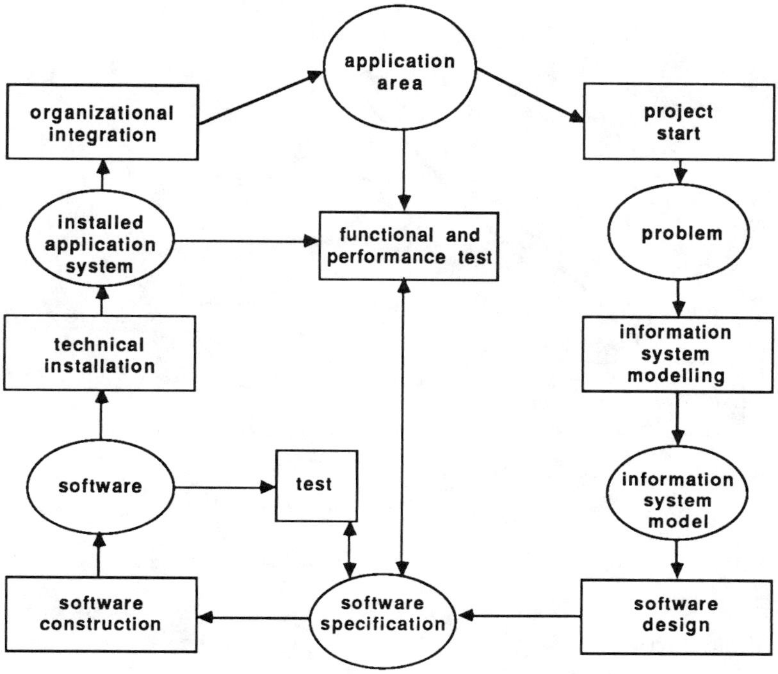


**Fig. 3.** Feedback by function and performance testing

The basic elements of software development are, then, construction *and* evaluation activities, together with the relevant input and output documents.

Evaluation activities consist in comparing documents, which are considered the basis for a particular activity, with the results of that activity and bringing them into line with these. In other words, the implementation of a particular model has to be checked against the specification of that model. Evaluation activities are identifiable as feedback from construction activities. They are performed by reference to documents that constitute a direct or indirect basis for construction.

We must take a more detailed look at these evaluation activities in order to identify the problems associated with traditional approaches. Following Lehman (see [Lehman81]), we distinguish between *verification* and *validation* as possible types of evaluation:

- *Verification* checks the correctness and consistency of each model in relation to itself and the preceding models (see Fig. 4). Ideally, this means checking the correctness of a transformation between two models. Provided that the models to be checked are described in terms of a formal calculus, verification is a formal process which can be performed locally, i.e. without knowledge of

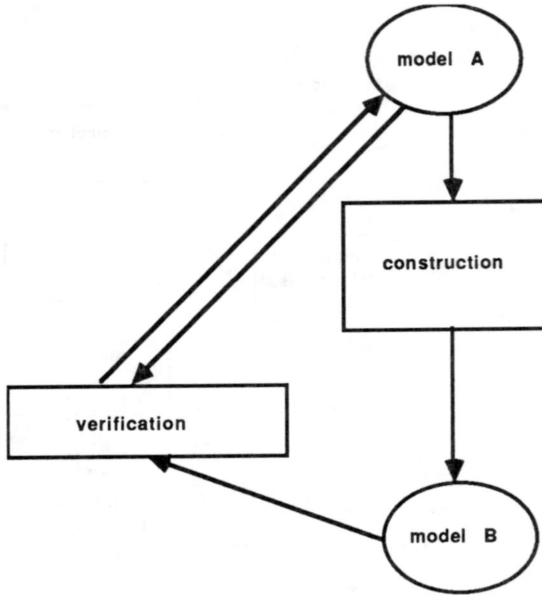


**Fig. 4.** Verification

other models or the context. Techniques for formal specification, automatic verification and program transformation make precisely this assumption. In certain application areas (compiler and operating system construction), formalization of models is state-of-the-art, allowing verification techniques to be used.

- *Validation* is the evaluation of models based on measurements and human judgement (see Fig.2 5). We are concerned here with the question of whether a model B (the resulting implementation) developed from a model A (the specification) still meets the requirements of the persons involved. A test of this sort cannot be a formal process since it is essentially characterized by human assessment and judgement based on knowledge of the application situation. For our purposes, we take validation to mean evaluation of the suitability of models by their users and developers, for which application knowledge is a basic prerequisite.

The evaluation activities in software development *always* involve both verification and validation. Many of the problems associated with traditional concepts are, in our view, due to the fact that efforts are made to establish verification activities where in actual fact validation is needed.

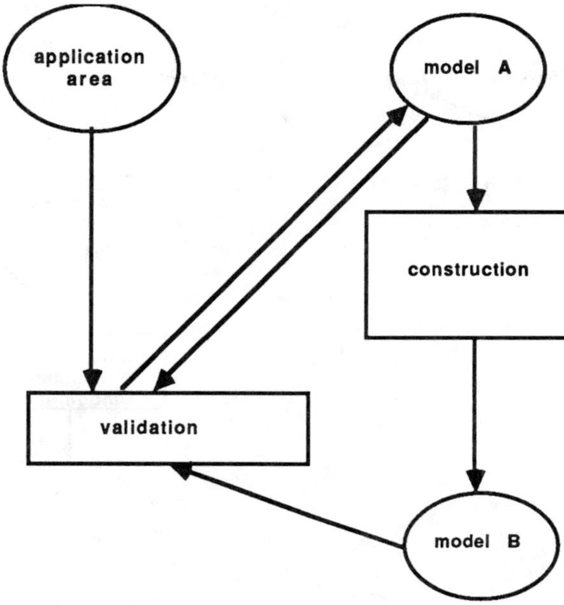


**Fig. 5.** Validation

**Summary**

In software development, we represent activities and documents by means of informal nets. The basic elements of our models are construction activities coupled with evaluation activities providing feedback. There are two types of feedback:

- Verification:
  - Checking the consistency and completeness of a model in relation to itself and the preceding model.
- Validation:
  - Evaluation of a model with respect to its usability.
  - The evaluation is based on measurements and human judgement.

## 2.3 Software Development Concepts

In this section, we take a look at the basic elements of software development by describing the *development process* using the construction and feedback elements introduced in the previous sections. To begin with, we focus on the construction activities with their accompanying input and output documents. These elements of software development are traditionally arranged in a simple cycle (see Fig. 6). The cycle shows the interdependencies between the elements, but does not prescribe a temporal sequence. We then turn our attention to the evaluation activities which provide feedback.

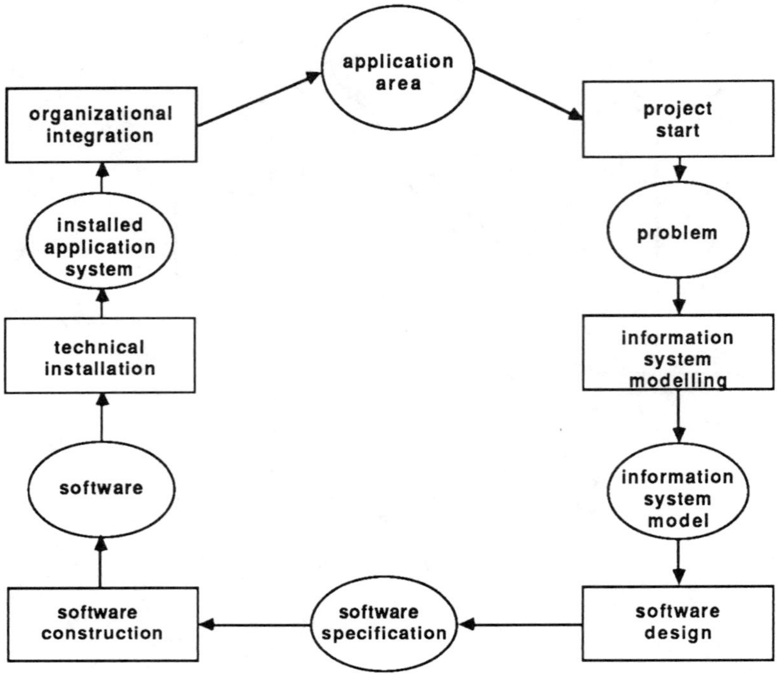


**Fig. 6.** Basic software development cycle

- *Project start* means that an application area within a particular organization initiates a project aiming at further development of existing organizational procedures and work processes in the organization and provision of computer support for them. Before a project can begin work on a sound organizational and personnel basis, the problem in hand must normally be set down in written form and considered "project–worthy". We call the resulting document the *business needs* or *problem*.
- The changes in the information flow which the project aims to bring about are described in a process known as *information system modelling*, the result of this activity being the *information system model*, also termed the Statement of Requirements or Procurement Specification. This is a written document frequently assuming the nature of a contract for the subsequent development activities. The information system model is still largely rooted in the world of the users and is mostly formulated in the terminology of the application area. The users' representatives play the major role in elaborating the information system model. The model includes both ideas about the future software system and a description of the existing information system with its personal interaction structures, organizational arrangements and working and communication activities.

- *Software design* involves specifying the parts of the information system model that describe the desired application system. The resulting document is the *software specification*. Even if this is written in a formal language,[6] it is not normally executable. It is during software design that the crucial transition from the application area to the world of data processing takes place.
- *Software construction* is the step during which the operational *application system* is built. Software construction includes activities such as coding, module integration and program documentation.
- During *technical installation*, the application system has to be adapted to the conditions existing in the application area. The result obtained is the *installed application system*. The process of adapting the application system to the target machine is frequently called "generation".
- *Organizational integration* is the activity during which the application system is introduced in the application area. From now on it is known as the *integrated application system*. This activity is of particular importance because it brings about organizational changes in the application area, the consequences of which are difficult to foresee. It is during organizational integration that the users' ideas (the "requirements") come face to face with the constructed application system.[7]

The various activities involved in the development process are assigned to the developer and user groups as follows:

- Software design, software construction and technical installation are traditionally the job of software developers.
- Project start, information system modelling and organizational integration are carried out jointly by users and developers, but are, in substance, the responsibility of the users.

After looking at the construction activities, let us now go on to consider the evaluation activities:

- Software testing involves checking the constructed software against its specification. This process of feedback may entail an additional software construction step in order to correct the software in compliance with the specification. It also gives rise to further construction steps if the specification is changed as a result of experience gained during construction.
- In the case of functional and performance testing, feedback covers several construction activities. The essential thing about such feedback is that the evaluation of documents or products of the development process leads to construction activities being carried out again. Evaluation activities are characterized by the documents that are incorporated in the evaluation and those that are changed as a result of the evaluation.

---

[6] By this, we mean a language with defined semantics. In commercial data processing, the term "formal" is frequently applied to *formatted* documents, e.g. forms, as well.

[7] No matter how well a computer department succeeds in screening itself off from the respective application area, organizational integration is the "moment of truth".

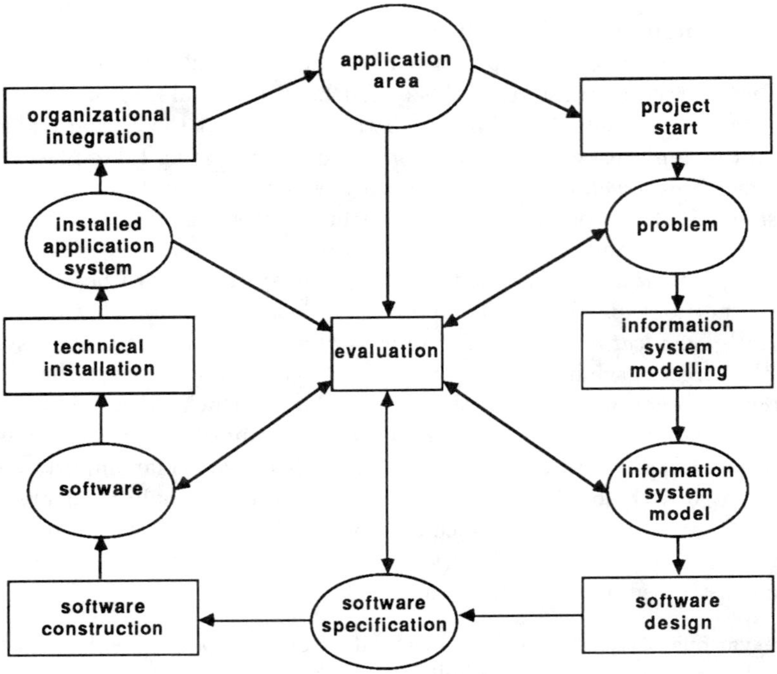


**Fig. 7.** Software development cycle with evaluation activities

The basic elements of software development are to be found in all descriptions of it. Figure 7 shows the interdependencies between activities and states in software development.[8] Evaluation correlates software development states and changes them. For the purposes of the diagram, we have subsumed evaluation activities under the single activity "evaluation".

We have now identified a number of activities and results of the software development process and incorporated them into a simple schema. This schema can now be used to characterize different approaches used in system development. Our attention focusses here on the evaluation activities. In the following examples and the chapter on evolutionary process models (Chap. 6), the activity "evaluation" is refined into specific evaluation activities.

## 2.4 Examples of Software Development Concepts

In this section we look at typical software development concepts and their different representations, such as they are to be found in textbooks and other software engineering literature. We set out to elucidate these concepts using the terms

[8] The diagram does *not* indicate the temporal sequence of activities and states. The assumption of such a temporal sequence in the diagram is inadmissible, as is illustrated by the possible feedback cycles.

defined above, indicating each concept's strong and weak points. At the same time, we use these examples to check whether our terminology is sound and how the various concepts can be represented using the means chosen by us.

To begin with, let us take a traditional concept based on a temporal sequence of activities and results (see [JensToni79]). This concept was originally adopted by the Hughes Aircraft Company and is in compliance with DoD procurement practices. The first thing that strikes us about the *original representation* of this concept (see Fig. 8) is the fact that it only shows activities.

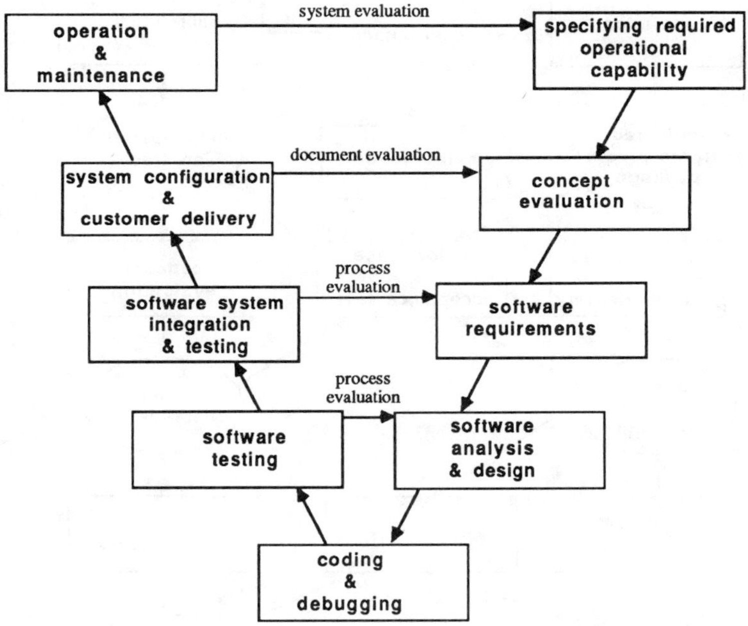


**Fig. 8.** The V model of software development according to Jensen and Tonies

The various activities are assigned to two complementary processes: problem decomposition and system recomposition. The characteristic feature of this concept and its original representation is the V–shaped arrangement of the two complementary processes.[9] This arrangement is meant to indicate that the system recomposition activities also serve to evaluate corresponding problem decomposition activities. There are different kinds of evaluation; these can be recast in our terminology as follows:

[9] As we are concerned here only with the characteristics of this development concept, we have, for the sake of clarity, included in our diagram only a few of the numerous activities shown in the original.

- The evaluation of the system is designed to ensure that the operational system also functions properly in its application area.
- The evaluation of documents by means of tests and reviews is designed to ensure that the requirements set out in a document are met when constructing the respective part of the system.
- The evaluation of the design process is designed to ensure that the respective documents are compatible with their immediate predecessors.

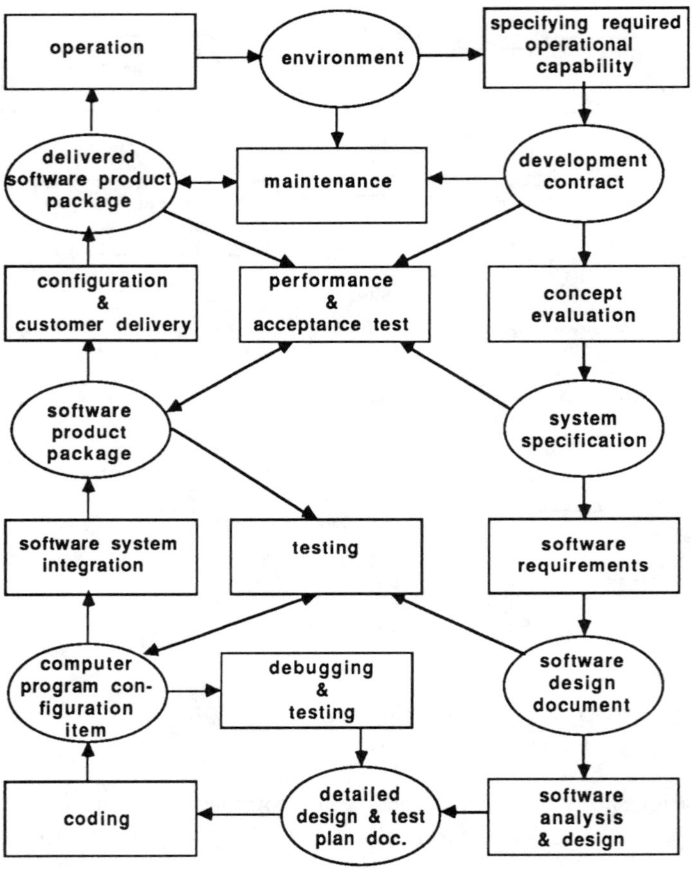


**Fig. 9.** Reconstruction of the V model

In order to acquire a better understanding of the special features of this V model, let us now translate the original representation into our own diagrammatic terms. To do this, two things are necessary: firstly, the results of the various activities must be incorporated into the diagram; and secondly, some of the original activities must be decomposed into a constructive and an evaluative part in order to illustrate clearly the various feedback cycles (see Fig. 9).[10]

The explicit representation of feedback cycles indicates that design decisions taken in the so-called early phases are not evaluated until relatively late on: for instance, software system requirements are checked during system integration. This temporal gap between construction and evaluation activities accounts, in our view, for the frequent observation that errors which occur in the early phases are particularly difficult to detect and expensive to eliminate (see [Boehm79]). If such errors are detected, i.e., if a discrepancy is found between specification and implementation, this may have two different consequences:

- The deviation of an implementation from its specification is eliminated "locally", as far as this is still possible. In terms of our example, this might mean that attempts are made to improve the system subsequent to its integration, the previous documents being left as they are.
- The development process is taken up again at the point where the deviation first occurred. In our example, the reason for the discrepancy between the software system requirements and the integrated system version might turn out to be an inconsistent specification. In this case, the development activities would have to begin again with the reframing of the concept in order to be able to take account of the necessary changes in all subsequent documents.

We do not wish to pretend that the authors of the software engineering textbook from which this concept is taken are unaware of the problematical nature of their model. In fact, they explicitly emphasize the importance of project reviews, particularly for the activities of problem decomposition. This does not, however, constitute a general solution to the problem.

Our next example looks at a development concept for a military real-time system that was one of the earliest of its kind (see Fig. 10 and Sec. 4). We have translated the original representation into our own diagrammatic terms. Although elaborate feedback cycles are provided for in the diagram, we find that the "range" of these feedback cycles is extremely limited and relates in each case only to the current phase. This means, for example, that the operational specification *is* incorporated into subsequent tests (assembly testing and shakedown testing), but that no provision is made for feedback to the specification itself. Since the development of large systems using this "local feedback global linear" technique is not yet possible at present, the model is unrealistic.

For our last example, we have chosen a development concept that includes prototyping as a feature for clarifying system requirements (cf. [Boar84] and Fig. 11). Here, different prototyping activities are embedded in a conventional software development framework. We wish to emphasize that – in addition to the concept discussed here – Boar does, in his textbook, propose another prototyping

[10] This footnote also applies to the following two examples. It is, we feel, a remarkable fact that only very few representations of software development concepts actually achieve a clear division between phases and their results.

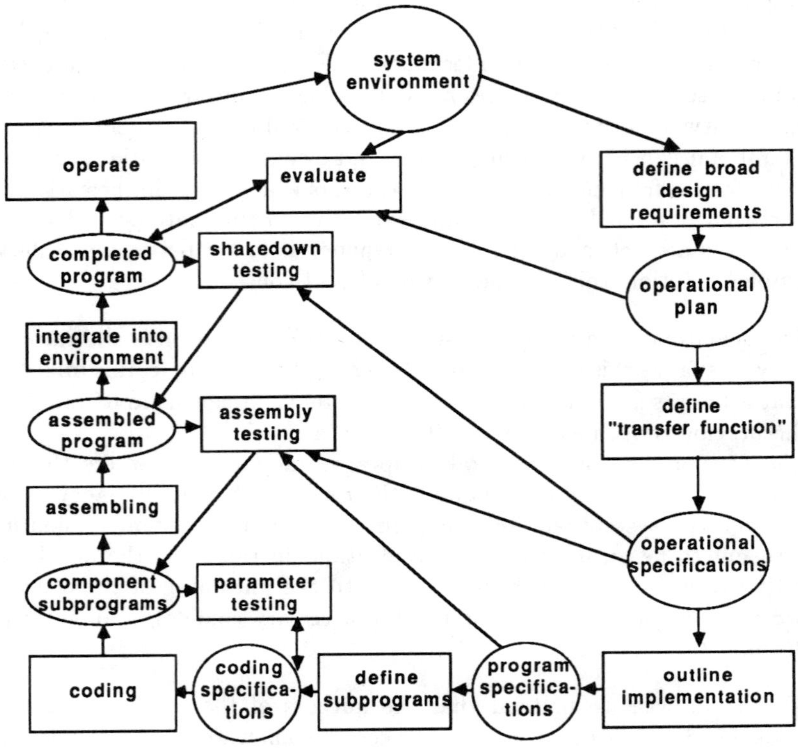


**Fig. 10.** Basic elements of software development according to Benington

strategy that comes close to our idea of *evolutionary prototyping* as elucidated in the following chapter.

If we consider the representation of this concept (which we have, again, adapted to our own diagrammatic form), we find there are three feedback cycles:

- The Prototyping Cycle – designed to clarify user requirements with respect to the application system.
- The Testing and Verification Cycle – designed to evaluate the implemented application system.
- The Maintenance Cycle – designed to adapt the running application system to changing organizational constraints.

The diagram shows that user participation in the development process is confined to the phases of prototyping and subsequent system use. Software construction, in the narrower sense, is carried out as an (almost) linear process.

To conclude, let us summarize some important aspects of the three concepts outlined above:

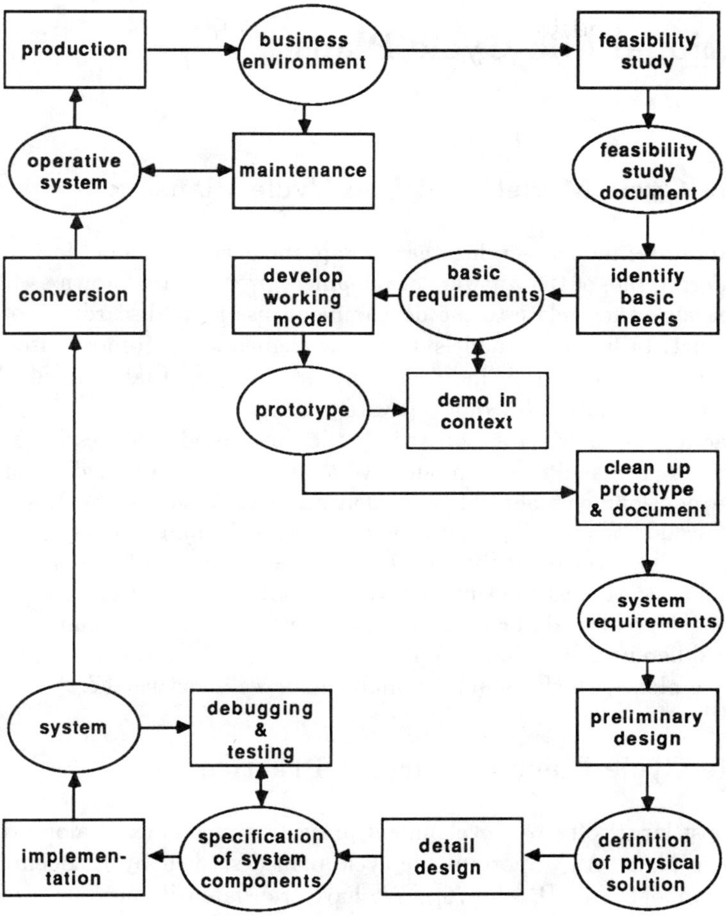


**Fig. 11.** Basic elements of software development according to Boar

- The general principle for dividing up development activities is: *First specify as completely as possible, then implement as linearly as possible.*
- The problems encountered in software development usually occur during requirements specification; and it is there that elaborate feedback cycles are provided for.
- Development concepts that do not include prototyping make no provision for evaluation of so-called early activities until late on in the development process.
- Software construction proper confines feedback to testing and verification cycles in which only the software developers are involved.

# 3
# Traditional Life Cycle Plans

## 3.1 Life Cycle Models and Life Cycle Plans

In the literature, models serving the same purpose as our model in Chapter 2, i.e., the *description* of the software development process, are known as life cycle models because they relate to the development, use and "discarding" of a software product. In life cycle models, the basic elements are in most cases merely put in sequence, the cycle being degenerate in the sense that it is, ideally, run through only once in the life of a software product.

In practice, we come across software development models possessing a *normative* character. Unlike life cycle models, which we use to *describe* different forms of system development, normative models serve to *prescribe* the behaviour of those involved in the development process. Besides defining and assigning activities and results, they prescribe the temporal sequence and form of the results to be produced. Models used in this way for project control are known as *life cycle plans*. A great deal of confusion arises if we fail to take account of the fundamental differences between descriptive models (which must be flexible) and prescriptive plans (which should, normally, have a restrictive effect).

## 3.2 Life Cycle Plans in Current Practice

Today, most large software development projects are conducted along the lines of life cycle plans. An important life cycle plan described by B. Boehm is the "waterfall model" (see [Boehm76]). We have translated it into our own representational terms (see Fig. 12). Boehm developed this plan to enable a software project to be planned and conducted according to engineering standards. It was conceived as an ideal strategy for project management. Right up to the present time, the "waterfall model" has continued to exercise considerable influence on project management in industrial practice, even though practical experience with the model soon made it clear that this is *not* the way to develop software.

The "waterfall model" is ideally suited for demonstrating the characteristic features of life cycle plans; they are sets of directions for solving the problems associated with software construction. The gist of these directions, for the software engineer, is as follows:

- In the application area, i.e., the world of the users, there are requirements which are to be met by a software system. These user requirements have to be translated into a system specification and implemented in the form of a software engineering product. If the software product meets the determined requirements, then it corresponds to the users' ideas.

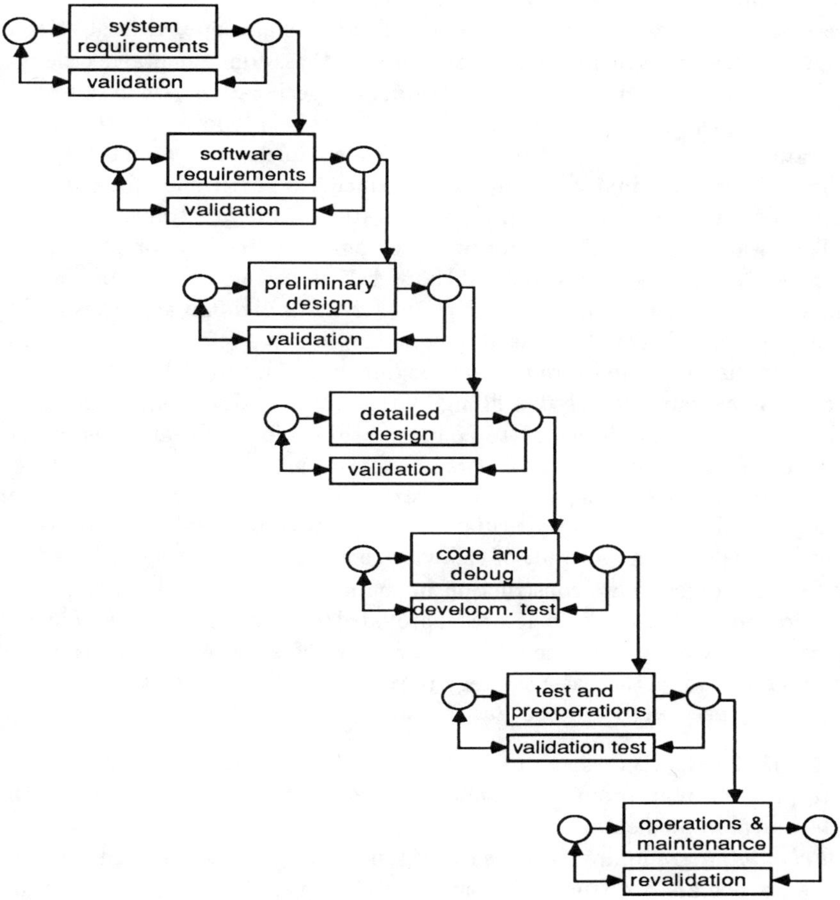


**Fig. 12.** Boehm's Waterfall Model

In the "waterfall model", the cycle is cut open to form a sequence. The software engineer's activities are fixed and arranged in a temporal sequence. The basic assumption behind this is that a problem can be presented in a well-defined form and an optimal solution reached step by step. Software development is seen as a predominantly technical problem – that of transforming the problem description into a problem solution – and not as a communication problem with users from the application area.

In the "waterfall model", the activities are arranged in such a way that, first, the (for the computer professional) abstract or general problems (i.e., those relating specifically to the application area) are dealt with, and then the (for the computer professional) concrete or particular (i.e., technical) problems. The idea here is to provide an answer, by means of these "early" activities, to fundamental questions relating to development aims and functional scope without reference to the technical implementation. In later phases, these fundamental decisions are elaborated in greater detail until programmable specifications are obtained. The technical implementation of the individual elements is followed by the stepwise integration of the overall system. In this way, a complex but abstract description of the problem is gradually decomposed into increasingly simple subdescriptions. Their subsequent reassembly yields the operational software solution.

The "waterfall model" was conceived as an ideal strategy for project management, though there was little likelihood of its being realized in the short term since the technical processes required for the individual activities had not yet been perfected. For this reason, it was adopted as a reference model for the newly established discipline of software engineering. This model made it possible to identify the gaps that needed filling by research and development in order to enable "software practitioners" to conduct projects on a linear basis, without the need for much feedback, and at reasonable cost.

Viewed from this angle, software construction is a mere process of hierarchical decomposition. Once a particular design process is complete, changes to it are to be ruled out. As a result of this view, software engineering has traditionally focussed on software construction in the narrower sense. Activities carried out prior and subsequent to it are – provided they are given any consideration at all – looked on as necessities, not as part of software construction. This still remains, today, the basic strategy of software engineering. It is outlined by David L. Parnas (see [Parnas85]) as follows:

- Requirements with respect to a software system should be documented *prior to* programming proper and should be *complete* but independent of their technical implementation.
- *Prior to* programming, a software system should be decomposed into modules, which are constructed according to the principle of information hiding.
- A module should not be programmed until a precise formal specification is available.
- Formal methods should be used for specifying software design.
- The programs themselves should be written in accordance with the principles of structured programming.

In industrial practice, hierarchical problem decomposition and project management based on life cycle plans are seen as a decisive means of improving software construction. Here, the establishment of sequential work steps goes a long way towards facilitating project management.

Life cycle plans have doubtless made it possible to build systems of high technical quality (with respect to robustness, error handling facilities, efficiency and modularity). However, as computer applications have expanded, considerable problems have become evident. These are looked at in Section 3.4.

## 3.3 The Origin of Life Cycle Plans

In life cycle plans, the principle of proceeding "from the general to the concrete" or "from the problem to the solution" is applied to the organization of a software project. Each activity is viewed as an input–process–output step. Advocates of life cycle plans (cf. [Born86, Rook86]) describe the respective input and output documents for each activity. Only minimal provision is made for feedback cycles. In each case, the input documents are compared with the output documents. Such comparisons may necessitate revisions of earlier documents, but these are seen as unwelcome and, in principle, avoidable deviations from the proper path.

If we consider life cycle plans from the angle of the software developer, the proposed approaches strike us as being quite reasonable and "natural". We have, after all, been accustomed to tackling problems in this way ever since our school days. One of the basic skills we were taught in mathematics was to translate a clearly defined problem into the language of mathematics, and to use the techniques of hierarchical problem decomposition, analysis, construction and recomposition in order to find the correct solution. Unclearly defined problems were considered to be the fault of the textbook or the teacher. There was seldom more than one way of arriving at the solution, and one particular way was always considered the "best".

Here, the – didactically useful – *presentation of a problem solution* is misinterpreted as a *problem-solving strategy.* The teacher's job is, first of all, to explain the problem, then to outline the basic way of tackling it, and finally to describe the individual steps that must be taken in order to obtain the solution. This approach presupposes that the problem is clearly formulated and that at least one solution is known; however, it rarely conveys how the teacher (or the author of the textbook) originally understood the problem and *arrived at* the solution.

In their standard works on structured programming (see [Dijkstra72]) and data structuring (see [Hoare72]), Dijkstra and Hoare have applied this problem-solving technique to software development. Hoare calls on the software engineer to

- concentrate on the relevant features,
- ignore irrelevant facts,
- choose a suitable form of representation,
- choose the appropriate axiomatization,
- start programming.

Dijkstra proceeds exactly in accordance with these principles developing a program for computing prime numbers through top-down refinement of the statement "print first thousand prime numbers".

The problem-solving method used in life cycle plans is based on a traditional world-view that Winograd and Flores (see [WinoFlores86]) call *rationalistic.* Let us summarize this view of the world in their words:

1 Characterize the situation in terms of identifiable objects with well-defined properties.

2 Find general rules that apply to situations in terms of those objects and properties.
3 Apply the rules logically to the situation of concern, drawing conclusions about what should be done.

Here, we come across the same view of the design and problem-solving process as that underlying the life cycle plans: the essence of the problem is identifiable and should be dealt with according to correct rules; the objective can be attained step by step, according to a predefined plan, through a process of gradual concretion. In this view of the world, the analyst is an onlooker, a neutral observer who acts logically and pragmatically, taking the necessary steps in order to bring about the predetermined final state.

## 3.4 Problems Associated with Traditional Life Cycle Plans

In the previous section, we looked at software construction based on life cycle plans. The traditional world-view underlying this fails to take account of the fact that designing something new presupposes referring back to what already exists. We arrive at a theoretical understanding of the world by acting in it. The basic question arising here is to what extent it is possible to design something fundamentally new without experience and action. Architects, for example, do not design buildings without reference to existing architecture; they have grown up in a specific architectural culture and, as a result of their professional training, are closely concerned with "handling" houses. The design of a new house is embedded in a world of tradition, experience and acquired knowledge.

Criticism of life cycle plans and their theoretical basis has been repeatedly voiced (cf., e.g., [Zave84, HekmatInce86]). It is summarized below in the form of a number of theses, each followed by a detailed elucidation.

**A complete and permanently correct description of information systems is not possible.**

Information systems are highly complex. Any description of such a system must confine itself to selecting certain elements and relations of that system. This selection shapes the rest of the development process. An information system is subject to continual changes, for example, because the organizational context changes, because communication processes are – explicitly or implicitly – organized on a different basis, or because there are changes in the persons or tasks involved. This has organizational, legal and, in particular, application-related repercussions.

A system description, then, is not only incomplete; it must also be continually updated. The problem can neither be completely described nor fixed for the duration of the development process. The traditional approach, however, assumes that a requirements specification, once declared valid, constitutes the permanently fixed basis of the software implementation.

**Specification and implementation of a software system cannot be performed as separate work steps in time.**

The specification describes *what* we expect from a system; the implementation prescribes *how* the system is to fulfil these requirements. Specification and implementation are distinct activities, but are closely connected with one another. The specification is indispensable and crucial to the implementation. But it is also true that the more we know about potential implementations, the more precise and abstract a specification can be. And the implementation helps identify inconsistent or unrealistic requirements and enhances our knowledge of potential system performance.

All software developers are familiar with the interdependencies between specification and implementation when programming "in the small" and recognize that it is impossible to draw a strict line between the two (see [SwaBal78]). And the fact that the ideas about how a system is to be designed (the specification) change during its realization (the implementation) is true to an even greater extent of system development "in the large".

Interesting in this connection are the conclusions reached by Parnas concerning software construction:

- It is possible to write system specifications in a formal language. The necessary methods and languages are available. There is, however, no method available for ensuring that a specification is complete and correct. Only if a similar system has already been built can a further system be consistently specified in advance with any amount of certainty.
- The decomposition of the overall system into modules is a simple matter in cases where the design decisions arising during implementation of these modules are known. This can only be the case, though, if a similar implementation process has already been successfully carried out.

The development of software according to classical life cycle plans runs into problems because, here, specification and implementation need to be carried out independently of one another in successive time phases. When developing new applications or when carrying out extensive modifications, stepwise decomposition of a software system into hierarchical descriptions – the implementation being fixed on one level, and then constituting the invariant specification for the next level down – is not feasible.

**Formal, nonexecutable specifications are largely unintelligible to users and developers.**

There is no doubt that formal methods for system specification can be applied successfully by developers in their work. The formal verification of critical algorithms is of significance in practical applications. However, formal, nonexecutable system specifications are found to be unsuitable for communication between developers and users (see [GomSco81]).

We go a step further: our experience has shown that formal specifications which are not suitable for experimental purposes are of no practical use to the present generation of developers either. In a project model divided up into phases, such formal specifications frequently do little more than evidence the fact that milestones have been reached. Before programming even starts, they no longer agree with the system under construction. Even at research institutions, specifications that can only be manually processed and evaluated seldom influence the implementation of systems .

For this reason, advocates of formal specification methods emphasize that their specifications can only be meaningfully handled if they can be evaluated by a machine (see, for example, [BerWin85, BalGolWil82] and [Smoliar82]). Efforts are underway to make available interpreters that will enable specifications to be made *executable*. However, if developers *experiment* with specifications, the boundary between this and simulation and prototyping becomes blurred.

**Traditional development strategies exclude the users from crucial activities.**

On the assumption that the users' ideas can be set down in written requirements once requirements analysis is complete, the users are excluded from the rest of the construction process. This means that the evaluation of the system by the users does not take place until after the software is completed and installed. Design gaps, conceptual errors or deviations from the original ideas are not identified until very late on. This frequently results in a polarization between developers and users since the differences in interests are, at this stage, difficult to reconcile. The developers would like to deliver what they consider to be the finished system promptly and unproblematically. The users, on the other hand, who will have to work with the system in the foreseeable future, are keen to have any necessary changes made before the project is concluded.

In numerous situations where software results in new work forms, it is impossible for users to formulate their requirements. They need material on which to develop their creativity. Without prototypes, user requirements remain vague, tentative and unable to offer inspiration to the software developer.

**The label "maintenance" conceals vital aspects of development work concerned with adapting a system to the application context.**

Once a product has been delivered, life cycle plans provide for a maintenance phase to eliminate errors that are not detected until the product is in use. Most of the "errors" reported by users relate to poor functionality or the desire for adaptation of the system to changed organizational constraints. "Maintenance", then, covers adaptation of delivered systems to take account of user wishes that were not previously realized or were not identified until during use. This means that a large portion of the development work is put beyond the control of management (cf. also [Gomaa83]). Here, the "linearity" of life cycle plans is carried to absurdity. Planning is replaced by an event–driven "muddling through". The premature fixing of user requirements in life cycle plans does not help solve the problems of identifying needs, but merely postpones them – their being lumped together, for simplicity's sake, under the general heading "maintenance".

Quality assurance, control and evaluation during maintenance are confined to a minimum. Depending on the gravity of the errors (whether only part or all of the software is unusable) and their implications (whether changes can be made easily or involve considerable effort), and taking into account the number of users and their potential influence, the developers draw up the system changes considered necessary, generally without feedback. It is quite normal for developers to test changes, even in critical parts of the system, "overnight", and then release them for use. The cases in which a "quick patch" has had devastating effects now belong to the body of software folklore and can be looked up in the relevant column of *ACM Software Engineering Notes*. The allegation made by advocates of life cycle plans that "prototyping encourages unplanned software construction" is not very plausible if we consider current maintenance practice.

**Life cycle plans are unsuitable for controlling software projects. Milestone documents are produced for the benefit of management only.**

Gilb (see [Gilb85]) and Brown (see [Brown85]) have pointed out that the main argument in favour of using life cycle plans, namely, their suitability for management and control, is largely untenable. Insofar as the projects examined by Gilb have any clear development goal at all, it is a predominantly product–oriented, not a task– and result–oriented one.

Control over the completion and success of the individual phases is exercised at fixed "milestones" by acceptance of documents such as the contract data requirements list, the system specification and the test plan. After acceptance, such documents are generally "frozen". As development progresses, the system is either built defectively (because changes are no longer permitted despite new findings) or the documents soon become obsolete.

The situation frequently arises that documents for project control and management are produced parallel or subsequent to the software system's construction documents "proper" (cf. also [Brown85]). On delivery of a system, many – in principle useful – documents possess at most "archaeological" value; they do not, however, describe the current system and its actual development.

One of the serious defects of software projects is the lack of reliable data about the costs involved and the benefits obtained. Even statements about a project's being concluded on schedule must be viewed very critically since the "termination" of a project is often a management decision and, in actual fact, merely marks the beginning of the maintenance phase.

Gilb emphasizes that far–reaching management decisions are taken at a very early stage on the basis of inadequate information. The revision of such decisions can only take place when the amount already invested (according to published data frequently up to 70% of total development costs; cf., e.g., [HenIng82]) means that devising alternative concepts or actually winding up an unsuccessful development project is no longer economically warrantable. To justify high investment costs, organizations are frequently adapted to a poorly designed application system.

## 3.5 Where Do Life Cycle Plans Work?

If we consider these problems and the fundamental criticism of life cycle plans outlined above, we find ourselves asking how it was possible to develop large operational systems at all. The answers are:

- The way software projects are conducted is *de facto* at variance with official strategies, the relevant project guidelines being in some cases circumvented, in others simply ignored. In many project plans, provision has since been made for feedback cycles; these, however, are generally looked on as "error recovery" measures rather than essential design activities.
- For many of the traditional application areas of software, sufficient knowledge is available about problems and their solution. Software development only ostensibly takes the form of a linear process starting with problem definition and ending with the operational software solution. Experience previously gained from similar systems means that, even at the stage of problem formulation, a fair knowledge of potential technical and organizational options is already available. To this extent, the problems involved in compiler construction, but also in the construction of operating systems or the development of inventory control and accounting systems are, today, considered to have been already mastered.
- Numerous software systems were initially built by developers for their own needs. This meant that during development there was constant feedback between requirements and their step–by–step realization. Software systems developed in this way have subsequently proved useful in other areas. Most editors and many word–processing programs are instances of this type of system; they often still "smell" of the computer department.

### Summary

The problems faced in software construction based on life cycle plans are:

- Information systems can be described neither completely nor permanently.
- Specification and construction must be interleaved.
- The phase–oriented, top–down "freezing" of models makes no sense.
- Formal, nonexecutable specifications are incomprehensible.
- Users are excluded from system development.
- Maintenance is unplanned system development.
- Life cycle plans are unsuitable for project control.

# 4
# Prototyping

In the previous chapter, we discussed the limitations of traditional life cycle plans. One fact which emerged clearly was that the major problems facing software developers today cannot be solved using life cycle plans. Equally clear, though, is the fact that prototyping can, *in principle,* solve these problems. The question that remains unanswered is that concerning the *practical handleability* of prototyping, and it is to this question that we now set out to provide an answer.

In the first part of the chapter, we look at prototyping from various different technical angles. Part two then gives a number of practical examples of prototyping in use. These examples are chiefly designed to help familiarize the reader with completely new ideas. We take a detailed look at the various concepts connected with prototyping and go into the question of its practicability.

In order to make a proper appraisal of the benefits offered by prototyping, it is worthwhile recalling once again the remarks of the "father" of life cycle plans, Herbert D. Benington, concerning the validity of his own model.

The first known life cycle plan (cf. Fig. 10 in Chap. 2) was used in the 1950s in MIT's Lincoln Laboratory for developing the military air defence system SAGE. The fact that a rigid approach of this sort was chosen was due to the following constraints: the system to be developed was a real–time system comprising a total of over half a million machine instructions; the team of developers was very large, consisting of hundreds of inexperienced programmers; the capacity and availability of the development computer for programming and testing purposes was extremely limited; and neither interactive test facilities nor machine-processable documentation were available (see [Benington83]).

Benington's own evaluation of the development situation shows that he considered the use of a life cycle plan to be a realistic proposition only because an elaborate experimental prototype was already available before the project officially began and the system itself was incremented step by step. He emphasizes that it is impossible to carry out a complete advance specification of a complex software system of this sort and stresses the importance of learning processes for all those involved in development. The insights and experience gained on this occasion were either ignored or forgotten. The life cycle plan has survived the intervening decades unaltered, except, as we have seen, for some changes in terms, and is still, today, propagated as a strategy for software development.

## 4.1 Different Aspects of Prototyping

In the following sections, we examine four technical aspects of prototyping:

- *The prototype in the software development process.* There are various kinds of prototypes required for the different activities in our model of software development.
- *Goals of prototyping.* Prototypes can be used to clear up a number of different problems.
- *Horizontal and vertical prototyping.* Prototypes can be used for experiments on various parts of the application system.
- *The relationship between prototype and application system.* Prototypes can be incorporated into the application system in different ways.

### 4.1.1 The Prototype in the Software Development Process

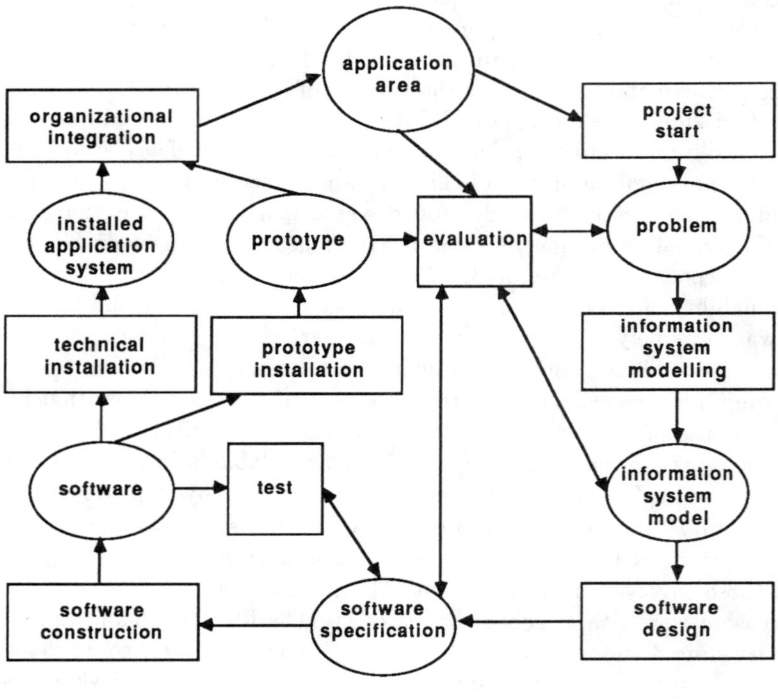


**Fig. 13.** Prototyping

The position occupied by the prototype in the software development process is important for the following reasons (see Fig. 13):

- A prototype is an operational model of the application system. It implements certain aspects of the future system.
- Prototypes provide a concrete basis for discussions between developers, users and management. They help in discussing difficulties, clarifying problems, or preparing decisions. Where necessary, prototypes are supplemented by written system specifications.
- Each prototype serves as a basis for subsequent prototypes or for the application system.
- At the user interface, the application system should, as far as system functionality and behaviour goes, be largely in conformity with the aspects evaluated using prototypes.

Three models influence the construction of prototypes: the problem or business needs, the information system model, and the software specification (see Fig. 13). To illustrate the way we see the relationship between prototype and model, we distinguish between the following *kinds of prototypes*:

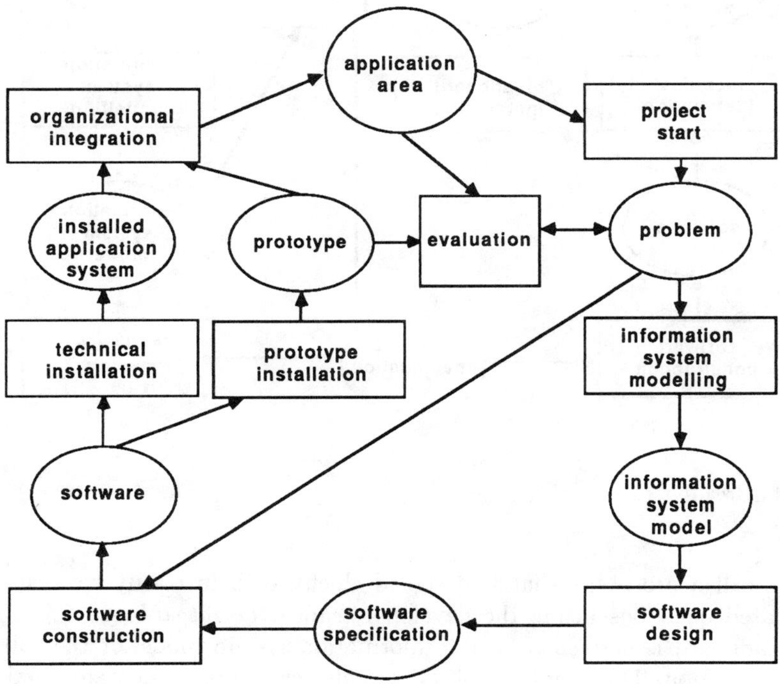


**Fig. 14.** Prototype

We use the term *prototype proper* to describe a provisional operational software system that is constructed parallel to the information system model (see Fig. 14).[11] A prototype of this sort is generally designed to illustrate specific aspects of the user interface or part of the functionality and thus helps to clarify the problem in hand. It is a better idea to build several "small" prototypes to deal with the various problems faced than to keep extending one and the same prototype because the problems involved are neither clear nor homogeneous.

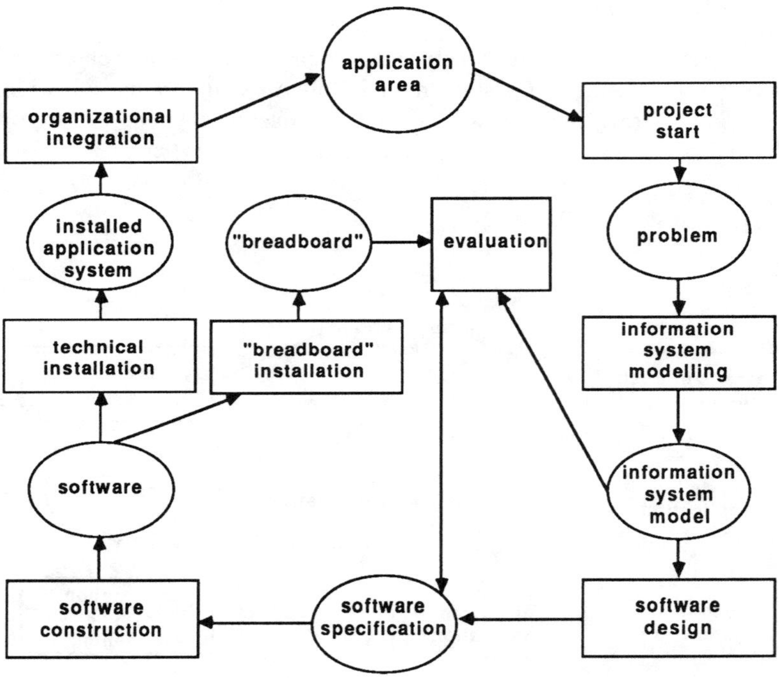


**Fig. 15.** Breadboard

– We call a prototype that is designed chiefly to help clarify construction-related questions facing the developer team a *breadboard* (see Fig. 15). A breadboard is derived from the information system model or the software specification. This kind of prototype is also encountered in traditional software projects, though the experimental approach associated with it is seldom given explicit recognition as such. Users are generally excluded from the eval-

[11] This and the following two figures include only elements and relations characteristic of the kind of prototype being looked at in each case.

uation of breadboards.[12] To this extent, the use of breadboards is a restricted form of prototyping.
Construction of a breadboard is based on different requirements from those of a prototype proper: the aspects modelled should be comparable with the future application system from a *technical* point of view. Depending on the particular problem in hand, this comparability may relate to the system's architecture or functionality.

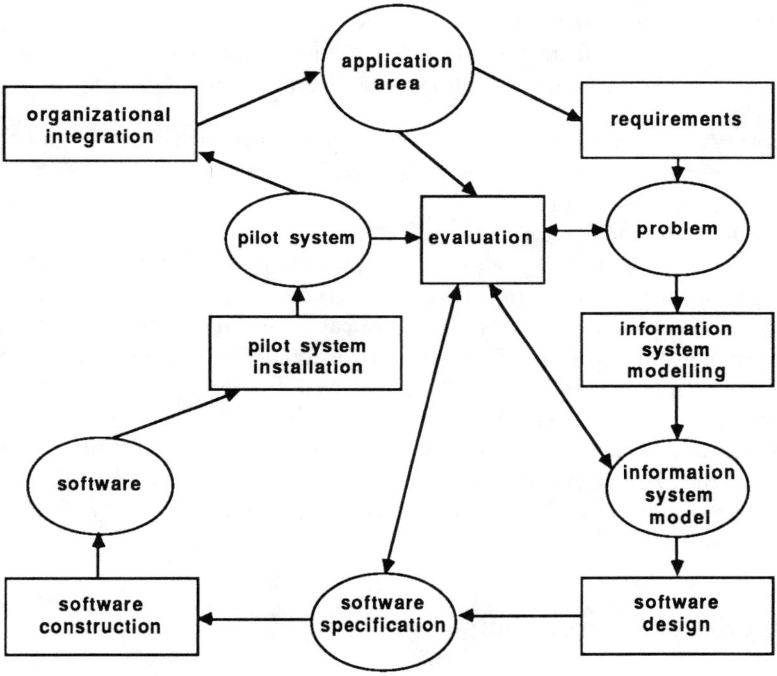


**Fig. 16.** Pilot system

- If a prototype is used not only for experimental testing of an idea or for "illustrative purposes", but is actually employed in the application area itself as the core of the application system, it is known as a *pilot system* (see [Rzevski84] and Fig. 16). In such cases, there ceases to be any clear distinction between the prototype and the application system. After reaching a certain degree of "sophistication", the prototype is practically implemented in the form of a pilot system and incremented in cycles. While defining the

[12] It is naturally an attractive prospect for developers to be able to use an operational system version as early as possible, even if the part modelled is unsuitable for testing or evaluation by users.

development framework, i.e., specifying the software development objectives, is a joint task performed by both developers and users, the various pilot system increments should be geared exclusively to user priorities. From the technical point of view, a pilot system requires a considerably more elaborate design than a prototype proper or a breadboard. After all, the pilot system is designed for use in the application area, and not only under laboratory conditions. Even where its use is restricted to a single department or to individual workplaces it is imperative that the system be easy to operate and reliable, and accompanied by a minimum of user documentation.

Prototyping may be used to support a variety of activities within a development project. This fact is highlighted by an examination of the relationship between the different kinds of prototypes and other elements in our model:

- Prototypes proper provide users and management with a "tangible" idea of the problem solution being sought, and hence support evaluation of the information system model.
- For the developers, a prototype constitutes an executable specification. It facilitates evaluation of the different models and helps narrow down the scope for interpretation in software construction.
- A breadboard demonstrates the technical feasibility of the system design. Experimental testing of it shows up the dynamic and restrictive features of the application system without the need to complete construction and installation of the system beforehand.
- Experimentation with prototypes helps prepare the organizational integration of the application system by giving the users a "foretaste" of the system. This applies in particular to pilot systems that allow the application system to be incremented step by step.

## 4.2 Goals of Prototyping

When constructing prototypes, we focus on the major problems arising in typical development situations, problems which prototyping is designed to help solve. We can distinguish several kinds of prototyping relating to different goals (cf. [Floyd84]):

- *Exploratory Prototyping.* This is used where the problem in hand is unclear. Initial ideas are used as a basis for clarifying user and management requirements with respect to the future system (see [HooHsi82]). Here, equal consideration is given to changes in work content and to the type and scope of computer support. Particular importance is attached to examining a variety of design options, so as not to restrict ideas prematurely to one specific approach (a problem which prototyping cannot eliminate; cf. [HenIng82]). The developers gain insight into the application area and into the users' work tasks and the problems they face. Discussions here may revolve around a number of different prototypes proper (see Fig. 14).

Exploratory prototyping is of particular importance in project acquisition if the developers and users belong to different organizations (companies). Here, prototypes assume the function of a "prospectus" or "tender", indicating to the management of the user organization how the future system might look.

- *Experimental Prototyping.* This form of prototyping focusses on the technical implementation of a development goal. By means of experimentation, the users are able to further specify their ideas about the type of computer support required. The developers, for their part, are provided with a basis for appraisal of the suitability and feasibility of a particular application system. An essential aspect here is the communication between users and developers on technical problems and questions relating to software ergonomics. Like prototypes proper, breadboards are also built to help clarify the technical problems facing the developers (see Fig. 15).
- *Evolutionary Prototyping.* Here, prototyping is not merely used as a tool in the context of a single development project; it is rather a continuous process for adapting an application system to rapidly changing organizational constraints (see [Duncan82]). This means that software development is no longer seen as a self-contained project, but rather as a process continuously accompanying the application. Since short development cycles are aimed at, it is useful to eliminate the differences between prototypes and application systems by developing pilot systems (see Fig. 16). Evolutionary prototyping is inextricably linked to the principles of evolutionary system development. One consequence of this is that the role of the developers also changes. They are no longer the "protagonists" of a self-contained project; instead, they become technical consultants working in close cooperation with the users to improve the application system.

## 4.3 Horizontal and Vertical Prototyping

If we view software development as the design and implementation of a number of layers, ranging from the user interface to the base layer – normally the operating system or a database query language, the subdivision into horizontal and vertical prototyping becomes meaningful (see [MayBeLo84]).

In *horizontal prototyping*, only specific layers of the system are built, e.g., the user interface layer along with its forms and menus, or functional core layers such as database transactions. In the literature, horizontal prototyping is almost invariably taken to mean prototyping of the human–computer interface.

In *vertical prototyping*, a selected part of the target system is implemented completely ("down through all layers"). This technique is appropriate where the system's functionality and implementation options are still open. This is usually the case when building pilot systems.

When considering the differences between horizontal and vertical prototyping, it should not be forgotten that it is the software development method that determines the layers of the software. It is, then, by no means "natural" for the user interface to constitute the top software layer, or for it to be located in precisely one layer at all. We have, nonetheless, retained the terminology because it is useful for denoting various approaches of practical relevance.

## 4.4 The Relationship between Prototype and Application System

A further criterion for classifying prototypes is the relationship between the prototype and the application system. Here, a number of different views are taken:

- **Prototypes are incremented to produce the application system**
  As the use of workstations and Very High Level Languages (VHLL) for commercial applications becomes increasingly widespread, technical differences between prototypes and application systems are gradually disappearing. Cheap hardware and efficient compilers or interpreters often make code optimization superfluous. The gradual transition from prototype to application system is becoming possible.[13]
- **A prototype is part of the application system specification**
  The application system is built on the basis of an accepted prototype. The prototype serves specification purposes only and is not used as a building block in the application system itself: it is a "throwaway". Prototyping consists in modelling and demonstrating selected aspects of the desired system. The individual prototypes are constructed as quickly as possible, making use of all the technical means available.
  Selection of the aspects to be implemented in the prototype generally focusses on the user interface and the system's functionality, questions relating to failsafe facilities and efficiency being practically disregarded. In conjunction with the development of standard software, Neumaier (see [Neumaier86]) has drawn attention to an extreme case: a prototype may implement full functionality, but differ considerably from the application system as far as user convenience is concerned, because it may have been designed originally for limited (personal) use only, its general utility being recognized at a later stage. Also, the technical implementation options for prototype and application system may be quite different (a prototype being implemented, for example, on a LISP machine, the application system with COBOL on a mainframe). The application system is rebuilt from scratch in order to ensure a sound solution by software engineering standards (see [DodRamAshPar82]).

---

[13] Perusal of the relevant literature has shown us that the basic idea behind this approach is as old as structured programming itself. As early as 1971, H. Mills suggested largely dispensing with nonexecutable written system specifications and conducting development on the basis of an executable but functionless program skeleton (cf. [Mills71]). Brooks saw in this an important idea for prototyping (cf. [Brooks87]). Mills, however, did not intend to use his executable program skeletons for such purposes. His aim was to solve correctness and debugging problems for large systems — the subject of discussion at that time in software engineering circles.

Prototypes forming part of the specification can be evaluated by experimentation; they lack important features essential for use in practical applications.

- **Prototypes serve to clarify problems only**
  One extreme view is the idea of constructing prototypes merely for the purposes of acquiring knowledge, with no intention of building an application system. This form of prototyping is frequently encountered at research and development institutes and universities (cf., e.g., [GiLiRoSaSoWi82]). Projects of this sort are designed to clarify problems or elaborate ideas. For instance, new concepts of user interface design can be tried out and evaluated, or the feasibility of construction ideas studied. The relationship between such prototypes and potential applications remains unspecified. Frequently, innovative or non-standard hardware and software are tried out in this way. Prototypes of this sort should not be confused with *breadboards*, which are designed to help clarify problems relating to a planned application.

## 4.5 Examples of Prototyping

In the following sections, we report on three different projects that used prototypes of differing *range* to clarify various problems encountered in the development process. A brief outline is given of each of the projects; details are given of how the use of prototypes was evaluated in each case; and aspects of general significance to prototyping are highlighted. We conclude by summarizing the examples looked at and assessing them in terms of the concepts presented in Chapter 4.

### 4.5.1 An Order Processing System

#### Background

A multinational concern decided to have an order processing system with a standard core built for use in all its subsidiaries (see [Rzevski84]). The biggest problems were caused by the differing requirements of the various national organizations: although orders were processed everywhere along the same basic lines, there were differences in the work processes and procedures in use in the various subsidiaries. For the foreseeable future, there was little prospect of coming to terms with these differences by means of written user needs analyses or system specifications, since for many of the subsidiaries the problems involved in understanding technical documents written in English were considered practically insurmountable.

Faced with this situation, it was hoped that prototyping would not only help the developers in building the order processing system, but, in particular, facilitate specification and acceptance by the various users and user organizations.

As the concern attached great importance to being able to adapt the application software swiftly and flexibly to its constantly changing range of products, it was hoped to use prototyping as a means to achieve shorter development cycles as well.

Each prototyping cycle covered information analysis, construction and evaluation of the prototype. In all, three cycles were run through. Each time, an increasingly large number of users and user organizations was involved in the evaluation process.

### Results

The *benefits* expected of a prototyping strategy were largely attained. There was good coordination between the different organizations and groups involved and active participation by the users. It proved possible to cut down construction time and costs, and the application system came up to the expectations of users and management. The authors of the report suggest using prototyping as a development strategy in other projects.

The *problems* that did occur were chiefly associated with the development team. Many of the developers were unaccustomed to cooperating closely with the users. In addition, the developers found it difficult to dispense with fixed specifications during prototyping and use new techniques such as program generators, although it was, in fact, precisely these techniques that enabled prototypes to be constructed and modified so quickly.

The major problem encountered in the project was the fact that the differences between the prototype and the application system remained obscure to both users and management. Once acceptable prototypes had been built, the remaining development work on the application system was underestimated. This meant that expectations concerning the completion date for the application system were too high. Lastly, during project planning, estimates of the amount of time required for evaluating the various prototypes were too low since the users demonstrated a greater degree of commitment and made more suggestions of their own than was expected.

Despite these problems, no doubts were entertained as to the validity of prototyping as a development strategy.

### Conclusions

Although acceptance problems invariably occur when introducing new methods and techniques, they are particularly in evidence when prototyping is first used since the success of a prototyping project is dependent, in technical terms, on the increased use of sophisticated tools. Moreover, many software developers are extremely wary about this new form of direct cooperation with the users.

This project also demonstrates how important it is to put across the "idea" behind prototyping to all those involved beforehand. This is the only way of preventing misconceptions occurring about the function of the prototype and the difference between it and the future application system. These misconceptions relate to both the functional difference ("What does and what doesn't the prototype demonstrate?") and to the development effort required ("How much effort is involved in providing error handling and help facilities, for example?").

### 4.5.2 An Office System for Planning Departments

**Background**

This project was conducted jointly by a software manufacturer and a research institute (Norwegian Computing Center). The idea was to develop a marketable system to support clerical duties in the planning departments of around 400 small to medium-sized Norwegian municipalities that had no previous experience of data processing. The system was to easily be adaptable to the local needs of the different planning departments (see [PapTho85]). It was to support the staff of the planning departments in performing complex tasks on a largely self-reliant basis and with only a limited degree of formalization. The project aimed to provide satisfactory solutions on two different levels:

- By developing a "common application system" that could be easily tailored to suit the local needs of the different user organizations.
- By taking into account the different organizational and social constraints in the various planning departments – due to differences in legal provisions, in the structures of the municipal bodies and in trade union co-determination rights.

Right from the outset, the project team recognized that the complexity of the problems facing them would necessitate the use of prototyping, among other things to promote learning processes on the part of users and developers.

The potential user organizations were classified by the project team according to the type of municipality they belonged to. Each of the three municipalities selected for installation and evaluation of prototypes was located in a structurally different region: Farmland, Coastland and Industryland. The prototyping process was divided up into three stages. First, a prototype was developed for the Farmland municipality and installed there. This prototype required considerable modification to make it suitable for use in a Coastland municipality. For instance, capacity problems arose and, as a result of the differences in working routines, previously unidentified errors were detected. The prototype installed in the third municipality was developed from the previous two. This time, only minor modifications were required. Finally, on the basis of all three prototypes, the nucleus of a common system for municipal planning departments was developed; this could be expanded by means of specialized modules to suit specific local requirements.

The prototypes ran on workstations and were based on standard application software that was tailored to meet the special needs in each case and then integrated. The experience gained using these three prototypes and the results of an accompanying across-the-board study together formed the basis for development of the common application system.

### Results

The close cooperation and coordination between the groups involved at the various different levels proved to be an *advantage* – a fact which soon became apparent once the first prototypes were in use. Both cooperation between developers and users and coordination with the various supervisory and decision–making bodies worked well. Coordination was less of a problem then expected. None of the groups involved entertained doubts about the use of prototyping.

The developers considered it a remarkable fact that a common system was developed from a prototype designed for a specific workplace. The usual approach – and the one initially advocated by project management – was to design, first of all, a common system, and then tailor it to local needs.

The user organizations (in this case: the municipal authorities), but also the trade unions involved in the project, were more attuned to the idea of using traditional life cycle plans. In Scandinavia, there are a number of technology agreements in force governing the introduction of data processing. These make detailed provision for co–determination and participation during the various phases of development. The trade unions made sure that the change in strategy did not affect workers' industrial rights.

### Conclusions

This example illustrates two important aspects of prototyping. By representing the "tangible" result of the software development process, prototypes provide an ideal basis for discussion and decision–making within the various bodies involved. Here, they constitute a great improvement on conventional written documents. On the other hand, there are often arrangements, provisions or established approaches that are geared to the traditional "milestone documents". This also applies to the drawing–up of contracts with software houses, such contracts being traditionally based on procurement and system specifications, etc. It is quite understandable that a change in approach to software development may give rise to uncertainties or fears about an "anarchistic" development process, to use Pape and Thorensen's words (see [PapTho87]). These problems can be eliminated by developing an explicit model of software development explicitly illustrating the different activities and results for each of the development cycles.

## 4.5.3 Software Tools for Graphic Workers

### Background

In the 1970s, the Scandinavian newspaper industries contemplated introducing computer–based text and image processing systems. Analyses of the American systems already on the market showed that they were not entirely suitable for the national newspaper industries in Scandinavia. The UTOPIA project, conducted jointly by various Scandinavian research institutes and the Nordic

Graphic Workers' Union, set out to develop a new technical concept for this particular application area (see [Utopia85, Boedker85, BoEhLyKaSu87]). The main idea here was to incorporate the graphic workers' know–how and skills in the development process in order to create a new professional profile and provide the necessary technical support for it. The aim was to develop the relevant tools in close cooperation with the users.

Between 1981 and 1985, experiments were carried out using various prototypes. These resulted in the specification of a graphic workstation. The graphic workers' participation in the development process enabled them gradually to gain insight into the new opportunities offered by computer support. The developers, for their part, were able to familiarize themselves with the application area. On the technical side, mock–ups and prototypes of various system components were built. In order to study the user interface menus and the use of display screen and pointing devices, simple simulation techniques were employed (paper models of the display screen lay–out, slide projection of interactive work sequences, plywood mock–ups of pointing devices). Some tools were implemented using graphic workstations.

## Results

The *advantages* of the chosen approach are obvious. The graphic workers have helped to create a new professional profile and new opportunities for technical support of their work. The developers have gained a profound insight into the work and problems of this particular profession.

*Difficulties* occurred because no suitable technical means were available for constructing a functional prototype of the overall system. Nevertheless, the opportunities offered by computer support were largely exploited. The detailed specification was passed on to a software manufacturer. Although this meant that implementation of the results was separated from the actual project itself, prototyping was seen as an indispensable and highly successful element for the analysis and specification phases. Criticism of the project came from various quarters, including Scandinavian journalists who saw this model of the application system as encroaching on activities which had previously been their responsibility.

## Conclusions

Here it is apparent that in specific areas prototyping may be highly dependent on the technical resources available. If, as in the case of this project, no suitable graphic systems or high–resolution display screens of the required size are available, a prototype can only implement certain limited features of the desired application system. This particular example, though, also indicates that creativity can help overcome technical constraints, even if plywood mock–ups and slide projectors may appear, at first sight, rather primitive means. In fact, this example from R & D practice merely serves to underline our previously expressed conviction that the limitations imposed by hardware and system software are no longer of any great significance today. As the UTOPIA project manager himself has pointed out (see [Ehn88]), a sufficient range of software tools has since become available for applications of this sort.

There is, however, one other point which we feel deserves attention. This is the fact that the participation of a single profession only in the development process evidently leads to conflicts of interest. Failure to involve other professions or user groups also affected by the system development is, in itself, enough to give rise to fears on the part of these groups about negative implications for their own professional status and influence.

### 4.5.4 Assessment of the Three Examples

In the case of the order processing system, the functional requirements and the technical implementation options were largely known in advance. An elaborate manual system for processing orders was already in existence; in other words, the functional specification of the software system was ready–provided. What remained to be done was to design the user interface and adapt the application system to the different user requirements and working routines existing within a multinational organization.

In the case of the Norwegian municipal planning departments, all the developers had to go on was an initial consensus among the groups involved on the need for an office system to support their work. The particular work area in question offered little scope for formalization owing to the complexity of the tasks involved. And the users themselves were not even sure about the desired functional scope of suitable computer support. One crucial constraint on the introduction of computer support was the need to take into account organizational and social factors as well as the industrial rights of those affected.

In the case of the Scandinavian graphic workers, predefined requirements and system specifications were almost totally lacking. The problem here was to redesign a particular work area, since rationalization measures had made it impossible to retain the existing professional profile. For this profession, then, new ideas were needed to develop technical support for new work tasks that it was impossible to define in advance. The search for suitable solutions also revealed that in many cases there were no suitable construction techniques available for the planned tools.

The three examples can now be looked at in relation to the different aspects of prototyping outlined in Section 4.1:

#### The Prototype in the Software Development Process

- In the case of the order processing system, a prototype was used to clarify design problems. The business needs and the functionality of the application system were largely determined in advance. To meet differing user requirements, alternative prototypes were developed; these were the subject of discussions between the various groups and user organizations. In this example, *prototypes proper* were used.

- In the case of the Norwegian municipal planning departments, a prototype was used to work out the desired scope and design options for an application system. Fully operational prototypes were installed in the application area itself, and these were used for step-by-step development of a common application system. Although the application area was limited at this stage, serving basically to test the system concept, the prototypes used were required to meet all the demands made on a *pilot system*.
- In the UTOPIA project, prototypes were used for experimental purposes. The aim of these experiments was to clarify, in a step-by-step process, the main problems associated with this work area and the introduction of new means of work. Evaluation of the technical options was only possible in conjunction with a comprehensive redefinition of work tasks. Here, the development process was not primarily geared to constructing a complete application system. The prototypes used served a wide variety of purposes and also differed in their technical characteristics. They ranged from *prototypes proper*, that served as a basis for discussions between the groups involved, to *breadboards*, that merely helped clarify questions of technical feasibility within the developer team.

## Goals of Prototype Construction

If we now consider the different goals pursued as a result of the different problems faced in each of the projects, we arrive at the following conclusions:

- In the case of the order processing system project, *experimental prototyping* was used. The basic concern here was with the technical design of the system and its user interface.
- The Norwegian municipalities focussed on the step-by-step development of a system within limited application areas. Here, a form of *evolutionary prototyping* was used.
- The Nordic graphic workers' project exhibits important features of *exploratory prototyping* – though, as yet, there has been no implementation of the prototypes and specifications in an application system.

## Horizontal and Vertical Prototyping

*Horizontal prototyping* was the main type of prototyping used in all three cases. Only in the UTOPIA project were specific tools built as *vertical prototypes* to enable questions of efficiency and problems of usability on workstations to be clarified.

### The Relationship between Prototype and Application System

In all three cases, the prototypes were viewed as part of the application system specification. The prototypes modelled important features of the target system. This relationship between the prototype and the application system might be considered typical of commercial applications programming for large and frequently used systems. Only in research projects or in the case of "single shot" developments are prototypes normally extended into application systems. The above examples show how prototyping can be meaningfully used for different purposes within a single development project, and they highlight the importance this approach may have for the project as a whole. By distinguishing between different aspects of prototyping, we hope to provide guidelines to facilitate understanding and support discussions on prototyping during software construction.

# 5 Evolutionary System Development

Prototyping is *one* approach existing alongside a number of others, such as the life cycle plan based on the "waterfall model". In our discussion of the different approaches, we have highlighted the benefits to be had from using prototyping to support project work as compared with classical project management strategies. So far, though, we have confined ourselves to looking at the individual software project, without mapping out a global view of software development. This is precisely what we set out to do in the following sections.

## 5.1 Evolutionary System Development

Evolutionary system development is a *view* of software development that – looked at in terms of its own development history – can be seen to have evolved from the critique of traditional approaches. It is not, however, a label for a new (or even better) process model; rather, it stands for a specific way of looking at software development in order to gain a better understanding of it.

For our present purposes, let us view software development with a certain degree of detachment and – instead of considering the mass of different–sized individual projects, each with its own specific approach – take a look at the evolving organization as a whole in which information systems and their technical core are embedded. Our interest does not extend to the evolution of an organization in general terms – for instance, how it reacts to changed market demands – but focusses rather on the changes brought about in the organization by information technology. After all, when we use the term *evolutionary system development*, we do not mean a mere "evolution of technology". Software systems can only be understood in the context of human society, so there is no point in talking about the (isolated) evolution of a program. What we mean by evolutionary system development are the changes occurring in an organization in correlation to the changes in information technology.[14]

To illustrate what we mean by evolutionary system development, let us take as an example the evolution of the automobile. The technical evolution of automobile production can, of course, be viewed as a process governed by economic and engineering factors. But the way society has evolved as a result of the growth of motor traffic is a subject involving consideration of such a wide variety of complex influences and effects that it is idle to attempt to explain the phenomenon in simple, straightforward terms such as: "People design cars and devise the means required for their use and further development". We must confine ourselves to the observation that both our urban and rural landscapes and the whole architecture of our cities have been transformed by the automobile, in the same

[14] This point is given detailed consideration in [Bahr83, Mumford77, MatVar87].

way as have our values, our patterns of behaviour and ways of looking at things in relation to this product of technology. This transformation has not taken place on an individual level only (even causing perceptible changes in the human physique), but has also given rise to phenomena such as commuting to work and mass tourism that have altered the face of society as a whole. An equally unforeseeable repercussion has been the retroactive effects these changes have had on the engineering disciplines involved in automobile production and on the automobile itself. In the field of software development, the example of Computer Aided Manufacturing (CAM) systems has served to show how developments of this sort can spark off such far-reaching changes in the user organizations that planners are frequently no longer able to control them (see [KerSchaff84]). However, the influence that the introduction of information technology (or changes in the way it is used) has on the working routines and interpersonal relations within a particular organization may take a less obvious form. We have already touched on the fact that the trend away from mainframes towards workstations has sparked off a wide variety of reactions in the organizations affected.

Adopting the evolutionary view, an individual software project may be seen as a relatively self-contained activity. It becomes evident, though, that by looking at an individual software project we are considering only a small slice of reality. What the "waterfall model" describes is simply what is considered to be the relevant period of time covering the actual (re-)programming of a software system. Such classical life cycle models fail to take any account of the way the organization reacts to a software system by adapting work procedures and paths of communication. Experience gained over the past twenty years has shown that this limited view of how information technology is manufactured, tested and used prevents proper attention being paid to the radical changes brought about in organizations by information technology. The negative repercussions of this situation even affect the technical production of application software. It has proved impossible either to form an idea of what "good software" really is, or for software developers to reach general agreement on sound ways of constructing good software. Hence the need to broaden our horizons with regard to software production, even where we are only concerned with software development "in the small". This is why the notion of *maintenance* from the classical process models acquires a new significance in our discussion. It not only accounts for approximately two thirds of the total technical effort required for developing and putting into use a software system, but also shows that far-reaching evolutionary processes are set in motion when a software system is installed, processes to which the developer is then obliged to react as part of so-called maintenance. Software developers tend to ignore the connections between the two. This would appear to be the only explanation for all the recent talk about "maintenance-free software". At the root of this notion is the old belief in the possibility of defining a problem completely and definitively and the idea that changes in information technology cause the human beings and organizations affected by them to *change in predictable ways only*.

Such beliefs are belied by the fact that it is impossible to describe the dynamic development and processes of change in human beings and organizations in terms of finite, discrete and fundamentally static software systems. Lehman has called this impossibility the "Principle of Uncertainty" (see [Lehman90]). Moreover, hopes of being able to reduce the influences exercised by the application area on a software system to the system's interfaces have proved illusory. Lehman points out that, according to conservative estimates, an external, application-specific assumption is made for every ten lines of program code written. Such assumptions can be invalidated by changes in the application area, and this in turn has a direct impact on the validity of the program. Thus, if "maintenance" is to be viewed as an evolutionary process, it is the developer's job to pinpoint and eliminate such unpredictable forms of what Lehman terms "software pollution".

The critique of traditional approaches and concepts presented in Section 3.4 can therefore be seen additionally from the perspective of evolutionary system development. It is not merely a technical question whether a project can and should be conducted along the lines of a classical life cycle plan. Since a software project inevitably sets in motion a process of organizational evolution, the question as to the methods and approaches to be adopted in software development needs reformulating in different terms: Which methods and approaches help to propel the evolution of an organization in a desired social and economic direction, and which approaches impede such an organizational evolution? After all, our objective as software engineers must surely be to enable people and organizations to achieve their goals more effectively *with the help of* and not *in spite of* the technical systems we develop.

Hence, the special perspective of evolutionary system development also involves posing the fundamental question as to the form meaningful support of the software development process should take:

- Communication between developers and users takes place throughout project run time and is not confined to the phases of user needs analysis and system installation.
- System development is a mutual learning process for all parties concerned, and not merely the process of transforming a specification into a target system.
- A system is built in a number of small work steps and parts of manageable size. This makes it possible to redefine or correct, step by step, the direction development is taking.
- Specification and implementation are connected, complementary activities. They cannot be divided up into consecutive phases.
- The development models are complemented as far as possible by operational software versions in order to allow and facilitate evaluation of the models early on in the development process.

## 5.2 Evolutionary System Development in Practice

In the following sections, we attempt to show that there are a number of procedures in use in practical software development in which the benefits of evolutionary system development become apparent. To illustrate this point, we have selected two examples of such procedures adopted during system installation. These are generally known as the *$\alpha$–$\beta$ test* and *versioning.*

### 5.2.1 The $\alpha$–$\beta$ Test Procedure

It is only over the last ten years that "off–the–shelf" application software has acquired economic significance. Today, most of the effort involved in producing such software focusses on desktop publishing, word–processing, spreadsheets and database–oriented application system generators. Compared with operating and database systems, for example, which hardware manufacturers and a few software firms have always supplied on a ready–made basis but which have only reached the user in the "guise" of application software, "off–the–shelf" application software must be much more easily adaptable to an existing organization. Consideration must be given, then, to the interaction between the organization and the application software. This means that manufacturers of such software can no longer close their eyes to the evolutionary view if they wish to be successful in marketing their product.

In the following example, we assume that a *manufacturer* undertakes to develop software for a *large number of users*, without being in a position, himself, to invest much effort in evaluation of the software once in use. Generally speaking, the manufacturer and the client are different organizations (in a legal sense), though in large institutions there are cases where internal cooperation between the computer department and various other departments of this type is handled in a similar way to the relations between a manufacturer and an external client. Difficulties in analyzing the application area and the complexity of the software involved make it impossible to use a life cycle plan, a fact that even software project managers are realistic enough to appreciate. On the other hand, it is unreasonable for a manufacturer to expect the whole of his clientele to try out for him software that has not yet been sufficiently tested. That is why software manufacturers are keen to find a "typical" user (or small group of users) to evaluate the software. The $\alpha$–$\beta$ test then takes the following form (see Fig. 17):

– The $\alpha$ version of the application system is tested internally by the manufacturer in the form of a prototype. Here, the developers anticipate the work of the users, performing what they consider to be typical working routines and modifying the prototype when errors or inconsistencies crop up. This is where a typical case of developer blindness occurs, due to the fact that they were the ones who constructed the software in the first place. Their knowledge of the way the software works makes them blind to the organizational context in which the future application system will actually be used. They use the software only in ways that appear plausible to them. Missing, unintelligible or incorrect parts of the documentation are frequently overlooked by the developers in the course of this internal evaluation. And, in our experience, this blindness cannot be remedied even when the developers themselves are aware of the problem.

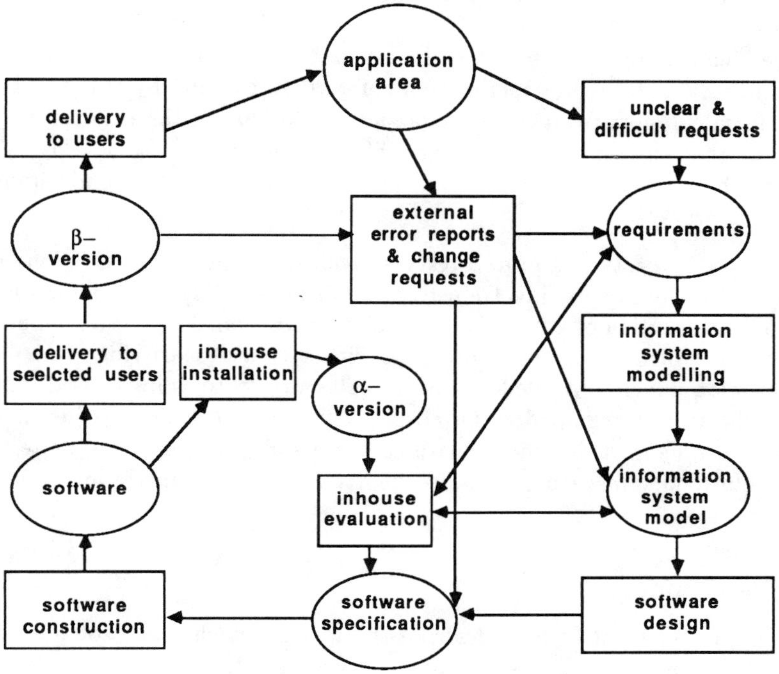


**Fig. 17.** The $\alpha$–$\beta$ test

– The $\beta$ version of the application system is tested by a small number of typical users. For this purpose, it is not unusual to create laboratory conditions and build a mock-up organization in which users pretend to go about their daily work. In many cases, though, the system is integrated directly in the users' daily working routines, after taking special precautionary measures. The users adopt different approaches from the developers in the way they use the new application system. They are unfamiliar with the "guts" of the software and are therefore obliged to interpret the documentation, and in particular the examples it contains, for their own specific purposes.
What is significant here is that the users are not merely being "misused" for the job of debugging. The whole point of the $\beta$ test is to determine whether the software supports the users' working routines, whether the users are able to cope with the system and keep track of what is going on, or whether the application system actually upsets familiar working routines and actions.

The $\alpha$–$\beta$ test offers benefits to both sides:

– The manufacturer gets software containing less errors and of improved quality as regards stability and usability. And he is able to refer other clients to

those acting as test users for information about the quality of the application system.
- The client acting as $\beta$ test user hopes to gain a lead over his competitors by being able to use a superior tool before they can and by enjoying better technical support from the manufacturer. In addition, the persons working within the test user organization are able to enhance their skill levels, because using the new application system helps them arrive at a better understanding of their work.

The use of prototyping in $\alpha$–$\beta$ tests is confined to internal evaluation of the system by the developers, involvement of "typical" users in the evaluation process, and construction of a "provisional" software version. There is no deliberate, planned experimentation with prototypes with a view to clarifying some predefined question under controlled conditions. The way prototyping is used in these tests might also be regarded as an abridged type of *pilot system* construction. On the other hand, this – on the whole successful – technique is quite obviously evolutionary in nature. It is frequently encountered in conjunction with *versioning*.

### 5.2.2 Versioning

Versioning is the term used to describe the way in which many software firms market their products and adapt them to the wishes of their clients. Development of a new software product is normally based on market analyses and client wishes or is originally inspired to a considerable extent by the developer's own needs.[15]

The difficult part is adapting the software product to user wishes, debugging the system after completing the $\alpha$–$\beta$ test if required, and delivering the product to a large number of users. This can only be done by subsequently delivering further updated versions, since it is no longer possible to modify each of the products originally delivered in its respective application environment.

With the increasingly widespread use of workstations and desktop computers, standard software products have acquired new significance. Whereas the normal price for big mainframe applications often exceeds the \$ 10,000 mark and installation figures even for a highly successful product are under 1,000 copies, the situation with respect to standard workstation and PC software is almost completely the reverse. Today, a good desktop publishing system for a workstation is to be had for around \$ 1,000 and the number of copies sold runs into the ten thousands. In order to be successful in this area of the market, developer firms have concentrated on attuning their products to user wishes and adapting their software to new requirements. An interesting feature here is that feedback takes place both on an individual level and in a broader context.

Direct feedback between users and developers is mainly taken care of via the usual written error reports. Numerous manufacturers do, however, also offer a hotline service enabling users to contact them directly by telephone. In addition, there are, for a number of products, established user groups that hold regular

[15] This is the case with Donald Knuth's TeX which was used to typeset this book.

national and even international meetings – generally in conjunction with conferences and exhibitions on the respective "computer family". It is quite normal, then, at meetings such as the MacWorld conference, for example, for the various suppliers of application software to present information and hold discussions on their particular domain of interest.

The forms of feedback mentioned so far are reliant on direct contact between the individual user or user organization and the manufacturer. Other – indirect – forms of feedback are, however, becoming increasingly important: for instance, the special magazines and journals dedicated to these types of computers which see themselves as relatively independent organs safeguarding the interests of the users and providing them with a forum to air their views. Lastly, there are the so–called newsgroups in the big computer networks such as *USENET* who see it as their concern to examine the pros and cons of new products for the various computer families that are currently the subject of international discussion. And it is not only the users who take an active part in this discussion, but representatives of the developer firms, too.

Around computer families such as the Macintosh and IBM PCs, user communities have grown up, each embodying a certain type of shared "computer culture". We see in this development the emergence of a special sort of tradition, evolving a collective reservoir of experience in the use of software systems that in turn shapes the future development of software.[16] One indication of this is the fact that the basic ideas behind these computers and the characteristic ways of handling them have tended to "rub off" on all the software products available for them and that the products themselves have tended to influence one another.

Let us take an example from the world of the Apple Macintosh. The features and functions of the editor and text formatter *MS Word* can scarcely be understood by looking at the current system and its documentation in isolation. It is important to know, first of all, that *MS Word* was originally developed for the IBM PC. The first Macintosh implementation therefore largely corresponded, in its functionality, to the IBM PC version. At the same time, though, *MS Word* was developed as a rival product to Apple's *MacWrite* and was consequently adapted to suit the typical Mac user interface and user behaviour. From there, we can trace a dense web of discussions in the corresponding *USENET* newsgroups (currently e.g. *comp.sys.mac.digest*) in the course of which the pros and cons of *MS Word* as compared with other similar systems were debated. However, it was not only these discussions that influenced the subsequent versions of *MS Word*. The success of systems like the so–called "idea processor" *More,* which allows tree–like structuring of texts, or desktop publishing software such as *PageMaker* has also played a significant role here.

If we now look at what we have just said from the point of view of evolutionary system development, we find that this form of version enhancement with its multifarious influences on software development is congenial to our own concept. But what becomes evident is the fact that, while we can talk about software

[16] We have discussed these ideas at greater length in [BudZue90].

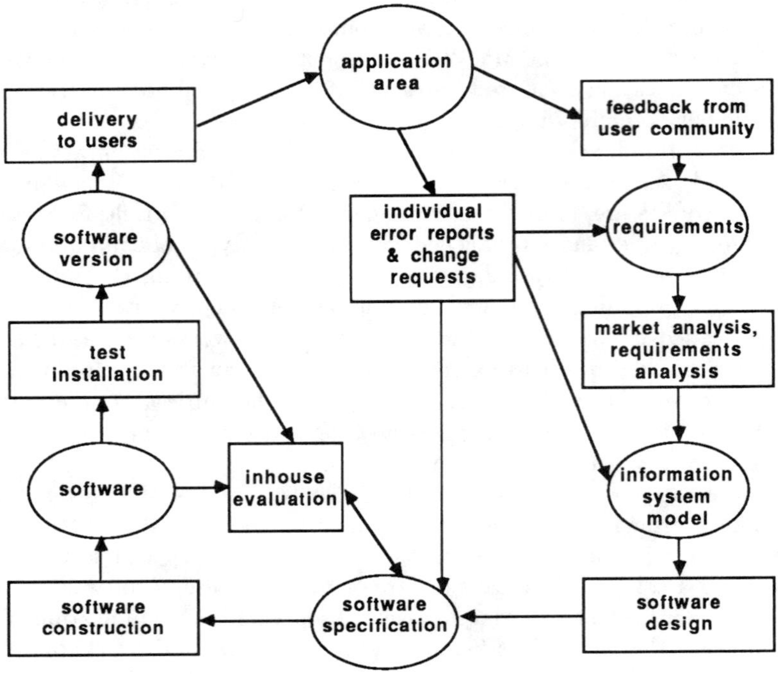


**Fig. 18.** Versioning

versions in evolutionary system development, we can no longer properly speak of prototypes. We illustrate this point in simplified form in Figure 18. Here, we attempt to show that both individual requirements and general trends and ideas originating in the user communities can act as a motor to system version enhancement.

The $\alpha$–$\beta$ test and versioning examples serve to illustrate the fact that, while prototyping may be considered an approach "in the spirit of evolutionary system development", the latter covers such a vast area of interaction between application systems and organizations that the term *prototyping* with its technical background and associations is inadequate to describe these phenomena. On the other hand, prototyping is an indispensable element in the software developer's repertoire if evolutionary system development is to be carried out successfully.

## 5.3 Problems Connected with System Development

In the early chapters of this book, we focussed on the problems encountered in software construction and showed that many of these problems can be overcome by using prototyping. We have now broadened our view of software development and found that it is invariably embedded in evolutionary processes. These processes must be given explicit consideration in the process model if we are to achieve better planning and control of them. The evolutionary system development perspective thus constitutes a frame for designing and organizing a software project with the help of concrete approaches and construction methods. Attempts to solve the problems in other ways are discussed in Section 5.3.1. The call for evolutionary processes to be taken into account can no longer be dismissed as a utopian demand: the social and technical "infrastructure" is already available (see Sec. 5.3.2).

### 5.3.1 Other Ways of Tackling the Problem

Let us now look at the attempt to deny the evolutionary nature of system development by buying ready-made software products from the manufacturer or a software firm. At first sight, this would appear to solve a number of technical problems by reducing the installation of software to a linear process. The success of personal computers has unquestionably given rise to a vast market for software products. Good-quality "off-the-shelf" software with sometimes excellent user documentation is available for a wide variety of applications. Selling software has become big business – Brooks describes it as "the most profound long-run trend in software engineering" (see [Brooks87]). He also points out, though, that the crucial question about the usability of this software still remains unanswered. Indeed, turnkey systems of this sort often prove to be unusable in the form they are delivered. Even if personal computers with ready-made application software are purchased, the amount of effort required to adapt these systems to the special features of the respective application is usually considerable. This effort involves not only making available "standard work objects" (in the case of word-processing these may be inhouse letter formats, address files or forms), but also modifying existing work procedures and responsibilities. In our example, this would mean sorting out who is responsible for address management, for drawing up and adapting forms, for purchasing printers and procuring material for them, etc. Irrespective, then, of the question "Buy or develop-it-yourself?", there is evidently a need to adapt and evolve information systems in organizations.

This means that "off-the-shelf" software needs adapting, too, and this can entail a lot of work. The effort involved here may, however, not be quite so evident at first sight since, in most cases, it relates more to the working routines and forms of organization than to the software itself.

Another instance of the endeavours to ignore the necessity of an evolutionary approach to the development of information systems can be seen in efforts to step up project control. Such efforts aim at restricting communication within the development team and focussing development work on a set of definitively defined tasks whose intelligibility is not limited to a specific context.[17] This view – governed by short-term economic considerations – is at the root of decisions to set up programming pools or assign responsibility for analysis, specification and implementation to separate project members or groups.

[17] By doing so it is also hoped to be able to employ less skilled software developers and thus do away with the effort needed to train them.

Characteristic of such endeavours to step up project control is the fact that they view feedback cycles, communication within the development team and with the users, and the continuous adaptation of the information system to changing requirements not as a matter of course, but rather as a problem. To minimize such "problems", extensive control and monitoring mechanisms are built into the development process – mechanisms that tend to acquire a significance of their own. Such mechanisms include the so-called milestone documents, which are designed exclusively for the benefit of the project management and which assess the work of the developers in terms of lines of code.

There is a danger here of project control degenerating into a sort of "parallel reality" where those affected are deluded into believing that the evolutionary nature of information systems can be simply ignored. We often hear from developers engaged in commercial software development that this form of project control exists, as it were, in a realm of its own, quite divorced from the reality of the organizations concerned.[18]

Let us consider the chief programmer team. Though seldom encountered in its "pure form", it may nevertheless serve as a good example of the attempt to implement the assumptions behind the classical life cycle models in terms of project organization (see [KiKoSiTo79]). In the chief programmer team, the hierarchical decomposition of a problem into specifications and solutions derived from them is reflected in the distribution of tasks among the following persons: the chief programmer, his direct subordinate the project assistants, the project secretary, and the programmers responsible for subtasks. The underlying assumption of the life cycle models that a project can be decomposed into completely self-contained subtasks is implemented here in practical terms by the chief programmer or his assistant assigning precisely defined work packets to each programmer on the basis of a fixed specification. Each work packet involves complete programming or testing of a software module, and this task is to be performed without the collaboration of other programmers.

The attempt to minimize communication and cut down feedback within the team means that the individual programmers may only communicate with their superiors in the hierarchy and have no chance to reach agreements amongst themselves on the tasks assigned to them and the problems they face. In addition, the strict separation of design, construction and testing activities and the distinction made between productive and administrative tasks in the division of labour between the chief programmer, the project assistant, the project secretary and the programmers mean that each project "role" may only perform specific tasks. For instance, the project secretary may be in charge of the entire text documentation and program and test execution, whereas the project assistant is the only person authorized to supply the test data.

But what is the good of this sort of project organization? It is, we agree, an indisputable fact that clear task definition and controlled documentation produce better technical results than uncontrolled, undisciplined work. The work

[18] We know of cases where, for the benefit of management, already completed software projects had to be redocumented along traditional life cycle lines.

organization in the chief programmer team, modelled as it is on that of a team of surgeons, also helps enhance the efficiency of a single outstanding software expert directing a team of inexperienced programmers. The fact remains, though, that most software projects are not conducted along these lines. Moreover, this type of project organization is inconsistent with two fundamental considerations that we have previously emphasized:

- It is essential to improve communication and feedback between all persons involved in software development, rather than attempting to minimize them.
- Software development must be seen in the context of changes in the overall information system of an organization and cannot be treated as an isolated technical problem.

It follows, then, that projects based on the idea of greater project control can only be successful *in spite of*, not *because of* the chosen project form. This is also the tenor of reports on the work of chief programmer teams or similar forms of hierarchical project organization. The projects either failed or were completed at exorbitant cost. The typical conclusion reached is that it would have been better to have the entire system developed by a small, skilled team working on a cooperative basis.

### 5.3.2 Evolutionary System Development is Necessary

Our reflections on how to overcome the problems outlined above are by no means new. Numerous system developers have long been aware that software cannot be produced along traditional life cycle lines. The problems connected with the initial development and subsequent enhancement of information systems cannot be solved by simply streamlining project organization, by efforts towards formalization or the use of new tools. What we choose to call a process of rethinking in software development (cf. also [Floyd89]) is not a "revolutionary" concept. Quite the reverse: evolutionary system development and prototyping stand for a way of thinking already "secretly" adopted by numerous successful developers, despite project guidelines to the contrary. If this is so, we are justified in asking why large companies still insist on refining and implementing classical life cycle plans. And it is, at first sight, rather puzzling that criticism of such concepts should only have met with any real response in the last few years.[19]

If we consider the current situation of commercial data processing, we find that here discussions on development methods have only just begun. A computer department or software firm is, then, going to be extremely reluctant to abandon overnight a life cycle plan it has only just adopted and switch to a concept of evolutionary system development with prototypes. In the way of such a move are also problems connected with training developers (see [Brooks87]).

The adherence to traditional approaches is, however, only one aspect of the current situation. The concepts behind evolutionary system development are not

[19] It is worth recalling that the few conferences held on the subject on prototyping did not take place until the 1980s.

merely the result of the criticism levelled at traditional approaches by a handful of theoreticians. As far as the software engineering discussion goes, the opposite is the case. In the past, it is true, software engineering was chiefly concerned with development strategies in which evolutionary system development had no place. But this situation has changed over the last few years (cf. [Boehm88]). In both the research and development and commercial data processing sectors, the pace at which workplaces and working routines are being changed by information systems, reinforced by the speed at which the technical base of the information systems themselves is being refined, has resulted in new situations and new ways of thinking. The arguments in favour of approaches such as object–oriented modelling are no longer of a merely technical nature, but are also influenced by the discussion on prototyping and evolutionary system development (cf. [Meyer88]).

In the following sections, we examine the changes in the technical base and use of information systems that have helped to make evolutionary system development concepts not only a necessity today, but also a real possibility.[20]

### 5.3.3 Evolutionary System Development is Possible

#### Hardware and Software Trends

Our look at the first life cycle plans (cf. Sec. 4) showed that, owing to the high cost and low capacity of hardware and software systems, software development was predominantly governed by technical constraints. Today, however, high–capacity hardware and good basic software have become so reasonably priced that they have ceased to constitute a limited commodity for the software developer.

There is no need to cast our minds back nostalgically to the 1960s and recall the IBM/360 (priced at around $ 500,000) in order to appreciate the drastic changes which have taken place in this sector. Comparison of a ten–year–old Z80 computer under CPM with one of today's 68030 PCs under Unix suffices to show how technological developments have raced ahead here. 1976 saw the launching of the Altair 8800, the first "off–the–shelf" microcomputer to come on the market. In 1982, an Apple II was priced at around $ 5,000. In early 1990, firms like SUN, Texas Instruments and Apollo were offering workstations with the same capacity as earlier mainframes for well under $ 20,000. Desktop computers like the Atari or Apple Macintosh can be paid for today out of the postage funds.

Also on the market are high–performance operating systems, modern programming languages, interactive programming environments and an abundance of programming tools. Operating systems like Unix are tailored to the needs of interactive software development. The command languages they provide are sufficiently powerful for constructing simple prototypes.

Very High Level Languages like Lisp, Prolog and Smalltalk are available as interpreters or with "interpreter-like" incremental compilers. And there are now

[20] Similar arguments are presented in [FriCor85, Floyd87].

so many so–called "4th generation languages" available for developing database applications that it has become practically impossible to keep track of them. There are also numerous application systems (such as dBase or Lotus1–2–3) on the market, providing various types of integrated packages for data management, spreadsheet programs, graphic applications and word–processing. The programming of interactive applications has been standardized and simplified by systems like X Windows or the Macintosh Toolbox.

Today, computing speed, storage capacity and software support have reached such levels that the fast development cycles and interactive software construction required for evolutionary system development no longer constitute a technical problem.

### Changed User Requirements

As we pointed out at the beginning of this section, evolutionary system development invariably involves the question of values, too. What this means, basically, is that the values held by the users of software systems are given greater consideration in the system development process. Today, interactive application systems are used widely on workstations. Their user interface is tailored to the specific application in hand and is graphic–oriented. At one time, the computer department constituted the only door to the world of data processing. Nowadays, though, workstations or microcomputers are often purchased and installed by the users themselves, without any direct involvement of the computer departments.

According to the findings of a survey carried out in the United States as early as 1984 (see [Canning84a]), personal computers were used by executives and clerical staff in three quarters of the 71 medium– to large–sized companies looked at, by management in approximately half of them, and for secretarial work in about a third of them.

Changes in the way computers are employed have caused users to make greater demands with respect to convenience of handling. Interactive user facilities are considered state–of–the–art nowadays. Smalltalk and the Xerox workstations may be regarded as trailblazers in user interface design, and, following in their footsteps, Apple Macintosh has set new standards in user convenience for professional applications as well. To begin with, pointer devices like the mouse were either ignored altogether or regarded as cheap publicity stunts.[21] Today, though, the "direct manipulation" principle behind them has acquired crucial importance in numerous successful application systems (cf. [NorDra86]).

But user requirements for software systems have not only changed in step with developments in the workstation sector. Whatever our opinion of computer games may be, there is no denying their influence on commercial software production. Today's users of commercial software systems have come to expect the same sort of ready intelligibility and easy handling of graphic elements provided by a microcomputer games program. They are, however, frequently confronted

[21] The first mouse–oriented Hypertext system was implemented by Douglas Engelbart as early as 1968. See [Conklin87].

by the situation that the systems installed at their workplace are – compared with the average games program – unintelligible and complicated to use.

The "user–unfriendly" image of existing "traditional" software is fostered by software suppliers with promotion slogans suggesting that the use of "new" software systems presents no problems at all. The current promotion trend is for computer systems and software products to be extolled as some sort of revolutionary panacea that eliminates the problems faced once and for all.

What these increased user requirements mean in terms of our discussion as a whole is that a great deal more flexibility is called for in adapting application systems to user working routines. It is understandable, then, that the current technical discussion on software quality criteria focusses on aspects such as user convenience, changeability and compatability with other systems (see [Meyer88]). In terms of the development process, this means that software development is no longer seen as taking the form of an isolated project, beginning with the user needs analysis and ending with system delivery, but as the process of constantly adapting software to the changing requirements and wishes of the users. There is, then, a close correlation between evolutionary system development and increased user requirements.

### New Influential User Groups

It is, however, not only the user requirements with respect to the design of application systems that have changed in recent years. There have also been changes in the structure of user groups within the individual organizational hierarchy. "Data processing" is no longer the sole reserve of data typists and a handful of computer specialists. The former group's influence within the organizational hierarchy is (and has always been) extremely limited. The latter group has largely been able to realize its demands on its own; and, being made up of computer specialists, it has shown little interest in the development of good user interfaces, dismissing efforts in this direction as "goodies" for the "non-professional" user.

As workstations become more widely available, they are also finding their way into the higher echelons of user organizations. Here, their function is, in most cases, not merely that of a desktop "status symbol": computer support has become an indispensable element in management's everyday work, not only in banks and insurance companies.

Today, batch processing of large quantities of data can undoubtedly still be encountered in commercial data processing – in accounting, for instance. The problems, however, are posed by new application areas for which general conceptual solutions have still to be found. Support is frequently required for activities that are difficult to formalize and that leave a great deal of scope as regards system design. These include: word–processing, support of clerical duties, communication systems and systems for processing information as a basis for management decision–making. The users working in these areas occupy positions of influence and have precise ideas about how computers can be used meaningfully to support their work.

Two important points are addressed here: the need to develop flexible, interactive systems for which, as a rule, no ready–made model exists; and the fact that developers are obliged to come to terms with user groups who, when faced with obvious system defects, are unwilling to be fobbed off by having their signature on the user signoff held up to them. This change in the structure of user groups means that evolutionary system development is not just a process necessarily taking place within an organization, but largely eluding control. Instead, we have influential users demanding continuous and controlled adaptation of software to their working environment.

## Software Construction Techniques

If we consider how software construction has changed in recent years, we find that the elaboration of concepts for evolutionary system development is closely tied up with this process of change. Traditional software construction was – as we have pointed out a number of times already – associated with batch processing on mainframes and paper producing. Inputting and compiling source code, combining individual modules to produce an operational software system and, lastly, testing this system were separate, time–consuming work–steps. In view of the type of work organization required by a mainframe, the amount of work that had to be performed prior and subsequent to each one of these steps was quite considerable. Moreover, the development effort required was such as to make it worthwhile producing detailed drafts of software systems on paper, reducing actual computing to a minimum in favour of code reviews and post–mortem dump analyses.

Batch processing is incompatible with evolutionary system development, mainly because repeatedly modifying software is a very expensive business. The same applies to prototyping: constructing "incomplete" experimental systems in a world of batch programming requires considerable additional effort. Prototyping involves writing special test environments, simulating the not yet existent system components by means of stubs. Here, special test case definitions and file management procedures are normally required.

In contrast, the developments in hardware and software outlined in Section 5.3.3 provide the basis for interactive programming. Interactive command languages were needed in conjunction with screen–oriented editors, fast compilers and linkage editors or interpreted programming languages before a work–style could emerge that allowed a swift succession of design, construction and testing activities. Interactive programming enables step–by–step documentation of the development process to be performed directly on the computer.

Interactive programming supports evolutionary system development as an explicit goal. Software developers tend to adopt the above work–style anyway, with its swift cyclical alternation between the various activities. What is still needed is the explicit integration of this new individual work–style into an overall development concept.

## The Professional Profile of the Software Engineer

So far, we have highlighted various factors relating to technical advances and system development requirements that underline the need for and implementability of new approaches. The question that remains to be answered is whether evolutionary system development is a realistic concept from the point of view of the software developers' profession as a whole. In the nineteen–sixties and seventies, two distinct groups of software developers were discernable, differing considerably as regards their training and the type of jobs they were required to do.

On the one hand, there is the group of "programmers by adoption" who came originally from other professions and were retrained during the period when computer technology was expanding rapidly. Generally speaking, their training was confined to learning a single programming language (usually Assembler or COBOL) for use on one specific type of computer. The assignments given to these programmers in the computer departments are normally restricted to "programming in the small" on the basis of detailed instructions. Their many years of experience with numerous, often quite similar, programs, their familiarity with every nook and cranny of the particular language they have been trained to use, and their detailed knowledge of application systems that are frequently undocumented but crucial to the internal functioning of the organization in question, make them indispensable members of that organization. The programmers belonging to this group are adherents of the traditional approach to software construction and are generally reluctant to adjust to basic technical changes or accept having to deal with end users.

The other group – quite distinct from the first – is that of the "computer experts" who have enjoyed proper technical training and see themselves as professionals specializing in computer applications and software development. This group is very limited.in size, most of its members occupying leading positions in computer departments. These experts – insofar as they are still personally engaged in the development of software systems – tend to cut themselves off from the users, their attitude being: "We know what the users *really* want".

The traditional profile of the computer professional began to change as courses of study in computer science were introduced at universities and the profession of the trained computer technologist became established. Basic knowledge about computers and software development has since become available on a much wider basis, and the command of a standard set of software engineering techniques is considered part and parcel of the basic skills of today's software engineers. Their training includes the practical use of a number of high level programming languages and also deals with the problems of project organization and communication between developers and users. This "new generation" of software engineers is accustomed to using interactive systems that can be developed incrementally, and the number of software engineers who see evolutionary system development as part of their everyday work is growing rapidly.

### 5.3.4 Restoring Instead of Demolishing

Prototyping as part of evolutionary system development is not confined to the development of new software.[22] The reason why prototyping has attracted the attention of so many scientists and practitioners is the dramatic change in the overall conditions for software construction over the last ten years. Today's software developers are no longer in the position of having to start again from stratch each time, as was the case in the sixties and seventies: consideration must be given to the numerous software systems already in existence. Indeed, existing systems – constructed with the help of various technologies – form an integral part of practically every information system in use in organizations today. The question arising here is how such systems may co-exist with new or restored ones in terms of an *ecology of computer science.*[23] Obviously, many of the older systems do not meet the requirements for state–of–the–art user interfaces, security standards and software architecture. On the other hand, it makes no sense – and it is scarcely feasible – to demolish the technical parts of an information system and construct a new one. Ecological insights suggest that reconstruction and restoration are the only ways of solving these problems, although this is an endless task that may involve the careful replacement of unmaintainable parts with new ones.[24]

Software reconstruction can only be carried out step by step and in conjunction with extensive experimentation. It is impossible to draw up a plan for, say, the next ten years and closely adhere to it. Experiments conducted during software reconstruction should be given technical support by prototyping; this would appear to be the only way of acquiring knowledge about how to replace outdated parts.

One particular problem here is the co–existence of many different technologies. Hopes that some day we may arrive at a uniform technological platform are little more than naive illusions. Professional computing and data processing in organizations must come to terms with this problem of heterogeneous technologies. To illustrate the point, let us consider the following list of systems and environments that might be encountered within a single organization:

- Hierarchical database systems, COBOL, and old-fashioned TP-monitors.
- SQL and relational database systems in conjunction with 4th generation languages on a mainframe.
- Workstations with Unix in a network, programmed in C++ and supported by the OSF-Motif graphical user interface.

[22] We are greatly indebted to Reinhold Turner of Delta Software Technologie AG for many of the insights incorporated into this section.

[23] Brooks follows a similar line of reasoning when he states that the more appropriate type of incremental development strategy employed today can best be paraphrased by the metaphor "growing software".

[24] Note the similarity to city planning: in Central Europe at least, it is no longer considered a responsible policy to demolish whole urban districts and build new blocks on top of the rubble.

- Desktop computers allowing the representation and publication of sophisticated graphics. Hypermedia systems with "esoteric" peripherals like scanners, compact–discs incorporating databases, animation, speech, etc.

Each of these co-existing technologies has its own specific application domain and user community. Attempts to simplify this situation by standardizing software have failed, mainly because the influence of software engineers has been considerably weakened in recent years. Preplanned software development within a technically uniform frame is playing a losing game in commercial software development. What is needed is careful, step–by–step cooperation with all the parties involved. The communicative, organizational and technical problems encountered during system development can only be solved in a practical, experimental manner. The prototypes used in evolutionary system development are not fancy novelties, soon destined to disappear behind new buzzwords. In our view, they constitute a practical step towards ecological thinking in software development.

## Summary

Evolutionary system development is possible and necessary because:

- Small, high–capacity computers are available at a reasonable price.
- High–performance languages and development tools are available.
- Interactive application systems are "standard" software on workstations.
- Users have become more demanding in their requirements.
- Influential users groups have begun to voice their demands.
- There is a clear trend towards interactive programming.
- A new professional profile is being created by a new generation of software engineers.

Evolutionary system development makes sense because:

- Software systems evolve and are no longer constructed from scratch.
- Restoration instead of demolition is in keeping with the spirit of the times.
- We are faced with the co–existence of different technologies.
- Experimentation enables us to construct interfaces between systems built using different technologies. There is no other remedy to the problem.

# 6
# Evolutionary Process Models

So far, we have looked at system development *analytically* in order to highlight the problems associated with software construction and their proposed solutions. We now go on to translate the results of this critical analysis into *constructive* development strategies. Here, a number of ideas have been put forward by computer scientists, all of them designed to avoid the weaknesses of traditional life cycle plans (see [FloyReisSchm89, Boehm88, BjerEhnKyng87]). We attempt to integrate these ideas into our own process model of evolutionary system development which emphasizes the conscious process of changing a user organization. Like any other model, our process model is based not only on technical and task–related considerations, but also on the personal values and views of those involved as to what software development is all about:

- Software developers should base their design decisions on the wishes and conceptions of the future users of an application system.
- Since it is impossible to completely anticipate the requirements and implications of a software system, design must focus on the modifiability and integratability of a system as well as the reusability of the parts already developed.
- To enable those involved in the development process to make a better assessment of the changes brought about by the installation of a software system, thus allowing them to react as swiftly as possible to undesirable changes, a software system must be developed step by step and be installed and tested on an experimental basis.

Thus, our process model of software development is subject to the following organizational constraints:

- The various activities forming part of the development process should not be seen as following a strict temporal sequence, but rather as different activities that are interlinked. Explicit provision must be made for feedback.
- The different models generated during the development process have to be checked with respect to their correctness and suitability. Feedback therefore means verifying the models and comparing them with the users' requirements and knowledge. Design, construction and evaluation are all equally important activities, and this fact must be taken into account when specifying the intermediate results of a software project.
- The software development models should be available not only in the form of written documents, but also as provisional operational software systems. A software project's overall concept must provide for the construction of such software and the stepwise introduction of software components.

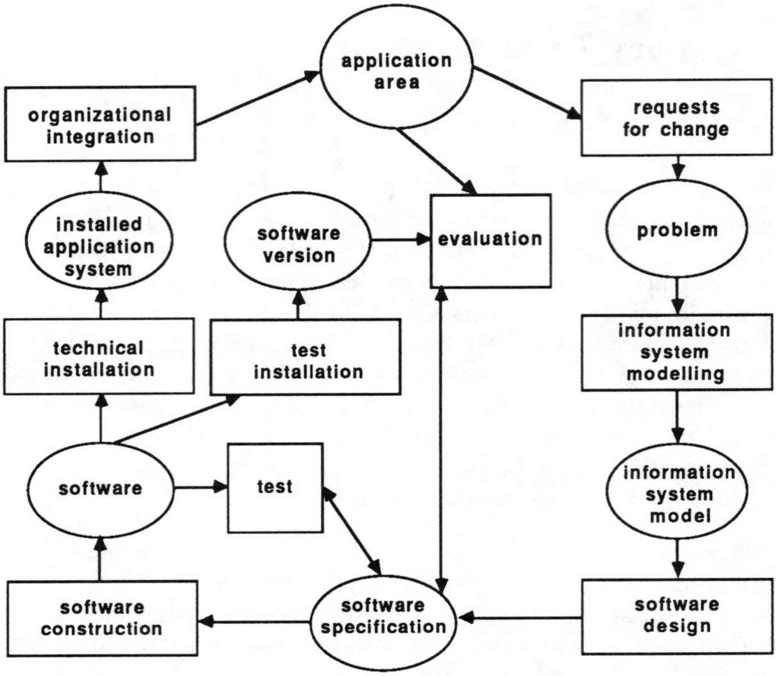


**Fig. 19.** Software version

In order to visualize this, we re-interpret the schema previously used to illustrate what we mean by the term *prototyping* (see Fig. 19). In evolutionary system development, we are not only concerned with the stepwise development of prototypes, but also in the long term – as we have shown in Section 5.3.4 – with the step-by-step further development of an application system. We use the term *software version* to indicate these common features of prototype and application system:

- Selected requirements for a software system are incorporated into an executable program, taking the form of a breadboard, and tested by the developers.
- The tested software is installed for evaluation by the users and developers: depending on this software's completeness and consistency, its validation is carried out either by the developer team on a development computer under "laboratory conditions" or in a selected part of the application area, at a particular workplace, for instance. This is why we use both the term *prototype* and the more general term *software version*. The different software versions are tried out by the users and then modified and extended by the developers.

- Software versions that are judged to be usable[25] are ultimately integrated into the application system, either by re–implementation (where the prototyping aspect is to the fore) or by mere organizational integration (where the evolutionary aspect is predominant).
- During integration, further components usually have to be added, e.g., error handling, (re–)start routines, help functions, etc. Frequently, the differences between the development and the target computer have to be taken into account. It is mostly not until this phase that the system is connected up to the respective technical environment, e.g., the "real" database.[26]
- The application system is, then, ultimately built and evaluated on the basis of the revised software specification and the software versions. Its use in an everyday working situation gives rise, on the one hand, to user wishes for improvement of the system – these relating to the faulty implementation of the specification – and, on the other, to new requirements concerning the enhancement of the information system as a whole.

The development and further development of a software system are not, then, confined to software construction in its restricted sense (see Fig. 20):

- Testing and evaluation of software versions clarifies and changes the original problem. Aspects relating to the system's dynamic behaviour – scarcely conceivable on the basis of a static specification – now become the subject of discussion. What appeared useful at the beginning of the development process may well turn out to be impracticable in the concrete application situation. This leads to changed requirements. The evaluation of a software version by the users is often the first clear indication the developers get of how the problems that have been articulated are connected with the working situations in the application area. The relations between a number of different factors, which have so far remained implicit (and which it is scarcely possible to make explicit), now become manifest for the first time.
- By handling operational versions, users and developers are able to visualize and assess the organizational constraints and implications of the system's future installation and use in the application area. Test installation of a system at a particular workplace can often help to show whether there is any real possibility of the system's being meaningfully employed by its future user. A number of other more general problems, too, such as access rights, data protection, the division of labour and rulings on working hours, only become evident as a result of handling a concrete software version, the perusal of lengthy specifications having failed to make these issues explicit. To this extent, evaluation by the groups involved in the development process helps to pave the way for the organizational integration of the future application system.

---

[25] Such a judgement can be arrived at in different ways, for example, by users and developers reaching a consensus, or by a management decision.

[26] The tests and technical checks carried out during this phase have been omitted to avoid overloading Figure 20.

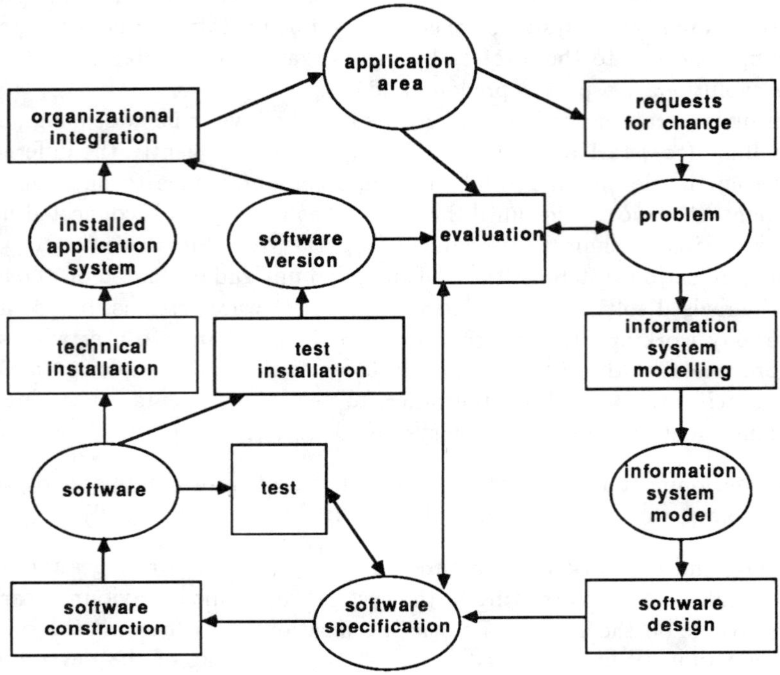


**Fig. 20.** Evaluation of software versions

- The conceptual basis of many newly developed systems and extensions to systems already in use testifies to a certain blindness to similar existing and contiguous systems. Only once the system is installed on a trial basis in a realistic working environment does it become obvious that the new version has indirect implications for existing systems. Frequently, its practical use on an experimental basis helps to reveal relations and incompatibilities that the specifications have failed to pick up. The more sophisticated the information technology installed within a particular organization, the more serious the implications of these relations are.

Our *process model of evolutionary system development* does not, then, merely describe a process aiming at technical optimization of software design and construction, but also an approach focussing on the continuous adjustment of requirements on different technical, organizational, economic and social levels and a process of pondering on the changes that gradually become apparent. To help illustrate this in diagrammatic terms, we have added to our figure feedback cycles that are necessary for interlinking the various specification, construction and evaluation activities. The result is a graphic representation of our process model of evolutionary system development (see Fig. 21).

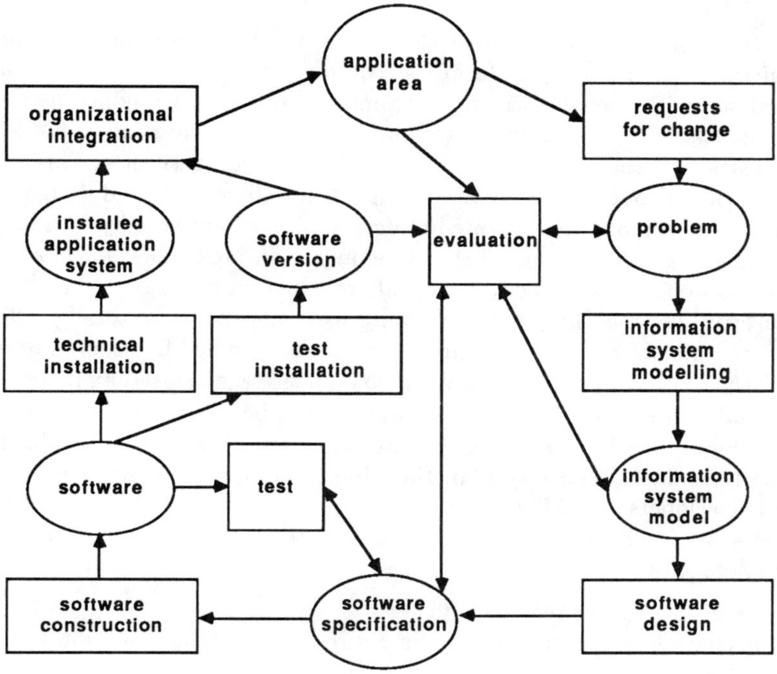


**Fig. 21.** Process model of evolutionary system development

## 6.1 Technical Implementation of Software Versions

In the previous section, we proposed a general approach to evolutionary system development. We now go on to clothe this conceptual framework with technical substance. Recent years have seen the development of numerous concepts and tools for software construction that have not focussed explicitly on the production of software versions. Nonetheless, we find that quite a number of these are well suited for what we consider to be efficient and technically sophisticated software construction. Before proceeding, in part two of our book, to examine the techniques and tools that play an important part today in "pure" prototyping, we have singled out a few of these that we consider to be particularly well integrated and relevant for evolutionary system development. These are:

- object–oriented design,
- the client–supplier model,
- the separation of interaction and functionality,
- the model–view–controller paradigm.

### 6.1.1 Object-Oriented Design

*Object-oriented* design can be used to describe the structure and development of a software system, starting from its requirements definition to its final operational state. Within the scientific community, object-orientedness is viewed predominantly as a programming technique: data representation is hidden by using classes, and code redundancy is avoided by using inheritance. This view is no doubt correct, but there is more to it than that: object-oriented design opens up the path to a more user-oriented understanding of software by focussing on ways of handling objects, while at the same time retaining the developer-oriented aspects of an object as part of a technical construction process.

The term *object* is the pivot connecting what appear to be totally different aspects: objects are *conceptual entities* that can be handled by users in order to perform their everyday work tasks. An invoice, a letter, a printer, an index-card, a chart – all of these are work objects that have to be represented in a software version (and eventually in the final application system) if we wish to enable users to properly evaluate such a system. But objects are also *technical entities* that software developers are able to work with.[27]

Object-oriented programming is usually characterized (cf. e.g. [Wegner87, BuKuSyZu89]) by

- message-passing between objects,
- encapsulation of design decisions in classes (comparable with the principle of abstract data types),
- inheritance among classes.

If we go beyond programming to take a more general look at object-oriented design, we find there is a way of formalizing the concepts and terminology of an application field in terms of an inheritance structure.

Object-oriented design means, first of all, deciding on the objects needed to design the software system. This modelling activity usually starts from "real" objects in the users' working environment. As we reconstruct these objects into objects in the software system, we group similar objects into classes. Features shared by different classes, i.e., similarities in the behaviour of their objects, are incorporated into a common *superclass* whose behaviour is *inherited* by its subclasses.[28] Many of the similarities that we express as inheritance structures among classes are also encountered in the application area. This approach to object-oriented modelling frequently leads to a simulation of entities from the application area in a mimetic "computer world". Within certain limits, mimetic software systems enable users to retain a considerable portion of their skills and knowledge about their own work area in a changed environment.[29]

[27] For a more precise definition of object-oriented terminology and modelling, we recommend consulting the literature on object-oriented languages[BiDaMyNy79, Goldberg84, Strous86, Meyer88], and on the appropriate concepts[CaWe85, WirfsWilk89, KraPop88].

[28] A detailed discussion of this approach and its advantages as compared with conventional modelling procedures may be found in [Meyer88].

[29] We have examined some of the problems behind this metaphor in [BudZue90].

Going beyond these already existing similarities, the attempt is made, by a systematic reconstruction of terms, to arrive at additional classifications facilitating the design of the technical aspects of the software system.

Object–oriented design may provide the key for solving the notorious communication problems encountered in system development. And it can help to reshape requirements engineering in such a way that it is understood by all parties involved. A modelling technique must, after all, provide a basis for talking about software both as a formalism (when attempting to *explain* its functionality) and as an element of our work (when attempting to *understand* its use).

This is the key to understanding the close relationship between object–oriented modelling as a technique and evolutionary system development as a strategy. From a methodological point of view, entities are designed as classes and class relations that can be used by the developers as building blocks for a software system; these same entities, when implemented as stubs or as inefficient prototypes, can be evaluated experimentally by the users. Once we have decided to use object–oriented modelling, we have both the means for technical design of a software system and for representation of important aspects of the application area in terms that can be understood and handled by the users. Hence, the differences between an inefficient, and perhaps unsafe, prototype and a technically sound and efficient final system may be considered *representation details* without any serious side–effects on the technical development process.

### 6.1.2 The Client–Supplier Model

In contrast to object–oriented design, which constitutes more of a general perspective and approach to application system development, the *client–supplier model* (see [Meyer88]) offers an *interpretation* of the relationship between the different software components of a system, thus supporting understanding of it on the part of both the developers and users.

The basic tenor of this model is that the components of a system both supply operations and make use of the operations provided by other components. This results in a network of client–supplier relations. Questions such as "Who supplies what?" and "Who is responsible for meeting a specific requirement?" can be answered by using this model. What this means for the developers of software components is that, when building a component that needs operations from other suppliers, only minimal interfaces of these other components should be known. Following the principle of information hiding, an interface of this sort should be designed in such a way that, wherever possible, the changes to a component remain hidden in its "interior", without being noticed by any of the clients.

But the model can be given an even broader interpretation: the operations provided by a supplier and, under certain conditions, made use of by a client may be expressed in terms of a contractual relationship. What we are concerned with here, then, is the reliability and soundness of system components. The conditions that the client must fulfil in order that the supplier can guarantee the operations it provides and the operations the supplier must provide in order that the client can get on with its work can be expressed in terms of a contract between the components, and thus formally specified as well. The greater the degree of independence of the individual components, the greater the importance of the client–supplier model. It is not surprising, then, that this model has met with an extremely positive response in object–oriented design. The object–oriented language Eiffel, for example, allows a client–supplier contract – or parts of it – to be expressed formally in terms of pre– and post–conditions of message–passing and class invariants that must be guaranteed by all objects of the class. In this way, parts of the requirements definition and system design, which can normally only be formulated in natural language, acquire an understandable interpretation. It is of particular importance for evolutionary system development that the contracts forming part of the client–supplier model can be specified prior to implementation of the respective operations. When using a language like Eiffel for object–oriented design, such contracts are also integrated into the inheritance mechanism, which means that subclasses are bound to the contracts concluded in superclasses.

The client–supplier model thus fulfils two seemingly contradictory requirements: on the one hand, it offers support in building a complex system incrementally from small comprehensive parts, each of which may first be implemented as a prototype; and, on the other, it serves to ensure the safety and integrity of the overall system, being able to provide declarations about the interconnection of the different parts.

### 6.1.3 The Separation of Interaction and Functionality

For interactive application systems, the *separation of interaction and functionality* is becoming a predominant construction scheme. Its major advantage is that a functional kernel can be supplemented by various different user interfaces which can be attuned to individual user needs and requirements. This obviously supports the idea of building several different software versions as design options. But it also enables us to provide different front–ends for a single system kernel without the need for far–reaching changes to the software.

In software versions, we draw a distinction between the part controlling the *interaction* and the part implementing the actual *functionality*. This is the main requirement for a division of software development into these two components, and thus for a (from the software engineer's point of view) clear separation of the software's handling characteristics from its functionality.

- The *functional component* is the effectuating and probing part of an interactive system. It implements the *services* and *operations* provided. If a suitable programming language is used, the functional components can be constructed "close" to an intelligible formal calculus.[30] In this case, the functional component can also be viewed as an executable specification. This meets the requirement of "easy" validation.
- The *interactive component* governs the way in which the user is able to *handle* the software. As we shall proceed to show, the interactive component

[30] The most important languages and their calculi will be dealt with in Chapter 10.

should be based on predefined building blocks, so–called interaction types. There are, it seems, few programming languages that provide as part of their standard repertoire the necessary constructs for supporting construction of the interactive component. Such sets of interaction types for the technical implementation of interactive software are, however, available as part of development environments or recent window systems.

In the field of interactive systems, uniform design of the user interface has acquired particular significance. Workstations like the Apple Macintosh have established a baseline for their successors, and developers should, today, think along the lines laid down by systems of this sort. Such systems are, it is true, only gradually finding their way into industrial practice, but we see here a trend to which, in the foreseeable future, there is no alternative.

State–of–the–art for users working with application systems means using mouse technology to handle pull–down menus, fill–in windows and acknowledgement buttons. These standard *interaction types* are provided with many current workstation computers, and there is a certain unifying trend towards the X Windows' version OSF-Motif. Interaction types support both the construction and use of interactive software. On the one hand, they enable users to draw on their own experience in using the software when it comes to evaluating the software versions, allowing them to quickly familiarize themselves with a new software version. And, on the other, they support implementation of system versions on different target computers, which was traditionally an awkward task owing to the machine-dependent features of earlier interactive components.

### 6.1.4 The Model–View–Controller Paradigm

The separation of interaction and functionality called for in the previous section is a general principle supporting the construction of interactive software. In this section, we set out to describe an architectural model that is suitable for integrating predefined building blocks into an interactive component and then mounting this on to the functional component without any major problems.

In our view, the most suitable candidate here is the *model–view–controller* paradigm (see [KraPop88, BudKuhlSylZue87]) first implemented in Smalltalk. We assume that both software versions and application systems are built according to this paradigm. The context in which this architectural model is employed consists of workstations with bitmap displays and window systems.[31] This model for the interaction balances out two contradictory requirements:

- Maximum flexibility is required when constructing the interactive component of a software version so as to ensure optimal adaptation of the system to user needs. Also required are simple facilities for interchanging different interfaces.
- The standardization of the interaction types used here allows the users to transfer the experience they have acquired in using a software version to the future application system and to other systems.

[31] Interpretations of this model can also be found in the context of mainframes and screen generators. We do not, however, propose to elaborate upon this here.

In addition to the general division of interactive software into an interactive and a functional component, the interactive component can be further decomposed into three parts (see Fig. 22):

- The *model* controls the *functional component* of an interactive system. The *model* keeps track of the state of the interaction between user and system, but possesses no information about representational details. Depending on this state, the *model* decides how the interaction is to proceed. It knows the interface to the functional component and activates it when this is required by the interaction state. The *model* also provides the *controller* with data on the situation–dependent activation of interaction forms.
- A *view* defines and controls a *window* along with its subwindows. This affects the part of the physical screen that is needed for representation of application data. A *view* computes the division of a window into subwindows in accordance with the specified size, this defining window sizes, their positions and the relations between subwindows. In the same way as a window is divided into subwindows, a *view* is divided into different *subviews*, each of which contains rules for computing the parameters of its subwindows. A *view* also assigns specific interaction types to the subwindows.
- The *controller* governs the *interaction* between user and interactive system. Its function here is to control the elementary interaction types. It interprets user inputs via the keyboard or mouse buttons as well as the position of the cursor or the mouse pointer. All input data is either processed, producing changes in the data representation on the screen, or an applications operation is called via the *model.*

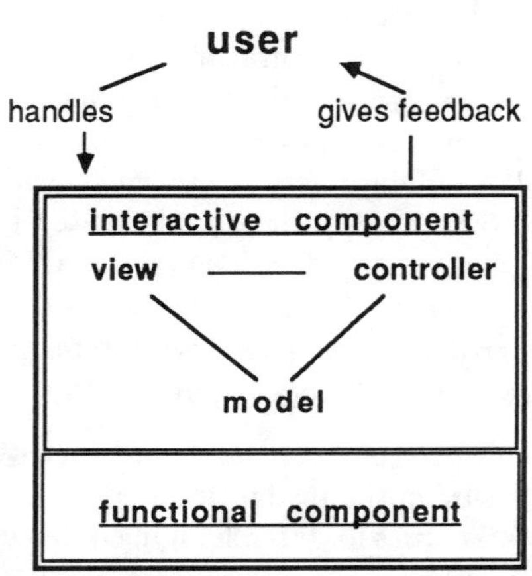


**Fig. 22.** Model, view, controller

The various parts of the interactive component hide different *design decisions*:

The *controller*:

This hides the actual implementation of the different forms of elementary system handling such as

- moving the cursor by means of the mouse
- or by using the cursor keys,
- selecting windows by means of an explicit command for activating a labelled window
- or by *clicking the mouse*
- or by pressing a key (such as ESC) after a sequence of cursor commands.

A well-designed *controller* allows more sophisticated handling of a software version on a workstation equipped with bitmap terminal and mouse than is possible on a traditional alphanumeric terminal. The software version can, however, be used on an alphanumeric terminal without modifications to the program.

The *view*:

An interactive system normally requires more than one single window pane to display data and receive user inputs. In addition, each individual *view* must take into account specific minimum requirements, such as the fact that a selection menu should contain the minimum amount of space required for its options. The minimum requirements for the whole interactive component of a system are defined by combining all the individual requirements of the *views* and allocating the interaction an appropriate window. Thus, the *views* are responsible for optimal presentation of the data, irrespective of the different screens or window sizes.

The *model*:

Depending on the state of the interaction – whether, for example, an element of a one–from–n selection menu is selected or a mouse button clicked – the *model* calls the functional component. How and how often data are displayed on the screen or whether data are hidden – these things are unimportant and unknown to the functional component. The *model* thus standardizes the interface to the functional component.

The functional component is called exclusively by the *model*, and not vice versa. It has no I/O interface of its own.

## 6.2 Our Assessment

We consider the following techniques and tools to be state–of–the–art for building interactive software capable of smooth transition to technically sound and effective application systems: *object–oriented design* based on concepts such as system construction with the help of classes and inheritance, the *client–supplier model*, the *separation of interaction and functionality*, and the use of predefined interaction types as part of the *model–view–controller* paradigm.

This set of models and concepts has not yet found its way into industrial practice, but discussions have begun on the subject and initial findings are available, not only within the academic community.

To support the conceptualization and technical implementation of software versions along these lines, it is useful to adopt one of two approaches, depending on the specific problem in hand:

- For applications whose functionality is still uncertain, the developer can concentrate first of all on the functional component. The different versions of the functional component can then be equipped with simple interactive shells. Questions concerning the functionality are gradually clarified in discussions with the users. And, as "spin–off" from this process, requirements for the design of the interactive component are formulated. Finally, on the basis of a sound functionality, the interactive component is built, with special attention being paid to the questions of easy usability and uniformity.
- For applications whose functionality is known or actually prescribed (as is the case with many database applications), the developers and users can jointly tailor the interactive component to the respective work requirements and working styles, and subsequently add the functional component to it. This approach only makes sense in cases where the functionality is well–defined. It is, after all, possible to develop the functional kernel of a system, while largely disregarding the interactive component; but conversely, the interactive component cannot be designed without knowledge of the functionality.

# Part II

# Technical Support of Prototyping

# 7
# The Tool Landscape

In Part II of our book, we consider how the construction of prototypes can be supported by tools. The tools currently in use are divided up into distinct classes. The following four chapters take a detailed look at each of these groups. The subsequent two chapters of Part II report on experience gained with prototype construction in software engineering projects conducted in industry and research. We also examine the interplay between the software development strategy, the groups affected and the tools used. Finally, we summarize the essentials of the book.

By tools, we mean the software engineering aids needed by a programmer in order to build an application system. It is of no consequence here whether the programmer is an end user or a computer expert. Editors, formatters and file transfer programs are tools in this sense. But our notion of tool also covers, say, a compiler for ANSI COBOL, an interpreter for a database query language, or a spreadsheet program.

If we look at software development in the commercial, technical and scientific sectors, we find that prototypes are already widely used today, either as part of a development strategy, or because of the urgent need to clarify the requirements for a particular software system. There are scarcely any instances of prototype construction without special tools or toolkits, merely on the basis of a COBOL compiler, for example. The tools and toolkits currently in use can be divided up into four classes: *screen generators, database-oriented development systems, Very High Level Languages* and *programming environments*. Before looking at the way tools are used and their respective advantages and disadvantages, we set out to characterize them and classify them into distinct groups by considering the following questions:

- What activities can the tools be used for?
- Which perspective is adopted by the tool developers and users?
- Where are the tools installed?
- What are the major objectives pursued in using the tools?

## 7.1 Screen Generators

Screen generators are the main tools used in the so-called early activities of the development process. They are used to build prototypes for *screen design*.[32]

[32] A *user interface* defines how a software system reacts to user inputs. This covers the whole of system behaviour. By *screen design*, we mean the sequence of screen maps that can be linked up to one another for demonstration purposes by means of user commands. Some screen generators are, in actual fact, only suitable for the "prototyping" of screen layouts.

Screen generators have been in use for several decades now and are part of every computer department's standard repertoire.

Screen generators allow screen design to be carried out quickly and easily. In many cases, however, a great deal of effort is required on the part of the users to familiarize themselves with the system. The generated programs are reasonably efficient in execution and are therefore frequently incorporated into the application system. Discussions on screen maps with the end users help the computer experts to obtain important information about the *function* of the future system. That is the whole point of building such prototypes. Another argument in favour of their use is that they allow the gradual introduction of (new) standards for user interfaces.

Screen generators were originally designed for use on mainframes.[33]

One of the standard application environments for screen generators is a TP-monitor, with COBOL as programming language and an underlying database. The functionality of the application system is generally fixed in advance in the procurement specification by a given database function. Only questions concerning screen design are discussed with the user. This has been the view adopted in building screen generators, and that is why they are relatively inflexible and limited in their range of applications. Most of those available are tied to a particular computer manufacturer.

## 7.2 Database-Oriented Development Systems

In practical software development, we come across a number of database-oriented development systems that are employed throughout the development process. They can be used by both the computer expert and the end user to build a prototype or an application system. Today, numerous companies use this type of tool to develop non-critical application systems (in particular "reports") quickly and efficiently, one important reason being that computer departments have, in many cases, reached the limits of their capacity. The following tools are encountered:

- So-called 4th generation languages such as *Natural*.
  *4th generation languages* differ widely: some of them can only be handled by professional developers; others are suitable for programming by end users. Some meet the demands made on a programming language, whereas others are problematical as regards both their conception and syntax. The systems available range from database manipulation and evaluation systems to enhanced report generators.
- Database systems with their corresponding query languages like *SQL*.
  Of the *database systems*, relational systems are the most relevant, all the other types of systems being too complex for prototype construction.

[33] On workstations, they are almost invariably encountered as *part* of a more comprehensive tool, especially in the case of database-oriented development systems (see Chap. 9).

- Application generators like *DBaseIIIplus*.
  *Application generators* were developed from the outset with the idea of providing a complete set of tools for programming database applications. These range from development tools for the user interface, through tools for data model normalization, to sophisticated data dictionary and word-processing systems.

What all these tools have in common is the fact that they were developed from a perspective focussing on data storage and manipulation. That is why we have subsumed them all under the heading database-oriented development systems. The developers of these systems generally proceed on the basis of the entity relationship model. Here, the area of concern is described in terms of entities, which are characterized by means of attributes and linked to one another by relationships. This form of representation can then be transformed into relations. Usually, the paradigm adopted is that of viewing activities as the processing of computer-based *card-indexes*. This paradigm is so deeply-rooted that it is difficult to develop software for other perspectives. Consequently, problems arise when dealing with application systems for office communication, where the object-oriented view is better suited. Another feature of the database-oriented view is the fact that the developers put themselves in the position of the end users, i.e., they are obliged to adopt the role of the user. This view is alien to traditional software engineering.

Database-oriented development systems are rooted in the world of both mainframes and workstations. Application generators are seldom used on mainframes; workstations are generally the development and target machine in one. The manufacturers of these systems aim to develop tools for efficient *programming* of standard database applications. A popular idea in this context is the integration of all the tools into a single *supertool*.

An important new development in this area are the so-called hypermedia or authoring systems (see [Conklin87]). Here, the idea of the "electronic card-index" is extended to include the view of index-cards as containers for all sorts of documents such as texts, graphics, photographs, video clips, sound, etc. (see [Veljkov90]). The individual index-cards are often not only kept in a "box", but are arranged into a freely configurable network in which the user is able to navigate. Thanks to their sophisticated user interface, the use of graphic elements and the integration of an easily learnable programming language, systems such as HyperCard on the Macintosh are likely to be trendsetters in this area for some years to come. We have not given them more detailed consideration in this book, since, as far as we are aware, little commercial experience has so far been gained with such systems – apart from their use for computer-aided instruction. Our own experience with hypermedia systems for presenting model solutions to software design problems has shown that they are extremely well-suited for prototyping.

## 7.3 Very High Level Languages

Where prototypes are built to model the functionality of an application program, we come across programming languages that are not designed for a specific application area, so-called general-purpose programming languages ensuring highly efficient program construction by means of *powerful function and data constructors.* Unlike conventional languages, here flow of control need not be explicitly declared at all points by the programmer (it may, for instance, be hidden in a pattern match). Such languages are known as Very High Level Languages (VHLLs). Some VHLLs, for example Lisp and Prolog are known as Artificial Intelligence languages.

With a little experience, prototypes can be constructed efficiently and compactly using VHLLs. Programs can be written in VHLLs in more general terms than in traditional languages. When using conventional programming languages, programmers are so aware of the constraints imposed by these languages that they confine themselves to "what is possible" as far as program functions are concerned. This means that design focusses prematurely on a low level of abstraction. The cycle *program modification, program loading* and *testing* can be run through much more quickly using VHLLs than with batch-oriented languages such as COBOL.

In commercial software development, there are very few programmers versed in VHLLs. However, the growing number of computer professionals in industry already familiar with these languages as a result of their training means that VHLLs are being increasingly used for the construction of prototypes (and target systems) in commercial data processing as well.

The view adopted by the developers of VHLLs is that taken by the "classical" computer scientist. Attention focusses on the development of a *programming language.* Considerable importance is attached to a powerful and easily intelligible model of the semantics of the language.

Most VHLLs are developed at universities, though some originate in the R & D laboratories of large companies. Hence, VHLLs are generally used at universities and research and development institutes. Their main use is for prototype construction. Such prototypes are helpful in illustrating ideas and conducting experiments. For this reason preference is given to powerful languages with simple semantic models. The languages most frequently used are Lisp, ML and Prolog dialects. Also of importance are *algebraic languages* (like ACT ONE) as well as set-theoretical languages like Setl .

## 7.4 Programming Environments

Developing highly integrated programming environments is the chief concern of most software engineering projects, whether they are conducted in the R & D laboratories of industry or at universities. One thing is clear though: we still have quite a way to go before programming environments may be considered as belonging to the standard repertoire of commercial software development. Only programming environments designed for use with specific languages – such as Pascal and C++, for example – are already in fairly widespread use today.

Since the aim in developing programming environments is to develop better software as quickly as possible, most programming environments include tools for constructing prototypes.[34]

Today, programming environments constitute the most important engineering-oriented approach to better software production. That is why they are of crucial importance in prototype construction.

The tools generally encountered are used to support the following activities:

- design,
- editing sources and texts,
- compiling, link-editing, loading and testing programs, and
- configuration and project management.

In addition to providing technical support for the construction of prototypes, programming environments may also facilitate the transition to the application system and its systematic enhancement over several development cycles.

The development of programming environments is influenced by analysis of the software development process. Starting from the development documents and activities, tools are devised for their support. The target group here is normally the professional software engineer. The point of departure is mostly a programming language, less frequently a language-independent method or life cycle plan.

Programming environments usually bear the mark of the research and development milieu in which they originated. They are designed to help develop better and cheaper software, mostly for the scientific and technical sectors, which is precisely where their developers come from.

Since programming environments mark important development trends, we also examine them from this particular angle – showing the sort of criteria that ought to be applied to prototyping tools.

## 7.5 Tools and Prototype Development

The differences between the various groups of tools are by no means clear. We see a growing tendency for the groups to overlap:

- Many database query languages have been extended in recent years by the addition of menu and screen generators. This means that the differences between them and application generators are becoming increasingly blurred.
- Application generators contain tools such as debuggers, compilers and tools for checking the consistency of data models, etc. This means that they are getting more and more like programming environments.

[34] It is only fair to point out that many programming environments are themselves prototypes. Their developers are keen to demonstrate their scientific findings quickly and for this (good) reason are interested in prototype construction with and for their programming environment.

- Suppliers of screen generators have recognized the fact that a mere sequence of screen maps without access to the underlying programs and database does not constitute an adequate basis for discussions between users and software developers. That is why many screen generators have been entended by the addition of (simple) data storage systems, thus coming close to the 4th generation languages.
- VHLLs are almost invariably supplied along with a programming environment.[35] Since many VHLLs offer excellent facilities for constructing prototypes for database applications, the differences between VHLLs and database-oriented development systems are also becoming blurred.

There are a number of correlations between who uses a tool and at what stage of software development a tool is used. These must be taken into account when selecting tools for prototype construction:

- If end users use the tools by themselves (i.e., program their own applications), several early activities coincide. The end users feel no need to inform computer experts about the system development objectives or describe the work environment to them.
  If the end users use the tools by themselves, prototyping is an indispensable software development method. Because of their limited experience in the computer field, end users lack the computer expert's ability to foresee what the future system will look like and how it will function. They are therefore obliged to determine a program's suitability by actually using it, making improvements where necessary.
  If, later on, it is found that the application program needs re-implementing – for example, because it is too inefficient or not robust enough – the software programmed by the end user is employed by the computer expert as a prototype of the target system. We have, then, a reversal of roles between those building the prototype and those evaluating it!
- If the *whole* development process is supported by a *single* tool, there is, for the area of commercial applications software, today (still) no alternative to the use of database-oriented development systems. If a comprehensive approach of this sort is opted for, a great deal of attention must be paid to the problems associated with such systems.
- If prototype construction is to be confined to *specific* technical software development activities, modern VHLLs like Prolog and Lisp are of crucial importance to the productivity of the development process. The use of a dedicated development system (normally based on Unix) further improves development productivity, even though compatibility problems occur when using mainframes.

To summarize: prototype construction without tools is of no practical significance in professional software development. In the following sections, we there-

[35] In the case of Lisp programming environments and Smalltalk, for example, the VHLL and the programming environment are, to all intents and purposes, inextricably linked.

fore take a detailed look at the scope of tool support and the advantages and disadvantages of the various classes of tools for prototype construction.

# 8 Screen Generators

In this chapter, we discuss the suitability of screen generators for prototype construction. To begin with, we outline the goals generally pursued when using these tools for designing and implementing user interfaces for interactive systems. We then specify some of the requirements for screen generators with a view to their use for prototyping. To conclude, we present tool components of generators currently in use and evaluate them with respect to their usability in conjunction with prototype-oriented development strategies.

## 8.1 Screen Generators and Prototyping

Screen generators have long been used widely in commercial data processing to support the development of user interfaces for interactive application systems. It is worthwhile considering the suitability of this class of tools for prototyping for two reasons: The first – a reason frequently given for the general use of such tools – is that they allow high-quality software to be *implemented quickly* and *simply*. By *separating* the interactive from the functional components of an application system and by largely *isolating* the interactive components from the application program, it is possible to improve the modular structures of the software. This allows the construction of easily intelligible and modifiable application systems that are also largely machine-independent, reusable and more reliable. It is precisely this aspect of reliability that is frequently emphasized in connection with the automatic generation of user interfaces (see [Myers89]). Another effect of this automation is that it relieves application system developers of a number of constantly recurring routine jobs when implementing user interfaces.

In addition to these arguments strictly pertaining to the developers' work in the technical implementation of application systems, there is another important aspect requiring consideration here. This is the fact that, despite numerous efforts in the area of software ergonomics,[36] there are at present no generally accepted guidelines for ensuring high quality of user facilities and acceptance of the user interfaces by the future users. The only way to secure this is to implement and evaluate the interactive components together with them on a participative basis (see [BalHopOppPesRohStr88]). In cases, then, where prototypes are used primarily for modelling user interfaces – the manipulation of data playing a secondary role – effective use can be made of screen generators (cf. Sec. 4.3).

*Screen maps* and *forms* – which can be generated and used in this way for *horizontal prototyping* – are designed to present the problem-oriented screen layout required for the input and output of the data objects to be managed by application systems. In addition, the use of simple dialog sequences, i.e., a

[36] Cf., for example, [Shakel85, BulShaKor87, BaecBuxt87, DiaGilCocSha90].

series of maps on the screen, is meant to help demonstrate simple computer-supported working routines. Here, the evaluation is not confined merely to the user interface *proper*, it also covers the objects that are to be represented and the functions operating on them. Prototypes of this kind may, then, – and are usually designed to – be used both for *defining* and *implementing* parts of the user interfaces and for *analyzing* and *specifying requirements* for other system parts.

## 8.2 Tool Components of Screen Generators

To give an adequate description and evaluation of screen generators, we must consider their origin and development history. They originated in the development and production departments of commercial data processing companies where the main concern was to relieve the developers of interactive systems of the constantly recurring, laborious standard implementation tasks involved when working on the level of detail required by traditional programming languages. Accordingly, they were designed as an extension to classical programming languages such as COBOL. Incidentally, their origin in the commercial sector is one reason why – unlike, say, general analyses of human-computer interaction carried out as part of software ergonomics – screen generators have been scarcely discussed at all within the scientific community and why there is so little literature on them.

The first screen generators were actually nothing more than simple *text editors* which used text commands to store field descriptions, line for line, as strings of characters in *text files*. It was possible to access these descriptions using the usual file operations. They were either highly machine-oriented or followed the syntax of classical programming languages. Nor were they subjected to any sort of checks while being generated. Checks on all input data were only carried out during interpretation of the complete descriptions once the application programs were being executed. While this concept ensured separation of the descriptions from the application programs' code, it failed to secure independence from a particular programming language or improved intelligibility and changeability of the descriptions – even by means of direct graphic representation. It was not until the mid-sixties, with the development of database systems (cf. Chap. 9) and related efforts to make data management and applications programming independent of concrete machines and classical programming languages, that advances were also made in the development of screen generators. From development aids used in the software manufacturers' own production departments, they evolved into sophisticated tools for supporting production and were marketed as such by the software houses.

### 8.2.1 Requirements and Characteristics of Screen Generators

To meet the above-mentioned goals of prototyping, screen generators must – in addition to providing facilities for describing maps and forms – allow

- simulation of data input and output on individual maps, and
- description and simulation of dialog sequences.

To enable parts of the prototypes to be used for the future target system, the screen generators must provide *interfaces* to *programming languages* for implementing the functional components. We now go on to take a more detailed look at these requirements with special reference to prototyping.

## Description of Screen Maps

In order to define screen maps, it must be possible to describe the screen area simply and quickly. This is why, to facilitate operation of the future application system, it is prescribed at which points on the screen data may be entered and displayed and through which points the cursor may be moved. The terminals still generally in use today in commercial data processing are based on alphanumeric representation, so that positioning is done via lines and columns. Adjacent character display positions are combined to *form fields.* A screen map consists, then, of the following elements:

- Input fields
  These fields are available to the users of the future application system for inputting data. They are usually specified by details of their position on the screen, their length and the value range of the input data. For form display, empty input fields are frequently marked by break characters (____).
- Output fields
  These fields are filled by the application system on data output as a result of the execution of functions. They are likewise specified by details of their position on the screen, their length and the value range of the output data objects. Some of these fields can also be used for data input by the users. For form display, empty output fields are frequently marked by break characters (____).
- Field identifiers
  These are strings of characters that are displayed as fixed texts for identifying *input* and *output fields.* These texts are protected and may not be changed during execution of the application system either by the system itself or by the users. The relevant fields are normally specified by details of their position on the screen and a text constant.
- Delimiters
  These are strings, generally consisting of special characters, that are used as fixed texts marking the beginning and end of fields or screen areas. They are usually specified by details of their position on the screen, the character that is to be used, and the length or extension of the character string.

## Input and Modification of Screen Map Descriptions

For first input and modification of specific description components and complete map descriptions, the usual editing functions are needed. Additional functions are also useful, especially ones for copying specifications or parts of them. These are, however, seldom all provided by a single system. Since the layout and structure of the different maps used in an application system is often very similar, such functions can help to reduce considerably the effort required for writing specifications. The editing functions must allow screen map design to be as simple and free as possible, and at the same time be as easily handleable as possible themselves. What has proved highly effective here is a mixture of *graphic* and *text* input and representation on the screen. This must, however, be independent of the internal program representation when storing the specifications by means of the screen generators. Graphic editing functions should be used for placing both the *delimiters* and the *field identifiers* directly in the positions provided in the maps and for editing them. It should also be possible, with their help, to fix the starting positions of input and output fields; the additional parameters required should be generated by means of text functions that are themselves *form-* or *table-oriented*. The form editors should also provide functions for *checking* the screen layout, to ensure that the fields do not overlap, for example.

## Simulation of Dialog Sequences

Support through editing functions is also needed for describing simple dialog sequences. This includes both the order in which the fields are to be processed within a map and the linking of individual screen maps to a sequence. For this purpose, screen generators should provide facilities for selecting "follow screens" by means of *text commands*, *function keys* and *menu options*, but dependent also on the content of the individual input fields.

To enable dialog sequences and input and output to be simulated on the screen maps using the descriptions generated, a number of additional functions are needed. Besides functions for interpreting the descriptions and displaying the maps generated from them, others are needed to provide computer support for

- positioning the cursor on the input fields,
- defining default settings of jump strategies for the cursor,
- entering and editing input fields, and
- displaying preset default values for data objects.

## Processing of Test Data

If screen generators are to be used effectively for prototyping, they must support not only the input, but also, to some extent at least, the "processing" of test data: fixing data types and value ranges directly upon description of the individual fields allows automatic generation of data structure descriptions and data models as well as effective consistency and plausibility checks during execution of the prototypes containing the user interfaces generated. In addition to such functions, support must be provided for storing data both for the duration of individual test runs and after completion of the test sessions. This enables test logs to be produced for test cases and allows the test data already obtained to be utilized for subsequent sessions. And this, in turn, helps to reduce considerably the effort required for the constantly recurring evaluation and analysis activities. Horizontal prototyping without the functions described above is practically impossible.

The editors in use today are form- or table- and screen-oriented. They can be used to enter and modify the descriptions on the screen in a problem-oriented representation. Such a representation is largely independent of classical programming languages and the internal form in which the descriptions are stored in files.

Owing to the vast number of such systems on the market – frequently differing from one another only marginally – it is impossible to give a detailed description of the various screen generators available. Still, our basic concern here is with prototyping, and we therefore focus our attention on the essential aspects common to this whole class of tools. These aspects are highlighted below by reference to examples using "fictitious" screen generators.

### 8.2.2 Tool Components for Building Simple Prototypes

Most of the screen generators in use today support the construction of prototypes by means of two mutually independent tool components: *form editors* and *form interpreters*.

The tools provide functions enabling the screen layouts for the application systems to be designed interactively and by means of direct visualization. Besides the input of text commands and the selection of commands from menus, the user interfaces also provide for other forms of input: on the character-oriented terminals on which most of the generators run, the maps can be generated "semigraphically" by simply positioning the cursor and using all displayable characters. Special commands can be used to enter additional parameters for specifying the fields. Figure 23 shows an example of a screen generator that allows semivisual design of the maps on the screen. The field identifiers and delimiters can, in the input mode, be positioned and denoted directly on the screen. In our example, the identifiers are `PARTICIPANTS`, `ADMINISTRATION` and `NAME`; the delimiter is the line under `ADMINISTRATION`. Definition of a writable input and output field is initiated by entering special characters, in this case the character # marking the starting position and the break characters (____) marking the field expansion. Execution of the command `DEFINE FIELD` causes a window to be displayed on the screen. This already contains positional details relating to the field, further parameter descriptions being expected from which not only the field structures but also the structures of the data objects that are to be subsequently managed can be derived. In this case, these are a `FIELDNAME`, a field `TYPE`, a data `FORMAT` and a value `RANGE` within this "format". In our example,

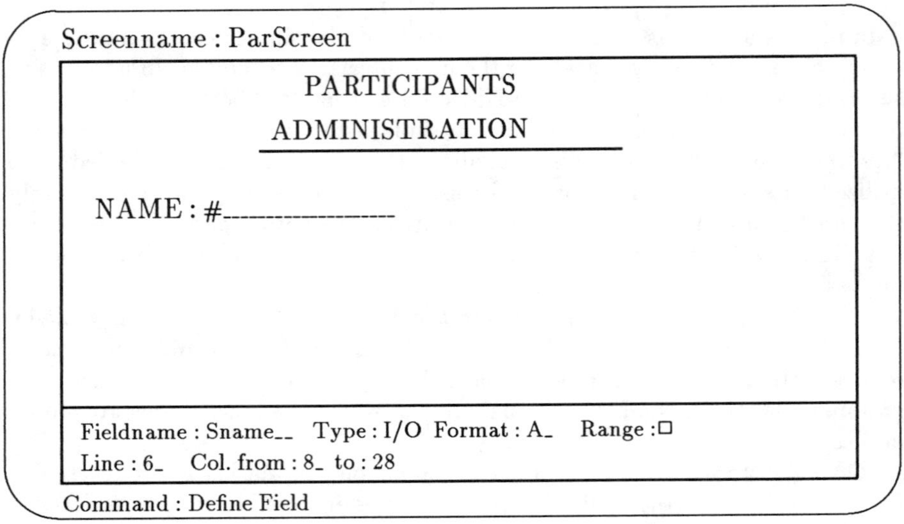


**Fig. 23.** Form definition using a screen- and form-oriented editor

alongside the field name **SNAME**, the field type is denoted as an input and output field by the identifier **I/O**. The definition of the format specifies that any strings of characters consisting of letters can be used. This is denoted by an **A** for alphabetic characters. A value range has not yet been specified. To enter parameters, the cursor – represented here by the symbol □ – is moved automatically from field to field.

Other predefined formats – such as numeric or alphanumeric characters – are, of course, also possible. Many screen generators provide more "advanced" formats, such as **DATE** for formatted representation of the date, and attributes affecting the field presentation such as **UNDERLINE**, **REVERSE VIDEO** or **BRIGHT/DARK**. An extension of this repertoire, however, is not provided for. There are two reasons for this: First, screen generators are not thought of being powerful programming tools; their emphasis is on easy use of predefined building-blocks. Second, the data types offered are considered to be sufficient for the applications in question.

The names given to the parameters and the values they may assume clearly indicate the tools' origins. They are not data type names of the sort generally encountered in mathematically and scientifically oriented programming languages, but rather identifiers such as are used in the world of commercial data processing.

Figure 24 shows another way of defining and representing screen maps. Here, the screen layout is described in a table; there is no visualization of the fields. The type of a field identifier is denoted by a **C** for text constant. A value range **'A-Z'** is also specified, indicating, for example, that all letters belonging to the alphabetic characters may be used without restriction.

Screen Layout : ParScreen

| FIELD | TYPE | FORMAT | RANGE | LINE | COL. FROM/ | TO |
|---|---|---|---|---|---|---|
| PARTICIPANTS | C | – | – | 3 | 37 | 48 |
| ADMINISTRATION | C | – | – | 4 | 36 | 49 |
| Sseparator1 | C | – | "_" | 5 | 30 | 54 |
| NAME : | C | – | – | 6 | 2 | 7 |
| Sname | I/O | A | A–Z | 6 | 8 | 28 |
| Sseparator2 | C | – | "_" | 22 | 1 | 80 |
| MESSAGE : | C | – | – | 23 | 2 | 11 |
| Smessage | O | A | A–Z | 23 | 12 | 79 |
| □ | - | - | - | - | - | - |

Command : Define Field

**Fig. 24.** Form definition using a table-oriented editor

Many of the screen generators available today provide a mixture of these different kinds of representation, enabling the users to choose the kind that best suits their purposes. In addition, the editors offer functions for copying, modifying, shifting, etc. field identifiers and I/O fields as well as for defining default settings for the fields. Though these functions are an essential prerequisite for prototype construction, we refrain from more detailed consideration of them at this point.

The procedures for defining forms implement a number of different concepts. Some form editors strictly prescribe these procedures. They require that all field identifiers be specified before writable fields can be defined. This practically rules out any subsequent modification of the forms. The editors available today, though, normally allow the tool users to select their own procedure. Various strategies are also encountered for checking field descriptions.

Some tools carry out checks based on the existing specifications immediately upon input of new field descriptions, thus directly preventing the generation of "faulty" forms – containing overlapping fields, for example. Others provide explicit check functions that have to be activated by the form developer. The situation is similar with respect to storage of the specifications generated: some tools only store internally consistent descriptions; others allow storage of all descriptions, irrespective of possible inconsistencies, but draw attention to the latter by issuing "warnings".

We go into the different development strategies and approaches in more detail in our discussion of database-oriented development systems in the next chapter. There are, however, two points concerning the definition of form descriptions which we would like to take up briefly here. One is the fact that, when giving field names, many generators are unnecessarily subject to program-language-based restrictions, allowing only very short – and thus often cryptic – names. Another problem is defining the order of the fields for data input. Some generators contain implicit strategies that determine the order of the fields from their position on the screen; others do so according to the order in which the specifications are entered. Both strategies can cause problems, especially in the case of modifications. An effective strategy is that provided by tools which allow the order of the fields to be defined by means of a separate function, independent of temporal or spatial sequences.

### Interpretation of Screen Descriptions

A necessary prerequisite for the implementation of simple prototypes is not only the generation of screen maps, but their interpretation, too. The form interpreter is an additional tool component that generates maps from the descriptions and visualizes them on the screen. In some generators, this function is integrated into the form editor, which means that the layout of the future form is visible directly upon definition. Figure 23 shows a form of this sort. In contrast, separate form interpreters, such as are provided by most generators, use the complete descriptions of the forms. From these, they generate forms on the screen, allowing data to be entered in the input fields by means of "built-in" functions for "moving the cursor" on the screen. Additional functions check the input data against the specified formats and value ranges. This allows implementation of simple ideas concerning the operation, handling and functionality of the application system under development. Figure 25 shows a simple screen form of this sort which can be used for evaluation and discussion by the developers and users.

The scope of such prototypes is, however, confined to the representation of simple screen sequences. The test data entered are not normally stored for reuse. This is why most screen generators are equipped with additional functions.

## 8.2.3 Tool Components for Building Complex Prototypes

To simulate dialog sequences, most tools are equipped with additional functions for linking screens. Such links are defined by means of special fields in the forms themselves or by corresponding allocation of function keys. Most tools, though, allow only strictly hierarchical dialog sequences. For the realization of the dialog sequences, a number of different concepts are implemented. In the case of the earlier screen generators, the developers frequently have to program on a machine-oriented file and data structure level, using a programming-language-based notation to laboriously "work out" the dialog sequence themselves with the help of text editors (see previous section). More recent tools allow this work to be done with the help of forms, providing for this purpose definition and menu facilities. Let us consider an example: Figure 26 shows a screen offering three "user functions" in one menu. The screen generator used provides a command for defining a dialog simulation. Figure 27 shows the screen form MainMenuScreen; on

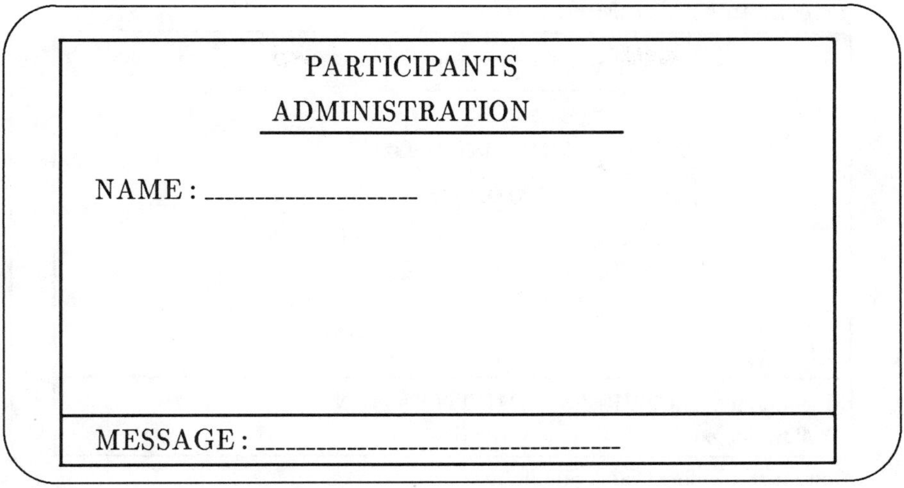


**Fig. 25.** Screen form generated with a screen generator

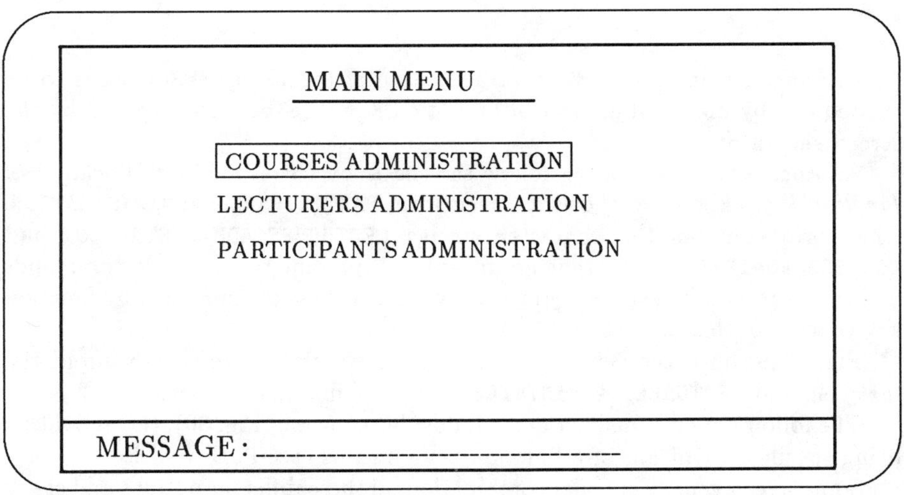


**Fig. 26.** A menu selection form

activation of the command `DEFINE DIALOG SIMULATION`[37] a window is displayed for input of the necessary data.

If the menu option `LECTURERS ADMINISTRATION` is selected, the follow screen specified is `LECSCREEN`; this is displayed on the screen during dialog simulation. There are various ways of activating such a screen. In our example, we specify,

[37] As demonstrated in the previous section, commands can be activated in different ways depending on the tool being used, e.g. by text inputs or by pressing a function key to which the relevant command has been allocated.

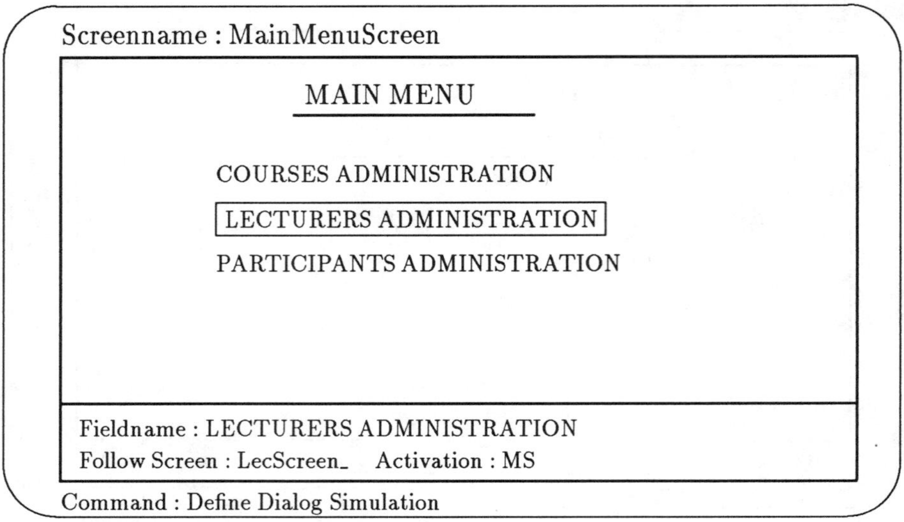


**Fig. 27.** Definition of a follow screen for dialog simulation in a menu screen

by entering the parameter **MS**, that activation of the form **LecScreen** is to be carried out by means of an activation option **Menu Selection** provided by the screen generator.

Another way of activating follow screens is by corresponding allocation of *function keys*. Figure 28 shows a screen form **PARTICIPANTS ADMINISTRATION**. This form contains the character strings **LECTURERS ADMINISTRATION** and **COURSES ADMINISTRATION** that are meant to represent two possible commands and the corresponding screen forms. Activation of these commands is by function key codes – in this case **F1** and **F2**.

Figure 29 shows the definition of the dialog simulation. In this example, the text constant **LECTURERS ADMINISTRATION F1** is marked and selected.

The follow screen is defined in a window (as shown in Fig. 30), the activation being specified by means of a function key – in this case **F1**.

Some screen generators offer combinations of these different options and check the resulting specifications before executing them. The dialog simulation itself is activated by means of additional commands; the form it takes is similar to that already described for single screens except for the additional execution of the specified screen sequences. As far as the modification and checking strategies are concerned, our remarks in the section on screen generation functions also apply here.

The various strategies for test data management should also be seen in connection with the simulation components. We have already pointed out the necessity of simple default settings as well as test data inputs and checks. Sophisticated generators also allow test data to be stored and reused, which considerably facilitates the construction and evaluation of complex prototypes.

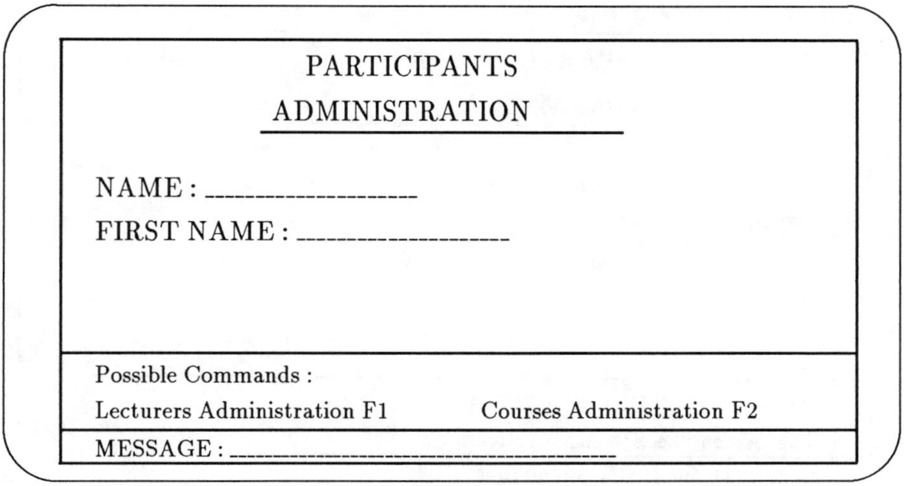


**Fig. 28.** Application screen with field identifiers for selecting commands

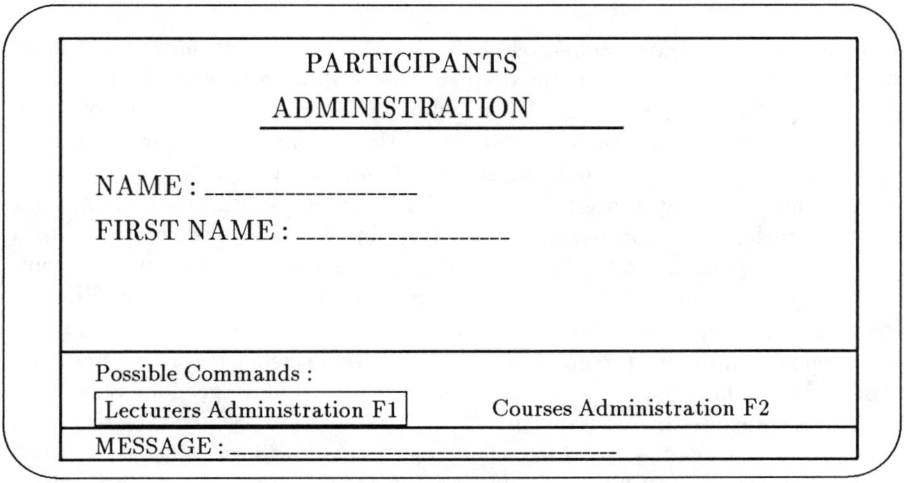


**Fig. 29.** Selection of a field identifier for defining the follow screen

### 8.2.4 Prototypes and Target Systems

Complex prototypes frequently constitute an "initial" version of a desired target system. Here, it is useful to ascertain which parts of the prototypes can be adopted for use in the target system and the amount of effort this involves. As a rule, it is possible to utilize them in cases where the screen generators provide interfaces to other tools, allowing the implementation of "missing" system components. Today's screen generators provide two different options here: they

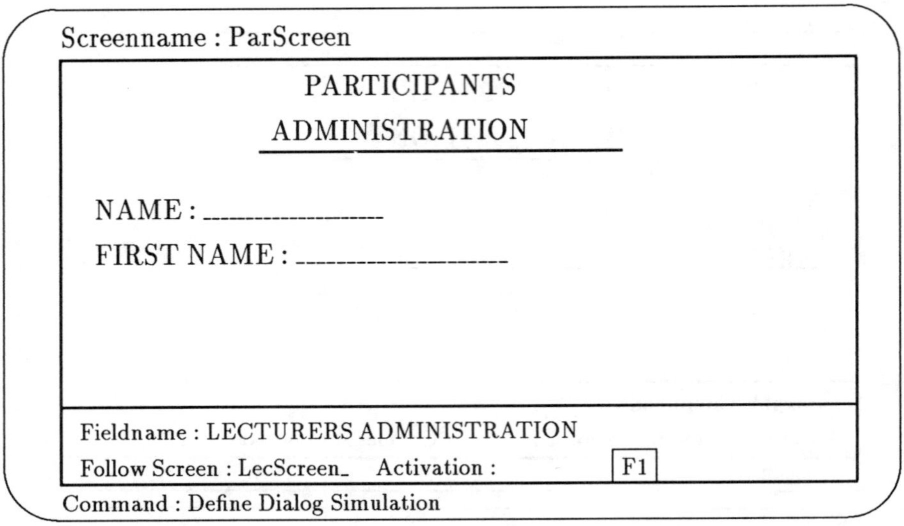


**Fig. 30.** Definition of a follow screen

either generate *program frameworks* in which the application algorithms must then be inserted, or they make the map and dialog descriptions available in such a form that they can be embedded in application programs. In both of these cases, the crucial point is the extent to which the system parts generated can be used independently of the tools generating them, and to which other classical programming languages interfaces exist. The classical programming languages do, it is true, require specialized knowledge, but they allow translation into a generator-independent code. Such programs can generally be executed as compiled programs without the screen generators. Here, some tools generate directly executable code in a "high-level" programming language such as C or COBOL, thus largely committing the developers to their use. Others generate source code in one of these languages, which can then be modified at target language level. Yet others translate the programs into "intermediate code", which then has to be transformed into the required target language by another tool. This last concept allows considerable flexibility in selecting the target language. In cases where the use of screen generators is not confined to prototype construction, consideration of such factors is of particular importance because they are decisive for the question of the reusability of the work results already obtained. It is, however, quite possible to implement even complex prototypes using the tool components described above.

## 8.3 Our Assessment

In their major application areas in commercial data processing, screen generators provide suitable support for the design and generation of the "classical" *standard screen maps* needed there. Since, as a rule, they also allow automatic generation of consistency-checking routines for data input, they are looked on by the system developers using them as quite effective and helpful tools, despite the fact that they fail to support more recent interaction techniques such as windowing and graphical user interfaces. We nevertheless feel that they should be submitted to a somewhat more critical appraisal by way of a summary. We do so by considering once again the various system components and the relationship between screen generators and "complete" target systems.

- Functions for describing screen maps
  Compared with classical programming languages, they allow a *simpler* and *quicker* description of the screen layout for screen map representation. Despite restrictions and problems — due both to prescription of the command sequences to be executed and the use of machine-oriented special characters as a command language for entering the descriptions, impairing — the flexibility and user-friendliness of the tools, the specified maps can be easily generated on an interactive basis and demonstrated for use as prototypes.[38] For the above-mentioned reasons, though, the tools are only suitable for handling by application system developers. There is practically no chance of their being used by the future end users.
  The kinds of prototypes described above support system development in cases where the main concern is with requirements analysis and the specification of user interfaces, and here more precisely with design of the screen layout. The undeniable advantage of such protoypes is their *visualization* of the screen maps on the terminal. Prototypes of this sort can already be used to clear up problems connected with the data objects that are to be managed and the functions operating on them during the so-called early phases of system development. They provide a suitable and helpful basis for discussion here. The implementation of system models relating to these areas and permitting a more detailed evaluation of the results of such discussions is a laborious business. This is also true of prototypes designed to contain user interfaces that do not form part of the standard repertoire of the screen generator being used.
- Functions for simulating dialog sequences
  The simulation components available allow only static linking of maps to be carried out easily. It is only possible to demonstrate alternative solutions for the course of human-computer interaction if different interaction types are made available, i.e., if, in addition to the input of text commands, selection via menus or function keys is also provided for. The dynamic behaviour of the desired application systems, resulting from the execution of data manipulation operations, can be implemented with the help of available access operations, but this requires a great deal of effort because the access operations and the necessary flow of control have to be implemented using

[38] Given the appropriate hardware and operating system software, which must ensure, during the construction processa, the short response times needed for rapid demonstration and modification cycles (cf. [Schmitt83]).

constructs from classical programming languages, and this leads to all the familiar problems encountered when using such tools for system development. For instance, detailed knowledge of the internal representation and storage of the map descriptions in the computer is frequently needed to enable the required access operations to be implemented. It is practically impossible to carry out swift development cycles under these sort of circumstances. The various concepts for handling test data must also be seen in this connection. Where the effort required for generating and managing such data is disproportionate to the effort needed for developing the prototypes, the benefits of such prototypes are extremely limited.

– Screen generators and target systems
On construction of the target systems in the later phases of system development, screen generators take over a large portion of the standard tasks involved in implementation of the user interfaces. What is more, with the help of the field descriptions it is, for instance, also possible to generate the declarations of the data that are to be managed in the later application program. This can, however, – where modifications are subsequently made to the declarations – lead to inconsistencies between the individual components of the application system, and these are extremely difficult to eliminate. Many screen generators also impose restrictions or establish dependencies when developing target systems through the interfaces of or to the classical programming languages available – which means that knowledge of these languages is a prerequisite for using the tools. Particularly where the functions for simulating the dynamic system behaviour are adopted, they prescribe specific structures for the system architecture and system implementation. Thus, the independence from the application system components – so often purported to be an advantage – is at least questionable. This is especially true where the course of human-computer interaction is directly mapped on to the software and each "user function" has to be implemented separately. This generally makes it necessary to combine input and output routines and access operations into program units, which, through the repeated coding of the access operations, results in redundant code and, at the same time, – owing to the blurring of boundaries between the different operations on the data objects – allows uncontrolled access, which in turn causes additional sources of error. Before using screen generators, it is therefore a good idea to check carefully the compatibility of such constraints and prescriptive elements with the implementation of the actual target system in order not to risk having to make changes on a large scale afterwards.

To sum up, it may be said that the use of classical screen generators offers a number of advantages for the construction of both *horizontal* and *vertical* prototypes in traditional data processing. However, the problems encountered when using these tools – problems which we have discussed above – should not be underestimated. We feel that both the use of these tools "in isolation" and their close coupling with classical programming languages limit their benefits. They can, however, be used effectively in conjunction with other integrated sets of tools. This is the idea behind *database-oriented development systems* which are increasingly finding their way into commercial data processing, ousting "stand-alone" generators. We therefore take another look, in the following chapter, at the use of screen generators in systems of this sort.

# 9 Database-Oriented Development Systems

This chapter gives an overview of database-oriented development systems which we discuss in relation to prototype construction. We begin by clarifying the terms and concepts used, and then consider the various system components, illustrating their use by means of an example. To conclude, we undertake an assessment of the systems with respect to their suitability for prototyping.

## 9.1 Concept and Features

Since the early eighties, development systems based on *database systems* have increasingly found their way into the development departments of commercial enterprises. Marketing efforts constantly emphasize that they are the appropriate means for coping with *all* the tasks arising in system development (see [Canning84a, Canning84b, Canning84c, Canning85]). The argument frequently used is that the various system components needed are integrated beneath a uniform, interactive user interface allowing controlled, incremental development cycles that require little effort for modification (see [FriQuiWer86, Bauer87b, Bauer87c]). Experience with these systems – above and beyond that gained when using them on the basis of traditional system development strategies – has been most extensive and most positive in conjunction with prototyping. However, far-reaching claims are made, and these are redeemed only in part. That is reason enough to take a more detailed look at this class of systems.

It is extremely difficult, though, given the diversity of the tools in this particular area, to give an overview of the range of products available and the facilities they offer. They range from evaluation and inquiry systems such as *AS, Focus* and *Nomad* to systems providing components for developing complex application systems, such as *Natural, Mantis, Ideal* and *Sesam/Drive* (see [Bauer90]).

There is a lack of transparency at present with regard to the different terms used to denote tools of this sort. A number of suppliers and authors speak of 4th generation languages (see [Martin85, Martin86, Bauer87a, WagKnoDis87, KnoDis87]), some of CASE (Computer Aided Software Engineering) environments (cf. [Balzert89], see also Sec. 11.1), others of end user systems (see [Bauer87a]) or application generators (see [Lobell83, Kuvaja88]) and yet others of program generators (see [Bauer84]).

### 9.1.1 The Conceptual World of Database Systems

In view of the variety of terms and notions used and given the importance of these systems for prototyping, we feel it necessary to begin by elucidating the basic terms and concepts of relevance here. In order to do so, we take a look at the historical development of the database systems at the heart of all development systems of this sort, and explain the terminology used.

The driving force behind the development of database systems was the desire for *physical* and *logical data independence* from technical storage media and the application programs that process the data (see [Date77]). In the early days of conventional application systems programming, the data required was managed in separate files which the various application programs accessed directly. In order to carry out such operations correctly, both the physical location and the structure of the files had to be known in the programs. If, in addition, different programs required similar data, but processed this data in different connections, the same data was frequently kept in several different files. This led, on the one hand, to data redundancies, and on the other, it meant that modifications to specific data could cause inconsistencies in the data stock as a whole.

To solve the problem of the strict allocation of files to application programs, the *physical data dependence*, program systems were developed that were embedded between the files and the application programs and that provided standardized file operations. Using such *data file management systems* in conjunction with application programs, it is possible to access data without knowing their physical memory location. Such access does, however, presuppose knowledge of the logical structure of the files and the individual data structures. The application program can only access complete data records – defined in the programming language being used – and must extract the required information from them. Moreover, it is impossible to add new data fields to the data in a file without regenerating the whole file and modifying *all* application programs that use it. In order to achieve this *logical data independence*, i.e., to obtain the desired information without knowledge of the memory structures and fixed sequences of data, more sophisticated data file management systems have been developed – the so-called *database management systems*, or *database systems* for short. Another of the objectives of such systems is to reduce the problems of redundancy and inconsistency still afflicting file management systems.

Database systems take account of the following points:

- The application works, independently of the physical structure of the data, only on the logical, abstract structures that are needed.
- The logical structures are managed by the database system and can be modified, deleted or have new elements added to them at any time by means of appropriate mechanisms; only the application programs affected by these elements have to be modified accordingly.
- Mapping of the logical structures on to their physical memory takes place in the database system only.
- To avoid redundancy, all data is stored in one large area, which can be divided up into different sections on the storage medium, but which is processed by the database system as one area, known as the *database*.
- Work on the data, i.e., definition and manipulation of data, is carried out by means of language constructs provided by the database system.

### 9.1.2 The Levels of Description in Database Systems

Data management with database systems is based on different levels of description:

- the conceptual data schema,
- the logical data schema,
- the external data schema, and
- the internal data schema.

Analysis of the problem area yields the set of objects that are to be managed with computer support. The description of the objects, as yet still independent of a particular implementation, together with their characteristic attributes and the latters' ranges of values and access rights – a description for which the use of a formal means of description may suffice – is known as the *conceptual schema* or simply *schema*. The implementation of the conceptual schema is called the *logical schema*. The views that are realized in the different application programs are in each case subsets of the complete set of existing objects; they are known as *external schemata*. Each of these views contains only the objects and descriptions that are relevant for a specific application. Finally, the *internal schema* describes the physical representation of the objects. Here, the data processing aspects are considered in relation to the storage organization (see [SchStu83]).

Description of the conceptual schema requires formal means of representation, both in order to describe the structure of the objects and to provide potential operations for processing such data. This function is assumed by the *data model*.

The modelling and description of the data itself are based on different concepts. A fundamental distinction can be made between two descriptive perspectives which have come to be known by the terms *datalogical* and *infological* modelling (see [VineRennTjoa82]). The *datalogical* description relates to technical aspects of the computing machinery that is to be used; accordingly, objects are known here as data structures with data items. The *infological* perspective, on the other hand, relates to the domain that is to be modelled. Here, too, it is *objects* that are considered, these also being known as *entities*.

Similar objects are combined to form an object class or an object type. An object is described in terms of characteristics that constitute its *attributes*. The values that an attribute may assume are limited by the range of values. The different objects of an object type are called *instances* or *extensions* of this type. To identify a particular object unambiguously, one or more attributes are specified as *key attributes*.

In order to relate classes of objects to one another, the relations existing between them must be modelled. A relation is a connection or mapping between elements of two sets. There are three classical forms of relations between object sets. If an object of set A is allocated precisely to an object of set B, we speak of a *1:1 relation*. If an object of set A is allocated to several objects of set B, we speak of a *1:n relation*. If several objects of set A are allocated to several objects of set B, we speak of an *n:m relation*.

Relations between data sets are represented in terms of their *key attributes*. Thus, an object of set B also contains as an attribute the key attribute of the object of set A to which it is related.

### 9.1.3 The Modelling Concepts of Database Systems

In addition to the descriptive perspective, three different modelling concepts can be distinguished: *hierarchical*, *network-like* and *relational* modelling. They are embodied in different database systems, also reflecting the development history of these tools (see [LocSchm87, ElmNava89]).

This goes back to the early sixties, when IBM developed the database system IMS (Information Management System; see [IBM71, IBM78]), the first database to find its way into commercial data processing. It implemented a *hierarchical* model. Here, the relations between objects are represented in strict accordance with the hierarchical principle in the form of sorted trees (see [Wedekind74, Date77]). Complex n:m relations that frequently occur in reality have to be represented "artificially" by several 1:n relations, which gives rise not only to modelling but also to redundancy problems. For addressing inquiries to hierarchical structures, knowledge of the point of entry into the tree and the paths to the individual objects is invariably needed. This approach is consequently not very flexible. Moreover, the implementation of this model is marked by a strong machine orientation. Even for description of the conceptual schema, details of the physical structure are required – and the means of description are accordingly machine-oriented, too. This leads to poorly intelligible application programs (see [Schneider83]).

A further development of hierarchical modelling, allowing the direct mapping of *network-like* structures, was presented in the late sixties and early seventies by the Data Base Task Group. This group had been founded at the Conference on Data Base Systems Languages (CODASYL) with the aim of developing a means of description for data modelling based on the programming language COBOL (see [Olle78]), which itself was a product of this conference. The network-like model has been incorporated into commercial databases such as *UDS, IDMS* and *IDS 2*. A major disadvantage of this model is the fact that to execute an inquiry precise knowledge of the current position in the network is required in order to be able to access the desired data via paths.

The hierarchical and network-like models and the database systems incorporating them were developed at a time when batch-oriented applications programming was the norm and are therefore unsuitable for the design, implementation and use of databases in an interactive mode. This, however, is accomplished to some extent by database systems developed along the lines of the third and most recent model, the *relational* model. Most of the work on the mathematical theory behind this model – a theory, however, that is not essential to a basic understanding of the model – was done as early as 1970/71 by E. F. Codd (see [Codd70, Codd71]). The only structure provided by the relational model is a two-dimensional table consisting of columns and lines in which the objects are represented together with their attributes. This table is viewed as a relation in the mathematical sense. Different objects are mapped in different tables on which powerful operations, based on the relational calculus, can be carried out. Though existing systems only realize part of the theory and the implementations are still rather poor from the point of view of run time, they are in widespread use in commercial data processing. They include systems such as *Oracle*, *Informix* and *Ingres*.

Owing to their simplicity, particularly as regards the comprehensibility and changeability of the schemata, relational databases are the only really usable systems for prototyping purposes.[39] We therefore take a closer look at them below. However, before going into the individual components of such systems in detail, we first of all give a general overview.

### 9.1.4 Language Constructs of Database Systems

To describe the logical schemata, so-called *Data Definition Languages* (DDL) are used. They contain constructs for

- the logical description of the objects and attributes,
- defining value ranges for the attributes,
- determining the access rights, and
- designating unambiguous attributes for identifying specific objects and defining classification criteria.

The physical description of the data is taken care of by *Storage Definition Languages* (SDL), though it is only in the earlier database systems that this has to be performed by the programmers themselves. More recent systems generate these machine-oriented descriptions automatically from the DDL descriptions. The manipulation and accessing of data is realized with the help of so-called *Data Manipulation Languages* (DML). These contain constructs for

- inserting,
- searching for,
- modifying, and
- deleting

objects and attributes, i.e., tables and entries within relational data models.

There are, however, very different types of such languages. In the first database systems, inquiries were addressed to the system using so-called *Host Languages*; for this purpose, the relevant language constructs were added to the compilers of commonly used existing languages. This approach, however, relies additionally on languages of which the respective user must have a command. Another approach is the Call-DML, providing procedure calls that "communicate" with the database. Here, we are not reliant on a particular host language

[39] Since non-standard databases like object-oriented database systems do not occupy a position of significance yet in the world of commercial data processing, we will not go into further details here. Overviews may, however, be found in [Kim90, KimLoc89].

since all possible languages can be extended by addition of an interface containing such procedure calls. Nevertheless, a sound knowledge of programming languages is needed in order to use the database. Database languages of this sort that are based on programming languages are called *nonindependent* languages.

Another branch of language development is that of the *independent* languages. These consist mostly of constructs borrowed from natural language. In the case of independent languages, a distinction is made between *procedural* and *descriptive* – so-called *declarative* – languages. A procedural language describes the procedure by means of which the desired results can be attained, i.e., the sequence of actions that leads to the desired result. In contrast, declarative languages describe the result itself. The sequence is then derived automatically from the description, i.e., a declarative language works out the procedure itself, all that needs to be declared is *what* is to be achieved by way of a result. Such languages are also known as *nonprocedural* languages. Here, independent system components, the *language interpreters*, process the user inputs and supply the results interactively.

Another way of addressing queries to database systems is by means of form-oriented, interactive components that enable data to be sought with the help of examples. In this case, the objects are represented graphically in forms and the functions are mapped on to function keys or a command language. This type of query is known as *Query by Example* or *Query by Form.*

### 9.1.5 Data Integrity in Database Systems

In view of the large quantities of data that database systems are designed to manage, two further aspects, *ensuring data access and data loss protection* and *safeguarding data integrity*, play such a major role that they are dealt with by separate system components.

The fact that vast quantities of data are stored in a database system – data that can be combined and related in all sorts of ways – means that there is a danger of the data being misused. To offer protection against such misuse, *restricted access rights* are installed preventing unauthorized users from accessing data. For this purpose, the data is protected by means of *passwords* or *encoding.*

To safeguard data integrity, *value ranges* are introduced, and automatic checks are carried out by the relevant system components to ensure that these are kept to. There are also facilities allowing the formulation of *simple transformation conditions* that may relate to individual fields or a combination of several fields. This sort of integrity is known as *semantic integrity.*

Another type of integrity that needs safeguarding is the *operational integrity.* Here, mechanisms are provided for solving problems that may arise as a result of the *simultaneous accessing* of the same data by different users. Another class of problems is that concerned with the processing of several connected actions that are to be executed consecutively – actions that are necessary to ensure consistent information. Such actions – known as *transactions* – must be marked as connected and executed accordingly. For this purpose, combination and allocation mechanisms are provided.

### 9.1.6 Developing Database Applications

To summarize, in database systems consideration is given to the following points:

- *data independence* and substantial *freedom from redundancy* by
  - realizing different views on the physical database, logical database and user level;
  - supporting the flexible use of data through suitable storage.
- an *infological* view that abstracts from technical aspects by means of
  - a descriptive model for the logical view of the data and the operations carried out on it;
  - the definition of a general inquiry language for describing and manipulating the data.
- *data integrity* by means of
  - protection mechanisms ensuring the error-free and consistent use of the data.

To design and construct database applications, they integrate the various system components for data definition, screen representation and manipulation under a uniform user interface. Since such systems vary wwith respect to their power and since no one development system contains all of the following concepts – which, taken together, would constitute an "ideal" development system – we speak, in view of their common basis, of *database-oriented development systems* when referring to systems that incorporate most of these concepts (see [FriQuiWer86]):

- The *data definitions* are specified in *data dictionaries* external to and independent of the application programs, and the instances of the objects are managed in a database external to and independent of the application programs.
- The *data definitions* and the *instances* of the *objects* can be generated and managed with the help of mutually coordinated graphical and form-oriented system components. This applies in particular to the design of input and report forms and the design of dialog sequences, but also to data access safeguards.
- The *instances* of the *objects* can be queried, evaluated, manipulated and displayed on the screen by means of operations that are available in the form of *nonprocedural language* elements.
- The *nonprocedural* operations for displaying and manipulating data can be combined with other language elements to form *transactions* or *procedures* with an explicit flow of control and in addition stored as repeatedly reusable programs.

## 9.2 Components of Database-Oriented Development Systems

In this section, we go on to look at the various tool concepts and components by reference to an example illustrating the interaction and dependencies between the different parts of database-oriented development systems. State-of-the-art in the area of commercial database systems are at present systems based on the *relational model.* As we have already pointed out, these are the only type of database-oriented development systems whose characteristics make them really suitable as a support for prototyping. In our example, we therefore confine ourselves to the use of concepts and tools from the "relational" world.

### 9.2.1 Example of a Conceptual Schema

We take as an application example the management of data for organizing and conducting seminars. In this problem area, we find seminars that are identified by means of a number and a title. Seminar participants are also given a number and are further identified by their surname, their first name, the company they work for, and the seminar they wish to attend. The important information about the company is the company name and a company number.

SEMINAR (SEMINARNUMBER, TITLE)

PARTICIPANT (PARTICIPANTNUMBER, NAME,
FIRSTNAME, SEMINARNUMBER,
COMPANYNUMBER)

COMPANY (COMPANYNUMBER, COMPANYNAME)

**Fig. 31.** The conceptual schema of our example

The conceptual schema consists, then, of the three object classes or entities **SEMINAR**, **PARTICIPANT** and **COMPANY**. They are first of all noted informally, their respective *attributes* being given in brackets. The *key attributes* are underlined, and the relations between the object classes are also expressed in terms of *attributes.* The object class **PARTICIPANT**, which is related to both the object class **SEMINAR** and the object class **COMPANY**, contains the *attributes* **COMPANYNUMBER** and **SEMINARNUMBER**. The conceptual schema in our example is shown in Figure 31. Our example is designed to illustrate the most important system components of database-oriented development tools. For this reason, we have deliberately kept it as simple as possible. For instance, it is only possible here for each **PARTICIPANT** to take part in one **SEMINAR**.

In order to implement operational prototypes on the basis of a logical schema, various system components are needed.

### 9.2.2 Integration of the System Components

All the system components of a database-oriented development system are integrated in a uniform user interface. From here, the various tools can be activated by means of commands or menus and the partial results already generated immediately made further use of (see Fig. 32 and 33).

```
    (entmenu)              UNIFY SYSTEM

                             Main Menu

 1. System Menu









    SELECTION : 1        □
```

**Fig. 32.** Main menu of a database-oriented development system

For the developer using an environment of this sort, this means that the tools available for performing a wide variety of tasks can all be handled in the same, or at least in a similiar way. Thus, some of the essential requirements for prototyping are met. Such a system helps, on the one hand, to simplify and speed up work, and on the other, it provides a set of tools that are so attuned to each other as to enable the development system itself to perform a series of checks to ensure the integrity and consistency of the solutions generated and to relieve the developer of some of the necessary routine work. What this means in specific terms is illustrated in the following sections.

(sysmenu) UNIFY SYSTEM

System Menu

| | |
|---|---|
| 1. Schema Maintenance | 9. Database Test Driver |
| 2. Schema Listing | 10. MENUM Screen Menu |
| 3. Create Database | 11. MENUM Report Menu |
| 4. SFORM Menu | 12. Reconfigure Database |
| 5. ENTER Screen Registration | 13. Write Database Backup |
| 6. SQL-Query/DML Language | 14. Read Database Backup |
| 7. SQL Screen Registration | 15. Database Maintenance Menu |
| 8. Listing Processor | |

SELECTION : 1 [0]

**Fig. 33.** Menu display /screen layout of an integrated user interface

Within a user interface of this sort, it is possible to work on a number of different levels. On the one side, data models, forms, menus and the resulting application programs can be developed on a largely interactive basis, and on the other, application programs or simple queries can be called and executed interactively. Thus, the *development system* also becomes the *application environment.* This constitutes an important advantage when implementing prototypes. For instance, once the logical schema has been implemented, application data can be entered to the database and managed by it without the need for other parts of the application to exist. This does, however, frequently mean that even when the application is completed the entire development environment is needed to execute the application, though there should actually be no real necessity for this. This is especially the case where the application itself is integrated into the development system and can only be activated from its user interface.

Such systems, in which integration covers both the development and application systems, account for only part of the products available. Other systems, in which the development components are integrated in the way described, contain additional system components that support the implementation of the applications in such a way as to enable them to be executed independently of the development environment. For this purpose, compilers are provided that generate executable code.

### 9.2.3 Components for Constructing Vertical Prototypes

Using database-oriented development systems, it is possible to construct prototypes whose functionality extends beyond the mere representation of user interface layouts on the screen and that enable objects to be manipulated. The basis for *vertical* prototypes (cf. Sec. 4.3) of this sort is the implementation of the *data schema.*

In database-oriented development systems, the logical schema is stored separately from other application system parts in a *data dictionary.* The structure of the data dictionary is dependent on the underlying file organization, the different concepts of which we described in the previous section. In relational development systems, the data definitions are stored in tables.

(schent) UNIFY SYSTEM

Schema Maintenance

DATABASE ID : 1

| LN | CMD | RECORD | EXPECTED | LONG NAME | DESCRIPTION |
|---|---|---|---|---|---|
| | ... | Particip | 40 | Participant | □...................... |
| 1 | *** | Seminar | 10 | Seminar | *************** |
| 2 | *** | Company | 25 | Company | *************** |
| ** | *** | ******** | **** | *********** | *************** |
| ** | *** | ******** | **** | *********** | *************** |
| ** | *** | ******** | **** | *********** | *************** |

(N)ext page, (P)rev page, (A)dd line, or, line number a

**Fig. 34.** Table editor for entering object specifications

The data model is entered by means of *editors.* As was the case with screen generators (cf. Chap. 8), here, too, a wide variety tools can be found. In addition to standard text editors, a number of systems also provide more sophisticated *table-oriented data editors.* A *table-oriented editor* is shown in Fig. 34 and 35. In this system,[40] input of the objects and their attributes is distributed over two screen forms.

[40] This and the following examples are taken from the database-oriented development system *Unify.*

(schent) UNIFY SYSTEM

Schema Maintenance

RECORD : Particip

| LN | CMD | FIELD | KEY | REF | TYPE | LEN | LONG NAME | COMB. FIELD |
|---|---|---|---|---|---|---|---|---|
| .. | ... | PCno | ... | Cno | numeric | 2 | Part_Comp_No | □ ... |
| 1 | ... | Pno | * | ... | numeric | 2 | Participants_No | ...... |
| 2 | ... | PName | ... | ... | string | 10 | Part_Name | |
| 3 | ... | PFName | ... | ... | string | 10 | Part_First_Name | ...... |
| 4 | ... | PSName | ... | Sno | numeric | 2 | Part_Sem_Name | ...... |
| .. | ... | ..... | ... | ... | ...... | .. | ........... | ...... |

(N)ext page, (P)rev page, (A)dd line, or, line number a

**Fig. 35.** Table editor for entering attribute specifications

The data definition editors and data dictionaries are interconnected in different ways in the different environments. This is reflected primarily in the different approaches used for checking the data models that have been input. Most tools attempt to ensure the consistency of the models directly on input and reject "faulty" inputs on the spot. This means that there are fixed procedures for editing.

Let us assume that the tool in our example belongs to this category. In this case, it is not possible to enter specifications of the object class `PARTICIPANT`[41] with this tool until the descriptions of the objects `COMPANY` and `SEMINAR` – to which `PARTICIPANT` is related – have been entered. This is because the key attributes of the other objects are also attributes of the object `PARTICIPANT`. This procedure is based on the assumption that a data model is inconsistent as long as the objects appertaining to the key attributes are not specified, for it seems pointless to describe `PARTICIPANT` without describing the objects `COMPANY` and `SEMINAR`. It is not, however, really necessary to couple this directly with the *input* of a schema, thus prescribing a sequence for editing operations that combines storage of data models with overall checks on their correctness. Another sound approach – and one which is desirable because it allows the sort of flexible strategies needed for prototyping – is based on tools that provide separate system

[41] In our example, this object is denoted by the identifier `PARTICIP` owing to restrictions in the length of identifiers used in the development system.

components for such checks and allow the developers a certain amount of freedom in designing their work.

Irrespective of the approach that may be adopted in implementing the schema, it is already possible to build simple prototypes once the data model has been specified.

### 9.2.4 Components for Constructing Simple Prototypes

Simple prototypes based on and also used for checking the data model can be implemented interactively with the help of *nonprocedural* language elements as well. Data-manipulating operations are available, for example, for inserting, modifying and deleting objects, without the need for the developer to bother about formulating instructions for positioning or searching for objects in accordance with the underlying storage organization. In the following examples, we present some of these operations from different development systems and languages.

The following examples are taken from *SQL/Unify*. The statement

```
INSERT INTO COMPANY:
< 1, Computing Company >
```

adds to the database in our example an instance of the object `COMPANY` that bears the name `Computing Company` and that is assigned the `COMPANYNUMBER` `'1'`. The statement

```
INSERT INTO PARTICIP
< 2, Smith, Peter, 10, 1 >
```

registers the data of a person called `'Peter Smith'` with the `PARTICIPANT-NUMBER` `'2'` who works for the `COMPANY` `'Computing Company'`, identified by the `COMPANYNUMBER` `'1'`, as `PARTICIPANT` in a `SEMINAR` with the `SEMINARNUMBER` `'10'`.

This example draws attention to a problem. As we have already pointed out, the database systems attempt to ensure maximum possible integrity and consistency of the data managed. For this reason, the execution of the above statement is rejected until an instance of the object `SEMINAR` with the `SEMINARNUMBER` `'10'` and the corresponding `TITLE` exists in the database. The statement

```
INSERT INTO SEMINAR
< 10, Evolutionary System Development >
```

for entering a `SEMINAR` must be executed before registering `PARTICIPANT`s for this `SEMINAR`.

A consistency problem also arises when deleting objects. In the following example, the statement

```
DELETE SEMINAR
  WHERE TITLE = 'Evolutionary System Development'
```

removes the instance of the object `SEMINAR` with the `TITLE 'Evolutionary System Development'` from the database. This may lead to inconsistencies in the `PARTICIPANT` data since it makes no sense to delete `SEMINAR`s for which `PARTICIPANT`s still exist. Some database systems therefore prevent the removal of such objects from the database as long as other objects exist to which they are related – in our example: `PARTICIPANT`. Others simply delete the respective attributes in the objects affected.

Another consistency problem arises when modifying objects. The statement

```
UPDATE PARTICIP
SET PFName = 'BILL'
WHERE Pno = 2
```

changes the `FIRSTNAME` of a `PARTICIPANT` who is identified by the `PARTICIPANT-NUMBER '2'`.[42] To ensure that during this operation no other operation accesses the object in question, most database-oriented development systems are equipped with so-called *lock mechanisms* that are automatically executed along with the modification operations and that prevent the object in question from being accessed by other operations.

Another class of data manipulation operations are the selection operations. They retrieve instances of objects selected on the basis of specific attribute conditions. In doing so, they abstract from the individual access operations of a search procedure to the objects in the database that are needed to supply a solution set.

In the following example of a data query, the data of all `PARTICIPANT`s known to the system and bearing the name `'Smith'` are returned:

```
FIND PARTICIP WITH PName = 'Smith'
```

This example is taken from *Natural.* The same applies to the operations for forming unions or intersections of sets that supply instances of objects or their attributes on the basis of join or difference conditions. The following statement is taken from *Sesam/Drive*:

```
SELECT PName, PFName
 FROM PARTICIP
  WHERE PARTICIP.PCno = '1'
```

retrieves the `NAME`s and `FIRSTNAME`s of all `PARTICIPANT`s who work for a particular `COMPANY`, namely the `COMPANY` that can be identified by the `COMPANYNUMBER '1'` – in our example: `'Computing Company'`. The results of such operations are formatted and displayed on the screen with the help of so-called *report generators* without any programming effort.

[42] The corresponding identifier in the above example is Pno. To improve readability, we have, both here and in the following examples, chosen identifiers from the conceptual schema. Many languages, however, require shorter identifiers.

This way of entering data manipulation operations gives rise to two problems. Firstly, the operations are specified and executed directly on an interactive basis. This means that they are not filed and therefore have to be re-entered whenever other data needs to be manipulated. Secondly, this way of entering is highly machine-oriented, the various attributes having to be specified in the order in which they are described in the schema. These functions allow the construction of simple prototypes designed primarily for checking the data model or clarifying technical problems. However, they offer little support in implementing prototypes to be used as a basis for discussion or for settling more substantial questions such as the design of the user interface or the system functionality.

### 9.2.5 Screen Design With Screen Generators

With the help of *screen generators*, which we have already looked at above (cf. Chap. 8), user-oriented screen forms can be generated. Most development systems provide two system components for this purpose. The first enables so-called "default" screen forms to be generated automatically for each object described in the data dictionary. Here, the attributes of the objects are allocated input fields on the screen. All the applications programmer has to do is name the screen form and give names, i.e., labels or "prompts", to these input fields so that the user can see on the screen where to enter which data. The forms generated in this way can then be used to manipulate objects, i.e., the data manipulation operations described above can be activated using a command language provided along with the screen form. Most screen generators also contain "built-in" functions for controlling cursor movements, which means that the developer no longer has to bother about this, either.

Nonetheless, automatic design of such screen forms is very rare and does not solve all problems. This is why the screen generators also support the free design of the maps for the application systems. Figure 36 shows a *map* and *form editor* that allows direct visual layout of the desired information elements for a form on the screen using a *screen painting* function. The visually-oriented functions for defining input and output field positions can be enhanced by commands for specifying additional design attributes, e.g., for underlining or reverse video display of particular fields.

The line `Data Base Field` in Figure 36 shows that this tool – like editors of other systems, too – is linked directly to the data dictionary, thus establishing the connection between inputs and their corresponding database fields. This already suffices for the construction of vertical prototypes that contain all the essential components of an application system. Other development systems implement concepts with which developers can or must establish the connection between maps and the data definitions themselves by activating separate functions.

### 9.2.6 Dialog Design With Menu Generators

The maps are now ready for use, but must still be activated independently of one another by their name. For this reason, *menu generators* are provided

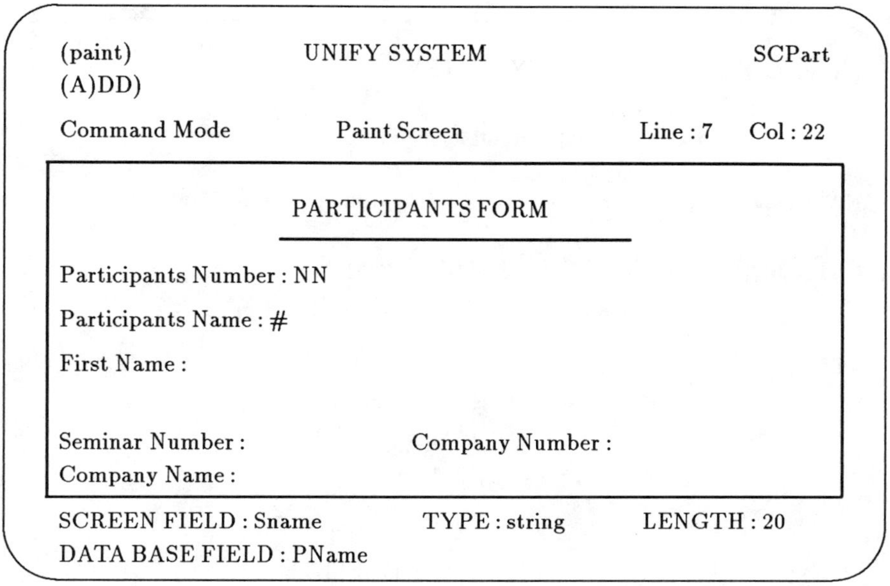


**Fig. 36.** Form definition with attributes from a data dictionary

for designing simple dialog sequences. With their help, it is possible to name application functions that can combine screen maps and the objects and access operations belonging to them and make application systems available at the user interface of prototypes with a minimum of programming effort. The instructions and the data required to realize a program are acquired with the help of *menu editors*. Figure 37 shows a detail from this sort of menu definition using a table-oriented *menu generator*. Here, three screen layouts already specified are declared as input forms for a menu called `Seminar Administration Menu`.

From this table, the menu generator builds a menu screen layout for the prototype. Figure 38 shows this generated menu screen providing, after selection, three functions for registering, checking and deleting data from our example by means of additional screen maps. This screen map is now available as part of an operational prototype for menu selection – with built-in selection functions, similar to those of the input forms.

If the development environment is necessary to execute the prototypes, the generated menu must be integrated into its user interface as well. Figure 39 shows this integration; Figure 40 shows the main menu of a system of this sort.

## An Intermediate Evaluation

Using the system components described so far, it is already possible to build prototypes for different purposes with a minimum of effort. We classify these as

```
(menumnt)                UNIFY SYSTEM
(A)DD)
                        Menu Maintenance

NAME : SemMenu      HEADING : Seminar Administration Menu

cmd   LINE   MENU/PROG     M/P   Prompt
...    1       SCSemi       E    Seminar Form
...    2       SCPart       E    Participants Form
...    3       SCPComp      E    Company Form
...    ..      .........    ..   ..................
...    ..      .........    ..   ..................

   (I)NQUIRE,    (A)DD,  (M)ODIFY,    (D)ELETE      [a]
```

**Fig. 37.** Menu definition for dialog design with screen maps

```
   (SemMenu)            UNIFY SYSTEM

                  Seminar Administration Menu

   1. Seminar Form
   2. Participants Form
   3. Company Form



   SELECTION : 2      □
```

**Fig. 38.** Menu of an integrated application system

```
(menumnt)                 UNIFY SYSTEM
(M)ODIFY)
                        Menu Maintenance

NAME : entmenu        HEADING : Main Menu

cmd   LINE   MENU/PROG      M/P   Prompt
...    1       sysmenu       M     System Menu
...    2       SemMenu       M     Seminar Administration Menu
...    ..      .........     ..    ..................
...    ..      .........     ..    ..................
...    ..      .........     ..    ..................

   (I)NQUIRE,   (A)DD,  (M)ODIFY,   (D)ELETE    [m]
```

**Fig. 39.** Menu definition for a prototype within a development environment

```
   (entmenu)            UNIFY SYSTEM

                           Main Menu

   1. System Menu
   2. Seminar Administration Menu

   SELECTION : 2     □
```

**Fig. 40.** Main menu of a database-oriented development system with an integrated application system

simple prototypes. But our examples also reveal some of the problems that these system components pose for the construction and use of prototypes:

- The manipulation operations are executed interactively, i.e., if applied repeatedly, they must be repeatedly entered; they are not stored as a recallable program sequence.
- It is not possible to combine several elementary manipulation operations into a procedure or transaction that can be repeatedly executed as a whole.
- It is not possible to combine a wide variety of operations in one program.
- Deviation from the work steps prescribed by the screen maps and manipulation operations is not possible. The system components described above only allow one or more instances of a *single* object class to be displayed on the screen at any one time. Activating a search operation, for instance, only allows a "search" to be carried out; to modify objects, a separate operation must be performed.

### 9.2.7 Components for Constructing Complex Prototypes

To solve these problems, database-oriented development systems provide additional system components allowing statements to be combined to form *procedures* or *transactions* and *programs* and to be filed in *libraries* for archiving, reuse or futher use.

For this purpose, the individual system components are integrated and enhanced by *flow of control* constructs in such a way that it is possible to program as in traditional procedural languages.

An important element of these means of expression are, in addition to the query and data manipulation operations described above, functions allowing the formatted input and output of data on the basis of externally defined forms.

The following examples are again taken from *Natural*. The statement

INPUT USING MAP participants_form

within a program results in the display of a previously defined form – in this example, the form **participants_form** – for registering **PARTICIPANT** data (see also Fig. 36) and allows the formatted input of data in such a form. The statement abstracts from all the individual steps of a standard text editor that are necessary for filling in forms. These include algorithms for moving the cursor inside forms as well as checking the value ranges of the input data. In addition to displaying data in individual form fields by means of simple WRITE statements, tables and lists can also be generated and displayed in programs. A table containing the data of **PARTICIPANT**s from our example (see Fig. 41) is generated with the help of a *report generator* and displayed on the screen by means of a statement sequence such as

```
WRITE TITLE UNDERLINED
     20x 'LIST of PARTICIPANTS'
     DISPLAY ParticipantName FirstName ParticipantNumber
```

The operation contains implicit formatting instructions for table generation with automatic line and column makeup. The table, i.e. the list, can be displayed either on the screen or on a printer, as required.

LIST of PARTICIPANTS

| ParticipantName | FirstName | ParticipantNumber |
|---|---|---|
| Smith | Peter | 1 |
| Miller | Bill | 2 |
| Jones | Peter | 3 |
| ........... | ......... | .. |

**Fig. 41.** List output with a report generator

### 9.2.8 Language Constructs for Flow of Control

To allow program-internal modification and intermediate storage of data, development systems also offer facilities for program-internal *declaration of variables*. For this purpose, various different concepts have been implemented. Some languages require – as is normally the case in traditional programming languages – an *explicit* declaration of variables for an object or its values, specifying the data type by denoting a keyword (**INTEGER**, **NUMERIC**, **STRING**, etc.). Others expect, the first time an identifier is used, an initialization from which the data type of the thus identified object can be derived, or declare a variable of a particular type by assigning it a particular identifier. This procedure may also be encountered in early versions of FORTRAN, for example, where the initial letter of an identifier could be used to determine the data type. The concept just described is also known as *implicit* declaration.

The execution sequence of the various statements and the flow of control can be programmed with the help of constructs for formulating *conditional statements*, *loops* and *logical operations*. In the following example, an implicit loop is combined with an I/O function.

If, on execution of the statement block

```
FIND PARTICIP WITH PName = Sname
IF NORECORDS FOUND
   'NO PARTICIPANT FOUND'
   REINPUT
ENDIF
```

no **PARTICIPANT** can be found in the database with the participant name **PName** that was given the value of the variable Sname, the message '**NO PARTICIPANT FOUND**' is issued on the screen and, in an implicit loop that is denoted by the keyword **REINPUT**, a new input is expected. The statement '**NORECORDS FOUND**' used in this example is also an instance of a *standard constant* provided by the language. Many development systems provide constants of this sort. In addition, the languages contain language constructs for formulating explicit loops (e.g., **WHILE**) and logical operations (e.g., **AND**, **OR**).

Numerical computations and text operations can be carried out with the help of "built-in" standard functions ($+, -, *, /, **$) and text operations (**SUBSTRING**, **CONCAT**). Many environments also provide additional functions allowing access to the system environment (e.g., **TIME**, **DATE**).

### 9.2.9 Language Constructs for Formulating Procedures and Transactions

The further structuring of programs is supported by concepts for combining algorithms into *procedures*. The following example taken from *Sesam/Drive* shows the declaration of a procedure *display* for outputting data about persons with the same name:

```
SUBPROC display
SELECT * FROM PARTICIP
            WHERE PName = &NAME
IF &SQLSTATE = 'EOF'
   THEN SET &MELDUNG 'No Participant Found'
END;
ENDSUBPROC
```

Depending on the respective value of the variable &NAME, the database is searched and a list of data is displayed.

In addition to these constructs, many systems also possess interfaces to other programming languages. This means that components built using the development system can be combined with traditional programming languages to help solve application problems that are difficult to tackle with the means available. The resulting programs are translated by means of *compilers*. Depending on the target language, it is then possible to modify application programs or add to them partial solutions in other languages. This applies in particular to compilers that generate from programs of this sort code in a traditional programming language like COBOL.

If, then, extensive prototypes are to be implemented – which are also to be gradually integrated or converted into the target systems aimed at – the availability of the system components just described is an absolute "must".

## 9.3 Our Assessment

As a basic principle, database-oriented development systems support prototyping strategies. They can be used for both *horizontal* and *vertical* prototyping and offer support in clarifying a wide variety of problems ranging from the *specification of requirements* to the *modelling of interactive* and *functional components* of the application systems under development. This only applies, however, to development systems that are based on *relational databases,* i.e.,

- that abstract from files,
- that directly manage relations and their connections

and thus make for less redundancy.

Database systems that fail to offer such support require considerable additional effort when programming application systems in order to achieve this objective.

Database-oriented development systems can be employed *throughout* the development process, especially for the technical tasks of design, construction and testing. They can be used most successfully where one – or, ideally, all – of the following requirements are met:

- the applications are not too complex or extensive,
- the applications provide support for task areas that are independent of one another,
- the applications are used primarily to carry out evaluations and inquiries and to generate reports.

This is the case, for instance, with a card file that is created and updated by a single staff member.

Database-oriented development systems and the programs generated with them meet some of the essential requirements for prototyping:

- They are *more problem-oriented* than traditional commercial programming languages such as COBOL. This means that the process of transferring working routines from the end users' working environment into computer programs is facilitated by the tools they provide.

- Their powerful nonprocedural language elements make the programs compact and thus *easier to understand.* This also enables prototypes to be converted and integrated into target systems.
- The construction of application programs is highly *efficient.* The separate generation and management of data dictionaries, screen maps, dialog sequences and application algorithms, and the implementation of concepts allowing early error detection support, as a rule, the *rapid* and *easy development* and *modification* of prototypes. Specific parts of the application systems under development can be implemented as prototypes.

For this purpose, complex algorithms for accessing the data are already available in the form of powerful operations. Simple and complex prototypes can be "built" by combining these operations with simple – and in some cases automatically generable – screen maps. By using control structures, more extensive applications can be defined. The fact that interpretive execution of partial algorithms and the use of automatic debugging aids like "trace functions" are possible means that such applications can also be easily checked and tested. Altogether, the interactive, integrated system components allow *rapid design, construction* and *evaluation cycles.*

After this generally positive assessment, we now go on to list additional criteria for the selection of development systems. By reference to the above-mentioned requirements for prototyping, the systems are given detailed evaluation with regard to the following points:

- use and handling;
- programming in the small and in the large;
- suitability for further use and target systems; and
- development strategies and approaches.

### 9.3.1 Use and Handling

At the user interfaces, most development systems provide strictly hierarchical menus for selecting system components. These offer useful support to the users in familiarizing themselves with a system of this sort. With growing experience, though, they are more of a hindrance than an aid. To perform certain actions with which the tool user is well-acquainted and which are offered in a submenu, it is invariably necessary to run through several menus until the desired system component is reached in the relevant submenu and can be selected. The selection is then frequently performed by the separate input of an identification key for the system component, mostly a digit. To call a component directly without running through the menus, a system-internal identifier for the component is often required. Users of the development system must therefore either run through a "cumbersome" series of menus or make a mental note of "cryptic" identifiers if they wish to perform specific tasks. Neither of these methods meets the requirements for a user-friendly tool interface. They make little or no use of convenient technical facilities such as mnemonics or function keys for sequences of long commands. Even less frequent is the use of technical developments such as the mouse, which can be used as an input device for direct manipulation of data on the screen.

It is important to note, however, that a number of development systems with user interfaces of this sort provide only a limited number of interaction forms and types for developing application systems, and these are often precisely the ones that are needed and implemented for the development system itself. In this case, the tools do support the – unquestionably useful – standardization of application system interfaces; they are suitable for constructing prototypes that are not primarily designed for implementing user interfaces, but, at most, for analyzing requirements or implementing functional components. They are, however, of only limited suitability for the development of prototypes with individual user interfaces. They require considerable effort for developing such an interface for the application system being constructed on the basis of a prototype.

Substantial differences are also found in the user interfaces of the various system components. These range from simple text editors, which expect complete textual description of the schemata, the screen maps and dialog sequences, to table-oriented and graphic tools such as we have described in the previous sections. These tools make a portion of the required data available in tables and forms and support input, for example, by automatically positioning the cursor in the input fields of the screen maps. User interfaces of this sort allow data to be entered more quickly and enhance comprehensibility of the application system components thus implemented. This helps support changeability and "checkability" – essential prerequisites for prototyping. However, here, too, there are certain restrictions that must be taken into account. In some cases, the editors are controlled by entering commands, the command languages themselves varying here as regards their power of expression and comprehensibility. In some systems, commands must be given as strings of special characters, which may impair ease of use and facility of handling. Other systems use more user-friendly techniques such as function keys and mouse control. Comprehensibility is also impaired by additional unnecessary restrictions, e.g., affecting the representation of identifiers for objects and attributes whose length is frequently limited so that only very short names can be used.

### 9.3.2 Programming in the Small and in the Large

If we consider the language constructs integrated as system components, we find that the incorporation of constructs for the declaration of variables and the use of control structures, as well as facilities for storing transactions and programs in libraries, support programming in the small and the reusability of algorithms. Since these constructs are, however, highly restricted in their syntactic forms, a number of problems arise. For instance, the implicit declaration of variables – quite customary in some languages – results in faulty programs and causes difficulties in fault location and debugging. Furthermore, the readability of the program code is considerably impaired by the use of numerous special characters. Similar problems are caused by the occasional failure to mark and identify program blocks. Such problems can, of course, occur when using such tools for prototyping, depending on the size of the prototypes being implemented.

In contrast, the powerful I/O and data manipulation operations represented by nonprocedural language elements allow the developers to formulate compact algorithms of manageable size. This is an important prerequisite for prototyping, though it is frequently achieved at the expense of longer execution times. Lack of knowledge about the implementation of what are sometimes highly elaborate operations requiring considerable computing time can, however, result in unreasonably long response times. While this is of only secondary importance for prototyping – depending on the size and purpose of the prototypes –, it can cause considerable problems for the target systems to be developed from such prototypes. Execution of the application programs is often inefficient, and the developer is at a loss as to how this inefficiency can be remedied.

For programming in the large, i.e., specifying the application system architecture, transaction, procedure and file concepts are normally available. Problems arise here if explicit parameter passing mechanisms are lacking for declaring or calling procedures, resulting in avoidable errors. Languages that make no provision whatsoever for such constructs are of only very limited suitability for prototyping. Most languages do not allow the definition of explicit interfaces between the different program parts. Module concepts – provided by and expected of high-level programming languages – are available in only a small number of languages such as *Natural*; they should, however, belong to the standard repertoire of every language. Without such language constructs, it is difficult to develop and implement architectures for the prototypes that are "sound" by software engineering standards. This impairs the correctness of programs and gives rise to additional obstacles to the development of prototypes and application systems on a participative basis. This, however, is imperative, especially when dealing with programs of substantial size. For such tasks, it is also useful to have a system component that manages the different versions of the application system under development. Not all development systems, however, provide such a component.

### 9.3.3 Suitability for Further Use and Target Systems

In the previous section, we have touched on the connection between prototypes and target systems a number of times from the perspective of the language constructs available. Since this connection plays an important part in the choice of a development system, we devote a separate section to its consideration.

In addition to the above arguments concerning the effort required to construct a prototype and the language constructs needed for structured programming, two further points are of significance for the transition from prototype to target system.

If a prototype using some of the system components provided by the development system is to be extended into an application system, it is of some significance whether or not the entire development system is needed to execute the application system. This is frequently the case where the implemented systems are executed by interpretive tool components. This takes up a considerable amount of storage space since, in addition to the application system's code, space is also needed for the development system's code. Apart from the general uneconomical utilization of the available hardware, this can also give rise to problems where the development computer is not the same as the application computer and the storage capacity of the two differs. Preference should therefore be given to systems that do not need the whole development system to execute application systems. Such systems have their own compilers that generate executable code from which the required data – whether these be descriptions of screen maps or instances of the objects managed in the database – are accessed. Here, the application system is executed largely independently of the development system.

The separation of development and application system is, of course, also supported by the provision of an interface between the development system and a classical programming language such as COBOL or C.

A further point on which the availability of such interfaces has a bearing is the frequently limited application scope of many development systems. In most cases, this is confined to the simple generation of reports by retrieving existing data. If the attempt is made to use them to solve problems peripheral to the application area proper, this often results in very "tricky" and unintelligible programs. No attempt should be made to solve application problems of this sort with such development systems, either in the context of prototyping or when developing application and target systems.

Nonetheless, a combination of development systems and classical programming languages can be used meaningfully in a case of this sort: using a database-oriented tool, it is possible to construct a prototype that can be viewed partly or wholly as a specification, and partly as an already existing component of the target system. Parts of the prototype, e.g., the logical schema, may be adopted and extended into an application system, for instance, by implementing an individual user interface and application-specific algorithms in a classical programming language.

A third point in favour of interfaces to classical programming languages is the resulting changeability and adaptability of the application systems. This not only allows optimization of the software developed, thus enhancing user convenience, it also enables the software to be ported to other machines on which the target language is available, thus bringing greater economic benefits.

Both changeability at target language level and viewing prototypes as specifications can, however, entail problems. If the prototype is not "frozen" in its function as a specification, but is further developed largely parallel to the target system, steps must be taken to ensure that the "specification" and the "implementation" tally. The ability to make changes in the target system that cannot be made in the prototype can easily result in the loss of conformity between the two and the impossiblity of re-establishing it.[43]

If we are to discuss the resulting application systems here, we must also consider the way database-oriented development systems affect the application system architecture from the point of view of software engineering quality cri-

[43] We will go into this problem in detail in Sec. 12.2.

teria. Many of the development systems combine the functional and interactive components of the applications in such a way that the algorithms for implementing I/O routines are embedded within the functional components. In the case of application systems with numerous different functions, this results in unnecessary code redundancy. Also, the interlacement of the various components impairs comprehensibility and hinders modification and checking operations during the development process. Our remarks in the previous section about "quick and dirty" architectures – that are highly questionable from the point of view of software engineering standards of quality – apply equally in this connection, too, perhaps even more so.

### 9.3.4 Development Strategies and Approaches

To conclude, let us consider the way development strategies and approaches support performance of the necessary development tasks. The interrelations between the various tools have a substantial effect on the way developers work. This is a crucial factor affecting job satisfaction and thus, implicitly, the developers' productivity. The coordination between the various tools has a considerable influence on the approaches adopted by the developers and their individual working styles.

The strategy of providing different tools for the different subtasks in system development and of managing the work results separately, outside the application programs, has, as we have already shown, a number of advantages, both for the work of the developers and for the products under development. The *integration* of the various tools in a uniform user interface offers support here on two different levels. Firstly, when changing tools, the developers remain in a world with which they are familiar; the use of a different tool within the development system does not require changes in operation routines. And secondly, the individual work results can be checked separately or all together before executing the application system. This facilitates development work and supports quality assurance for the resulting software.

Some database-oriented development systems, however, strictly prescribe the adoption of a uniform approach throughout the development process, especially during the design and modification of user interfaces, data models and dialog sequences. In systems of this kind, the various tools are interconnected in such a way that the use of certain components is a necessary precondition for the use of others. Some systems require a complete data model as a basis for designing screen forms and maps; others need the forms to generate the logical schema. Tools based on these strategies do, it is true, take over some of the standard tasks normally performed by the developers; however, they restrict the developers' scope for selecting specific approaches of their own and hinder the development of individual work styles.

Besides the question of individual work styles, prescriptive strategies of this sort also affect methods for carrying out the necessary revision cycles. Support of such revision cycles is, however, only meaningful if the individual work results requiring revision can be directly modified and updated without a great deal of effort and without the need to run through entire development cycles. If a fixed sequence is prescribed for performing the tasks here and if, as is frequently the case, this can be followed in one direction only – from the so-called early development tasks, such as generation of an information system model, to the so-called late tasks like implementation – then the flexibility in the performance of tasks required for prototyping is subject to considerable restrictions.

A number of systems therefore allow developers to use the various tools independently of one another. They ensure the integration of the partial solutions generated by the explicit use of *bridging tools* that preserve individual work styles and enable the tools to be adapted to the particular situation in hand. We consider systems of this sort to be better suited for prototyping. They do, however, also allow flexible development strategies to be used in development situations where prototyping is not employed as an explicit approach.

In addition, the various implemented concepts for *checking* the logical schemata and the specifications of the objects' screen representation when they are being defined and modified should be seen in connection with the approaches supported or prescribed by the development systems. Many tools take over the job of carrying out lexical and syntactical checks directly upon input, thus preventing the construction of an incomplete or inconsistent data model. In the case of closely coordinated tools, this concept is also frequently adopted for consistency checks on a "supertool" level. For the description of screen maps, for example, some tools require that for each screen field the corresponding attribute be given from the logical schema on a direct, interactive basis; they then check these data and, in the case of an error, demand its immediate correction. In some cases this concept is applied so rigorously that it is impossible to store incomplete and temporarily inconsistent schemata and screen specifications. This also means that development systems of this sort do not allow work to be interrupted at any desired point; nor do they allow pure editing operations to be carried out.

These strategies do, admittedly, reduce the danger of serious errors occurring and help avoid laborious debugging operations. However, they needlessly force developers to adopt work styles that no longer permit them to design their own work or carry out checks and corrections, or have these carried out, at their own discretion. Equally problematic, though, are system components that, owing to their poor coordination, do not carry out consistency checks until during run time. Such an approach results in nonoperational systems and entails a good deal of effort for debugging and correction. Development systems of this sort are of only limited suitability for carrying out the rapid, incremental revision and development cycles essential for prototyping.

We therefore consider a third concept to be the most suitable. Here, the tools draw the developers' attention to inconsistencies, but provide explicitly for the consistency checks to be performed or initiated by the developers themselves. This not only takes into account the above-mentioned concerns, it also helps to avoid errors during development, while at the same time supporting individual work styles. There are few development systems incorporating this concept, though it ought to be part of the standard repertoire here, since it provides an important basis for prototyping and evolutionary development strategies.

### 9.3.5 Outlook

The development history of database-oriented development systems, which has been essentially governed by pragmatic considerations rooted in the world of commercial data processing, serves to explain a number of the strengths and weaknesses discussed above. The constantly growing market in this sector leads us to expect a further increase in the number of application programs generated with the help of database-oriented development systems. There is also likely to be a continuing process of adaptation to the end users' way of thinking and usage of language. And this means that the importance of such systems for prototyping will continue to grow. The availability of better and cheaper hardware and the progressive decentralization of data processing – with personal computers increasingly ousting mainframes from the workplaces of both developers and users – are likely to accelerate this trend. And it will also be given momentum by the development of better and more efficient relational database systems, which in turn will encourage the development of new database-oriented development systems. The increasing popularity of these systems will lead to the growth of a pool of information and practical experience with their use, and to increasingly sophisticated demands being made on them. And this will eventually cause "pseudo"-database-oriented tools to disappear from the market and result in the elimination of the shortcomings described above.

# 10
# Very High Level Languages

This chapter gives an overview of Very High Level Languages, insofar as they are of interest for the construction of functional prototypes. We consider VHLLs from two different angles, examining whether they are used to gain a better understanding of

- design (i.e., the construction process) or
- implementation (i.e., the constructed product).

In both cases they enable prototypes to be constructed. We classify VHLLs into various groups and give an appraisal of the benefits they offer for prototype construction.

## 10.1 Concept and Features

The reason for using VHLLs is that the solution of a particular problem requires the use of means appropriate to that problem. A typical argument is: "All that remains for the programmer to do is to formulate *what* the problem is. *How* the problem is to be solved remains the secret of the VHLL". Unfortunately, it is not quite as easy as that to separate the *what* from the *how*. Depending on the level of abstraction, they may change places. The *how* of one level turns out to be the *what* of a lower level. And, even worse, *what* is possible is determined to some extent by *how* the problem is tackled. Every mountain-hiker knows that selecting the route (the *how*) is of crucial importance in order to arrive at the desired destination (*what*). The *what* and the *how* are, then, linked by economic considerations. That is why the notion of VHLL cannot be defined in context-free terms of the usual what-how antithesis or in terms of the "very high level" of the languages. We therefore confine ourselves to characterizing VHLLs in terms of *features* which many of them have in common. If the purpose of a VHLL is to focus the software developer's attention on describing a problem rather than programming the solution, a VHLL may be characterized as follows:

- Programs written in a VHLL should be *compact*. By this, we mean, for example, that the formulation of a graph theory problem in a mathematically oriented VHLL such as Setl should not be much longer than the mathematical formulation itself.
- VHLLs should have an *easily intelligible semantics model*; for example:
  - *Setl* is based on the set theory.
  - *APL* is based on matrix algebra.
  - *Snobol4* is based on Markov algorithms.
  - *Lisp* is based on the $\lambda$ calculus.
  - *Prolog* is based on Horn logic.

All existing implementations, however, contain constructs which cannot be explained in terms of the "easily intelligible" semantic model. VHLLs are *designed for use in specific application areas.* These application areas correspond well with their semantic model. If VHLLs are used in other areas, they are merely general-purpose languages, offering similar features to any other programming language. This may even result in programs becoming unintelligible.

- VHLLs contain as *little explicit flow of control* as possible. For example: Lisp uses recursion; Prolog, backtracking as well; Setl is equipped with powerful set constructors.
- VHLLs work with *highly powerful* data types whose manipulations are very efficiently implemented:
  - *Setl*: sets.
  - *APL*: vectors.
  - *Snobol*: character strings.
  - *Lisp*: lists.
  - *Prolog*: terms.

Today's VHLLs are usually delivered with the following support, which, in our opinion, is practically a must for prototyping purposes:

- A *programming environment* that facilitates project organization and provides an integrated set of tools. For Lisp, sophisticated programming environments have long been available. Most functional and logical languages are only supplied ready-equipped with a programming environment. Expert system shells are designed as programming environments.
- Means for conversion between data structures and programs (*reflexivity*). This, for example, enables tools for programming support to be implemented in the VHLL itself. In the case of Lisp and Prolog, reflexivity has proved a decisive factor in speeding up development work, especially in prototype construction.
- Means for their easy *combination* with other languages and tools.
- An *interpreter*, an *incremental compiler* or at least *small compilation units* in order to ensure sufficient speed of prototype development cycles.
- *Incomplete* programs written in a VHLL should be executable. This helps speed up the development and debugging cycles.

## 10.2 Benefits and Limitations

As in the case of *what* and *how*, it is difficult from a practitioners' viewpoint to draw a line between specification and implementation. We distinguish between them on the basis of the different purposes they serve:

- A *specification* helps us to understand a technical product and its application context. Specifications are therefore of interest to people (not only to software developers, but also to end users).

– An *implementation* is processed by a computer. Computers can only process formal descriptions.

An implementation, then, is almost invariably formal, regardless of whether the program is written in Assembler, Pascal or Prolog.[44] Unlike formal implementations, a wide variety of specifications can be found:

– informal (e.g., in natural language)
– formatted (with well-defined syntax, but vague semantics, e.g., pseudocode)
– formal (e.g., predicate calculus)
– executable (e.g., Prolog).

VHLLs are of interest for the purposes of both specification and implementation. We emphasize this fact when we call a VHLL an *executable specification language* or a *problem-oriented implementation language*. Both aspects highlight the benefits VHLLs offer for prototype construction.

But let us go a step further in discussing the benefits of VHLLs for prototype construction. In publications on the subject, complete *and* formal specification of an application system is frequently called for if software development is to be "state-of-the-art". We regard this view as being too restricted:

– It involves the implicit assumption that the functionality of a software system is the only aspect that needs specifiying. It is quite true that the functionality is the only aspect that can be formally specified without too much difficulty. There are, however, numerous other aspects also requiring specification, but their formalization is problematic, to say the least (user-friendliness, efficiency, robustness, but also the usability of a software system). The functionality is only a fraction of what goes to make up the specification of a software system.
– If we look at mathematics, a discipline that would appear to encourage a puristic, formal view of this kind, we find that there is hardly any complex mathematical proof that is presented in *completely* formal terms. Mathematical proofs consist of a conglomeration of formal and informal conclusions. If required, i.e., if uncertainties were to arise in following the lines of reasoning, these proofs *could* be further formalized. Even in the case of a simple statement, a completely formal proof does not facilitate understanding of the line of reasoning, and constructing it would involve unnecessary effort.[45]

These so-called "complete and formal specifications" differ from prototypes in two essential points:

---

[44] It is frequently the case that a specification of a program which is different from the implementation and meant to be readily understandable by human beings does not exist. Where this is so, the software developer must try to interpret the implementation as a specification.

[45] An excellent examination of the limitations of formal approaches can be found in [Lehman90].

- When constructing prototypes, *selected aspects* only are considered. That is less than would be obtained by means of complete and formal specifications: it means that a programmer is needed to construct the system and that no purely mechanical transformation will work.
- A prototype is *executable.* That is more than would be obtained by means of complete and formal specifications: it enables us to test the suitability of a system in the application area. Prototypes provide the unique opportunity of involving experts from a particular application area, who are not computer specialists, in software development at an early stage.

Prototypes are designed to clarify certain aspects of the system for the computer experts and the end users. For this purpose, the two groups (jointly) construct a program, analyze it, evaluate it in operation, and modify it. VHLLs are indispensable for this laborious trial-and-error process.

## 10.3 The Main Groups

In most cases, VHLLs are used today to implement prototypes. The simple reason for this is that, if the prototype requires modification, a VHLL will help to carry out the modifications efficiently. Thanks to the powerfulness of VHLLs, the design process is short, consisting mainly of programming work. In view of this, VHLLs are, today, already of interest for the commercial software developer's daily work.

Besides object-oriented VHLLs (which are considered later in Sec. 10.4), VHLLs based on *mathematical models* are frequently found in use at universities and in R & D laboratories. Their practical application in commercial data processing still remains the exception, though, despite their suitability for this sphere. We have subdivided them into four main groups:

- logical languages
- functional languages
- algebraic languages
- miscellaneous languages

### 10.3.1 Logical Languages

Logical programming languages are used mainly on the basis of theorem-provers for Horn logic. They stem from a discovery of Robinson's (see [Robinson65]). The most important language of this type is *Prolog* (see [ClocMell84]), which can also be implemented efficiently. Also available are implementations for the whole first-order predicate calculus. The most important dialects of the language Prolog are:

- *DECsystem-10 Prolog*: This defines the de facto standard for the language (see [DECsystem-10-Prolog]).

- *C Prolog*: This, along with its successors (Quintus Prolog, BIM Prolog, IF/Prolog), is the most widespread Prolog dialect (see [Cprolog]).
- *MU Prolog*: This allows delaying of unifications. Consequently, it contains a "cleaner" implementation of the *not* operator (i.e., logical negation) (see [MUProlog84]).
- On Lisp machines there exist *Prolog variants*, some of them with Lisp syntax (see [SymbolicsProlog85]).
- *PrologIII*: This allows processing of infinite term structures and systems of equalities and inequalities (see [Colmerauer87]).

None of the Prolog dialects in use today possesses modular design features facilitating the production of large Prolog programs in teams. They exist only in tentative form. Nevertheless, the existing implementations of the language are sophisticated and ideally suited to prototype construction, especially for language development – both for programming languages and "user" languages – and for the prototyping of database applications.

### 10.3.2 Functional Languages

In many areas of technology, systems are described with the help of mathematical functions, i.e., without side effects. The functions occurring here are not only between elementary types, e.g., *integer* or *string*, but also between types of a higher order, e.g. functions which map from type *string* to functions mapping *string* to *integer*: string→(string→int). If prototypes are to be built for system specifications of this sort, the most suitable languages – besides the logical languages – are the functional languages. They are, for the most part, based on the $\lambda$ calculus, in which higher-order functions are easy to define. The following is an (incomplete) list of functional languages:

- *Lisp*: The language from which functional languages are descended (see [McCarthyEtAl62]). In the course of time, during its evolution to Common-Lisp (see [Steele84]), Lisp has been extended by so many features that there is a danger of its becoming too complex. Nonetheless, Lisp and its extension to object-oriented programming, CLOS, must be regarded as the most widely-used language of this type.
- *Hope*: This language was used early on for demonstrating the benefits of program transformation (see [Bailey85]).
- *Scheme*: A Lisp dialect, not only ideally suited for training purposes, but also for demonstrating how object-oriented-style programming is possible in functional languages with the help of functional objects (see [SteeleSuss78]).
- *ML*: A typed Lisp dialect whose polymorphic type system detects a number of programming errors, but is not as restrictive as type systems of Pascal-like languages e.g. (see [Milner84]).
- *Miranda*: A successor of ML, based on the powerful model of lazy evaluation, with means for defining algebraic and abstract data types (see [Miranda]).

A feature shared by all of these languages is that they have either no type system at all or a powerful polymorphic type system.

### 10.3.3 Algebraic Languages

For some years now, algebraic techniques have played an important part in the specification of abstract data types. Proceeding from the fields of programming languages and software engineering, important work has been done here by Parnas, Hoare, Liskov and Zilles (see [Parnas72, Hoare72, LisZi74]). The mathematical foundations have been defined by the ADJ group (see [GogThaWa76]). The literature is full of algebraic definitions of stacks and queues. But even large-scale systems like a database management system (DBMS) can be dealt with today using algebraic techniques.

The implementation of an algebraic system causes some problems. Algebraic techniques are so powerful that they are difficult to implement efficiently. Todays implementations are mainly based on term rewriting systems. There are numerous scientifically oriented groups at universities and R & D laboratories implementing term rewriting systems; for example (see [KapJou87] for detailed information):

- *CEC* (University of Dortmund)
- *OBJ 3* (SRI, University of Oxford)
- *RRLab*, *TRSPEC* (University of Kaiserslautern)
- *RAP* (University of Passau)

Algebraic techniques provide a set of tools for tackling some problems of implementation-independent specification. They allow the construction of prototypes that do not anticipate the implementation in the target language, but at the same time are not too vague.

### 10.3.4 Miscellaneous Languages

This group consists of grammar-oriented languages, set-theoretical languages and query languages.

Over the last 20 years, numerous grammar-oriented VHLLs have been developed for compiler construction. Some of them are also extremely useful outside their actual application area: data structures, command languages for end users, and even algorithms of an applications program can be specified with the help of grammars. Using a grammar-oriented VHLL, prototypes can then be constructed.

Generators for lexical analyzers such as *lex* in Unix are, in themselves, of little interest since they are located at too low a level. Along with generators for parsers such as *yacc* in Unix, they constitute a kind of VHLL. As far as user convenience is concerned, however, there is still room for improvement here.

Mention should be made of two special approaches that are of particular interest when building prototypes for substantial languages:

- Attribute grammars: This technique is ready for practical use today. Attribute grammars may be visualized as context-free grammars that are supplemented by context-sensitive computations by attribution. An instance of such a system is the GAG System at the University of Karlsruhe (see [KaHuZi82]).

- Denotational semantics: This technique allows formal specification of highly complex languages in terms of a uniform – not exactly simple – mathematical formalism (see [Gordon79]). In addition to specialized systems such as *VDM*, functional and logical VHLLs are suitable for obtaining operational prototypes in the style of denotational semantics.

Among the VHLLs based on set-theory, Setl (see [DeSchoSchw82]), at least, is well-known as a language suitable for prototyping. Sets and (higher order) functions between sets are powerful constructors for prototypes. The first certified Ada compiler was implemented in Setl. The prototype was implemented before the language design was completed, all subsequent changes being incorporated immediately into the prototype. The ease of change of Setl programs forms the basis for such a successful prototyping activity.

Languages such as SQL (see [IBM81]) are built as query languages for relational databases. The relational algebra model underlying them is highly suitable as a basis for prototypes of commercial applications software. At this point, there is a considerable overlap between logical VHLLs such as Prolog, and database-oriented languages such as SQL, both of which are well-suited for building database prototypes.

## 10.4 Are Object-Oriented Languages VHLLs?

As we have pointed out in Section 6.1.1, object-oriented design is a way of viewing and constructing that can be used to give a well-ordered description of the application area, the problems faced, and their solution. It involves focussing on the way in which objects are *used* in the course of different activities, ignoring the so-called "implementation details" that go to make up these objects. This enables excessively implementation-oriented approaches to be avoided during conceptual phases (see [BuKuSyZu89]). Viewed from an object-oriented perspective, "computing is simulation" (see [Kay77]). Starting from the objects conceived in the application area and the activities performed on them, the behaviour of these objects is reconstructed ("simulated") in the application system. This helps to provide a better basis for discussions between software developers and other groups. In its conceptual approach, then, object-oriented design is akin to the experimental form of prototyping.

The classical object-oriented languages are *Simula 67* (see [BiDaMyNy79]) and *Smalltalk* (see [Goldberg84, GoldRob83]). The only form of communication offered by *Smalltalk* is message-passing between *objects*. If classes and inheritance are viewed as the data model of Smalltalk and message-passing is interpreted as a generic procedure call, then Smalltalk has a compact, uniform "data structure" that is very powerful, that can be easily adapted to problem-oriented a abstraction level (by designing a problem-oriented class-library) and it can justifiably be classified by its features as one of the VHLLs. In this sense, we generally subsume object-oriented programming languages under the notion of VHLL.

Typical instances of object-oriented design are the Smalltalk system's user interface based on the model-view-controller paradigm (cf. Sec. 6.1.4), and the *Macintosh's* user interface and applications like *HyperCard*.

VHLLs that are considered as belonging to the world of object-oriented programming are frequently encountered in ***process control applications***. The reason for this is that the simulation paradigm, which is akin to the object-oriented approach, underlies the construction of process control systems. In object-oriented design, prototypes are generated, so to speak, by simulation of part of the specification. G. Hommel (see [Hommel80]) has published a comparative study of different specification techniques, which also looks at simulation of the specification.

Well-known VHLLs used in process control applications are the specification languages:

- EPOS,
- Mascot, and
- SREM[46].

However, the decisive break-through for the object-oriented approach came with the development of object-oriented, general-purpose programming languages. Of the current languages descended from *Simula67* and *Smalltalk* – both of which continue to remain important even today – the following are of particular significance and already suitable for use in professional applications:

- C++,
- TurboPascal, and
- Eiffel.

In our opinion, C++ is the likeliest candidate for commercial applications, while Eiffel represents the "purest" implementation of object-oriented concepts in a ready-to-use programming language.

The benefits VHLLs offer for prototype construction depend significantly on the extent to which a VHLL enables those involved in software development

- to anticipate the target system in the proposed environment;
- to use the prototype as a model for the application system.

Particularly on this second point, object-oriented VHLLs are superior to other approaches.

## 10.5 Application Areas

It is quite straightforward, to think of a VHLL as an implementation language for the anticipated product. But there is a second possibility: that of using a VHLL

[46] Of these, SREM is probably the language with the highest degree of formalization. As a model, it uses sequential finite automata. Concurrency is thus introduced in the model by worst case assumptions.

to describe ("implement") the *design process itself.* In this case, a prototype can be implemented in any other language. If it requires modification, the VHLL allows efficient repetition of the design process, taking into account the necessary modifications. The powerfulness of the VHLL is not reflected in the implemented prototype, but in the "replay" of its design process. This view originated in research on the reusability of software: in an article on the limited benefits of so-called reusable software components, R. Balzer (see [Balzer83]) states that "*...the current paradigm deals with the products of processes rather than with the processes themselves...*". He consequently formulates two important demands: the software development processes themselves must be

- formal, and
- capable of replay after a development goal has been changed.

The call for complete formalization we consider to be unrealistic. The call for automatic replay of a design process is, on the other hand, an interesting research problem. It means that the following elements must be "largely" commutative:

$$\begin{array}{ccc} \text{specification}_1 & \rightarrow & \text{specification}_2 \\ \downarrow & & \downarrow \\ \text{implementation}_1 & \rightarrow & \text{implementation}_2 \end{array}$$

This enables part of the effort already invested in the design process

$$\textit{specification}_1 \rightarrow \textit{implementation}_1$$

to be dispensed with in the case of a new design process: most design decisions can be reused during replay; only a few need replacing. An instructive example of this technique is provided by Petrone et al. with their *Dual* system (see [PetSiLeCa83]) for Pascal. The application system is designed by stepwise refinement. The units refined are Pascal language constructs, which can be replaced by a valid sequence of other language constructs. Pascal-inherent restrictions hampering design (for example, Pascal does not allow sequences of statements in expressions) are eliminated by means of automatic program transformation. The design steps are stored in a database and can be reconstructed interactively by recalling them from the database and displaying them on the screen.

These ideas extend the narrow view of VHLLs. If, for example, we take a look at the Unix program *make*, we are able to illustrate how VHLLs can be used to improve the efficiency of aspects other than mere programming. In the Unix system, a *makefile* and its corresponding program *make* (see [Feldman79, Bradford79]) serve to describe the configuration of a software system. For example, the rule

```
target.o: source.c source.h
cc -c source.c -o target.o
```

indicates that the file `target.o` is dependent on `source.c` and `source.h` (declared in the first line). Whether `target.o` must be generated from the two files with the help of the C compiler *cc* (declared in the second line) is determined by *make* on the basis of the date of a file's last modification: if one of the two *sources* is more recent than the *target*, the compiler has to be called. The configuration descriptions contained in *makefiles* are abstract and compact. The descriptive model used rests on a rule-based system. Flow of control is implicit in *makefile* programs. *Make* thus exhibits numerous features of a VHLL. A system of this sort is practically indispensable for experimenting with system variants. It serves to make the design process more intelligible and effective and can thus justifiably be considered as belonging to the group of languages being dealt with here.

The idea that VHLLs can be used to implement a target system's functionality as well as to reflect on the design process of the target system should be kept in mind when considering the following transformation approaches. So far, none of these approaches is suitable for extensive use in commercial software development, but this may change. Two good surveys are given in publications by Feather (see [Feather85]) and Partsch & Steinbrüggen (see [PartStei83]). Work on transformation approaches can be divided up into four main areas, though it is hard to draw clear distinctions between them. In the following sections, we describe each of these areas.

### 10.5.1 Extended Compilation

Extended compilation is a generalization of conventional compiling techniques. Languages are defined with such general constructs that fully automatic compilation (i.e., selection of a low-level algorithm that implements a high-level algorithm) is no longer possible. That is why the compilers require information from the programmer about potential implementations. A classical instance of such a system is *RAPTS*. This compiles extended *Setl* programs (see [DeSchoSchw82]) to *Setl* programs. During this process, radical changes are made in the algorithmic structure (see [Paige83]). The high level of the languages enables them to be used for building experimental prototypes.

### 10.5.2 Metaprogramming

In metaprogramming, the programmer proceeds from an abstract description of a problem, which is transformed into more concrete terms using transformations that have been proved to be correct. The programmer selects the transformations from a catalog. They may be used, for example, to transform recursion into iterations or to introduce recursion. The programs generated during a series of transformations constitute the data on which the transformations work. Thus, the list of transformations used represents a formal description of the design process.

Darlington has demonstrated this technique using a number of small-scale examples, and R. Bailey (see [Bailey85]) has written a good brief introduction to the functional language *Hope* used by Darlington for this purpose. The sample programs can, however, also be rewritten in the easily available languages *ML* or *Miranda*.

The *CIP* project is likewise based on metaprogramming (see [HorschEtAl85]). At its "abstract" end, the CIP (wideband) language contains logical constructs, and at its "concrete" end, imperative language constructs such as assignments. The link between these two extremes is a catalog of transformations (proven to be correct) between program constructs. The software developer can choose from this catalog. If prototypes are developed from a specification by means of a series of transformations, we have, on the "abstract" side, a specification that is not necessarily executable, but compact and intelligible; and, on the "concrete" side, software whose usefulness can be assessed during operation. The correctness of the transformations ensures that both mean the same. If the specification changes, the stored transformations are, for the most part, reusable. This means that the prototype (re-)construction process is speeded up.

### 10.5.3 Program Synthesis

In program synthesis, the attempt is made to synthesize, from input and output data, a plausible algorithm whose input and output dataset includes the sample data. New sample data cause the algorithm to be either confirmed or rejected. In the latter case, it has to be modified in order to be able to compute the new data, too. Of course, the algorithm

```
proc synthesis( input, output ) is
if input = input_data_1    then output := output_data_1
elsif input = input_data_2 then output := output_data_2
...
fi
```

invariably constitutes an undesirable solution. The crucial problem in program synthesis is therefore a generator program that generates a series of algorithms to which the sample data are applied. The algorithm that covers all the old sample data constitutes, together with the new sample data, the input for the generator program.

Since a generator algorithm is always liable to reach a deadlock, it is never universally applicable, but only suitable for specific problem areas. The idea of synthesizing a prototype from data which can be taken from the application area is too good to be true. For the reader well-versed in Prolog, the doctoral thesis of E.Y. Shapiro (see [Shapiro82]) gives a very fine description of a program synthesis system.

### 10.5.4 Derivation

Starting from a variety of important, simple basic algorithms (sorting, pattern recognition), there are a number of variants for different applications, e.g., nearly sorted lists, very large numbers of data records, which bear scarcely any relation to the common basic algorithm.[47] Using a derivation, the attempt is made to

[47] For sort algorithms, there's a nice little saying: "If a sort is intelligible, it's inefficient."

demonstrate the common features of a class of algorithms. This approach is very useful for understanding the way optimized algorithms work and for preparing to establish program libraries. In principle, the approach is similar to that used in metaprogramming. This technique has been studied using sort algorithms (see [Darlington78]). It is not, however, relevant for the prototype construction process itself. A conceivable approach here is to construct verified sets of building blocks, from which, then, prototypes can be put together.

### 10.5.5 Summary

All the above-mentioned transformation approaches have three interrelated problems in common, and these would seem to suggest that transformation techniques are at present still unsuitable for extensive practical use:

- The number of transformation steps, i.e., the proof length, is very large.
- The transformations are – compared with the level of abstraction desired for design – performed at a very low level.
- It is very difficult to structure the transformation process plausibly; it appears amorphous and hard to follow.

For prototype construction, metaprogramming would appear to be the most important of the approaches. It allows different abstract, but operational, versions of a software system to be compared. The abstract early versions help to check the suitability of the software product, a concrete later version forming the application system. The correspondence between the prototype and the application system is established by means of intermediate versions and the accompanying correct program transformations.

## 10.6 Selecting a Very High Level Language

The chief criterion in selecting a VHLL is, of course, the particular problem in hand. VHLLs are tailored to specific applications and tend to be clumsy when used in other contexts. Prolog, for instance, is particularly well-suited for use in database systems, expert systems and language design. It would be unwise, however, to use Prolog for specifying communication prototcols, or Smalltalk for specifying the functional core of a database application. A software developer is likely to run into trouble when using a VHLL for applications it is not designed for – merely in order to stick to one VHLL.

Nearly all the VHLLs mentioned here have reached a considerable level of technical perfection. They are not, of course, as widely-used and well-documented as, say, Pascal, which is why their users must always be prepared for unexpected features limiting their use. In the research and development sector, recent years have seen an increase in the importance of *logical, functional* and *algebraic* VHLLs in particular, while object-oriented languages are currently considered promising in both commercial and research environments.

Almost all VHLLs – with the exception, perhaps, of Smalltalk, Lisp and several object-oriented languages – lack the libraries, along with their prefabricated building blocks, that are needed for the prototypical construction of interactive components.

VHLLs are particularly well-suited for implementing prototypes and application systems for single-user systems, especially scientific workstations and similarly organized technical systems. Today's VHLLs are unsuitable for constructing applications for multi-user systems offering simultaneous access to a common database, or for large databases with high requirements for transactions.

It is generally advisable to employ the strategy of developing application systems step by step from prototypes. If this entails transferring a VHLL prototype to an application system in a conventional programming language, provision should be made for porting only selected parts of a prototype – e.g., for reasons of efficiency – from the VHLL to the target language, and then integrating these parts as an extension of the prototype. The application system then consists of a VHLL part, and a compiler or interpreter that contains all the necessary target language extensions in the form of a runtime system.

Many VHLLs are, themselves, ideal for designing and implementing tools for program development with VHLLs. Tools for VHLL program analysis, synthesis and description are very easy to build using modern – especially logical and functional – VHLLs, because such languages

- offer facilities for converting data into programs and vice versa, and
- have a simple syntax.

This means that the programs are much simpler than those written in the classical programming languages such as Pascal, with their extensive syntax and their separation of compilation and execution.

# 11
# Programming Environments

In this chapter, we discuss the concept of programming environments as a technical framework for prototype construction. To begin with, we explain what we mean by a programming environment, and then go on to discuss the types of languages needed in a programming environment and the demands made on them. This is followed by an outline of what we consider to be an "ideal" programming environment for supporting prototyping, along with the set of tools it should provide. In the final sections, we assess the importance of available programming environments for prototyping.

## 11.1 Prototyping and Programming Environments

In their general outline of the subject, Houghton and Wallace (see [HouWal87]) draw a distinction between software engineering environments and programming environments.[48] They consider the following features to be characteristic of *software engineering environments*:

- They support system development during all activities of the life cycle.
- They "surround" the developers with tools for designing and enhancing software. Here, software is taken to include programs, data and documentation.

Software engineering environments generally provide tools supporting the following activities:

- design,
- editing, compiling and loading,
- testing,
- configuration management, and
- project management.

Of importance for our purposes is the fact that software engineering environments are often tied to a specific development method (e.g., SADT) or life cycle plan.

In contrast, *programming environments* are of limited range:

- They support software development during the "technical" activities of the life cycle.
- They "surround" the developers with tools for programming.

[48] Numerous publications have appeared on this subject. Further details and overviews can be found, for example, in [PEWorkshop86, Charette86]. A number of systems still of importance today are described in [Huenke80]. The journal *Software Engineering Notes* has a regular column on software engineering environments.

In Part I of our book, we outlined our view of prototyping as part of evolutionary system development. Important for our purposes is the fact that prototypes are constructed and evaluated for the different software development models. These prototyping activities require *technical* support. Depending on the form of prototyping used, it is also desirable to facilitate the transition to the application system and the latter's systematic enhancement.

If, in the light of these demands, we look at the software engineering environments currently available, we find that most of them are unsuitable for supporting prototyping. This is because restrictions in their approach and their commitment to certain types of results make the construction of prototypes difficult or even impossible. Also, experience gained thus far in software engineering has made a number of things clear:

It is not advisable to limit a development environment to *one* construction method, if this means that a process model fixes the *sequence* of activities in the environment, thus transferring control of the development process from the development team to the development environment. This form of "software bureaucracy" (cf. [Denert87]) exhibits all the points criticized by us in our discussion of traditional life cycle plans. In this connection, it seems appropriate to touch briefly on the current discussion of Computer-Aided Software Engineering (CASE) systems.[49] Here, we find there are numerous tools on the market today bearing this name which are designed to support the development process. We came across the following apt definition of such tools: "CASE is the most general term for a development tool that supports the software development process during some phase" (Axel Keller, cited in [Dreesbach89]). CASE systems that are not confined to specific activities or phases are much less common. Some two dozen systems of this sort – all of them from the field of database applications – have so far been widely adopted (worldwide sales figures ranging between 1,000 and 15,000, depending on the system). Initial studies have shown that the number of systems actually in use is much lower. Characteristic of such CASE systems is the fact that they support a specific design method (e.g., JSD or SA/SD), and mostly a fixed approach as well, by providing various more or less integrated sets of tools.

Frequently, the so-called "early phases" up to construction of the software model are supported. This support covers graphic editors, development and application data management in the form of data dictionaries, consistency checks for documents and generator tools for transforming one design document into the basis for a subsequent one. Thus, there are numerous tools on the market designed to help produce data flow diagrams, data structure diagrams and screen forms, and capable of generating program skeletons on this basis. For fixed life cycle plans, there are, in addition, tools designed to support project control and planning. Regarding the integration of their tools, their usability and methodological support, we come to the following conclusions with respect to their suitability for prototyping:

---

[49] We wish to thank Hannes Färberbök of SBG in Zürich for his valuable ideas on the subject.

- Many CASE systems "implement" a classical life cycle plan and are incompatible with cyclical software development. They are geared to the sequential production of milestone documents (cf., e.g., [Bleimann89]).
- There are few CASE systems combining the design and construction of application systems.[50]
- The conceptual basis of such systems makes no provision for the interplay between design, construction and evaluation or for the construction of prototypes during all phases of the development process; on the contrary, such interplay is, in most cases, actually obstructed.

Programming environments and CASE systems have their origins in different "worlds": the former in the world of programming language development; the latter, as we have already indicated, in database applications. Thus, programming environments have evolved from the technical core of programming "outwards", whereas CASE systems largely owe their origin to concern with the problems of data modelling and user needs analysis. And yet, given their considerable similarity with regard to the problems they address and the solutions they endeavour to provide, we are amazed at just how little there has been in the way of exchange between these two areas.

Despite growing sales figures for CASE systems and an aggressive marketing strategy, we feel that, for the foreseeable future, there is little that is likely to emerge from this quarter in the way of suitable approaches for supporting the evolutionary development strategy we advocate. There are, quite obviously, still a number of unsolved problems associated with the claims of such systems to universal usability, and with their claim to provide a uniform methodology and appropriate technical support (cf. [Simonsm88]). Furthermore, the expectations concerning the use of expert systems for software engineering have so far remained unfulfilled. Studies on the subject (see [Schoder87]) have shown that, as regards both state-of-the-art and capacity, such systems still fail to meet the standards required for professional software development.

However, this rather cautious assessment does not only apply to CASE systems and approaches using knowledge-based systems. It is also our contention that existing software engineering environments still fail to provide reasonable support for prototyping. We do not pretend that it makes sense to develop a software engineering environment for a *specific form* of prototyping. Fixing on a particular methodology and selecting the appropriate kinds of prototypes is something which is done from case to case and which cannot be embodied in a general process model. Moreover, we consider it one of the essentials of prototyping that control of a development project remain in the hands of the developers and users involved, and for this reason it should not be transferred to the development environment.

We therefore go on now to discuss the desirable features of a programming environment. Freedom of choice as to these features does not, however, mean that a programming environment can be reduced to a mere collection of software tools. For, just as the temporal sequencing of development steps constitutes

[50] Some promising ideas here may be found, for example, in [ZihlEng89] or [Kaptelna89]

too rigid a restriction, a toolbox, too, is in itself an inadequate guide to the construction process. In order to be able to establish a proper relationship between tools, languages and development steps, a programming environment must be based on a uniform *model* of (but not *approach* to) software engineering.

In the following section, we consider first of all the requirements for integrated support of prototyping with respect to the different language types that should be available in a programming environment. For practical purposes, we can derive from these requirements criteria for selecting languages that are suitable for supporting individual prototyping activities.

## 11.2 Languages in a Programming Environment

The fact that we view our model of software development as part of evolutionary system development has implications for programming environments. First of all, we must bear in mind that the activities performed in software development – beginning with the specification of user requirements, going on through the construction of various prototypes, and culminating in the transition from the prototype to the application system – should not be treated as separate, self-contained work packets to be processed in a particular temporal sequence. This means that the various models generated during the development process can only be described in terms of their relations to one another. But it also means that no rules can be laid down in the programming environment as to the *sequence in which they are to be processed.*

In Chapter 2, we referred to the specification, implementation and evaluation of a model as elementary software construction activities. The implementation of one model constitutes the specification of the next lower one. In a programming environment, then, it is imperative that different means of description be available: construction languages for specification and implementation, and process languages.

The *construction languages* are used to build the various models, including prototypes and the application system. We list below the various "language types" that are useful for supporting these activities:

- The *tool language* enables the tools of a programming environment to be built. It paves the way for further development of the environment.
- The *design language* is used for designing the system "in the large". It is a construction language for abstract system models and the architecture of software systems.
- The *programming language* is a construction language for the "actual" programming of the system "in the small".
- The *prototyping language* is used for constructing the prototypes.

In contrast, the *process languages* document the relationship between the different models, and do so in two different ways: firstly, they document the relationship between the different levels of abstraction, i.e., they describe how the various models are related with respect to their content; and secondly, they document the temporal relationship between the different software versions and options, i.e., they describe the development process and the project's progress.

Instances of process languages are:

- The *project language*: This is used to describe the software process itself.
- The *document language*: This serves to process documents. It must also be capable of use as a construction language, since the documents relate to both of these areas.

## 11.3 The Requirements for These Languages

By distinguishing between construction and processing languages, we have undertaken a fundamental classification of the languages used in a programming environment. We have to derive criteria for the selection and construction of such languages from the way in which they are used in the programming environment. We confine ourselves here to consideration of those criteria that affect prototyping. These often turn out to be in conflict with one another, which means that compromises have to be found. The points considered below each begin with a specific criterion, followed by a brief outline of its significance for prototyping. After each point, we list, in brackets, the languages on which the respective criterion has a bearing:

- The generated programs should be compact and easy to modify.
  This is a fundamental requirement, derivable from prototyping on a purely technical level. In addition to the prototypes, the dedicated tools and the approach itself must also be easily modifiable.
  (*Tool language, project language, prototyping language*)
- The language should allow flexible typing and the execution of incomplete programs.
  To allow swift development of models and prototypes, it is sometimes useful to dispense initially with redundant declaration. Besides, during prototyping, it is often unclear which types are most appropriate. In many cases, the developer will want to try out specific parts of the system design without the bother of having to write stubs.
  (*Design language, prototyping language*)
- The language should enforce typing and support information hiding, at least in terms of abstract data types and, where possible, in terms of object-oriented design.
  For developers, prototyping involves taking into account software engineering principles right from the moment they begin designing the various prototypes. This helps facilitate, on a technical level, the transition to the application system. Information hiding and the construction of abstract data types are design principles that are of significance for prototypes, too, largely irrespective of the language used. On the other hand, developers will, as a rule, want to add type declarations as outlined above.
  (*Prototyping language, programming language*)

- The language should be equipped with interfaces to external systems (i.e., languages "outside" the programming environment) and to other application systems, especially database systems.
  Few prototyping projects venture on to "new ground" in a technical sense. Whenever the application area already contains software systems, the new application system has to be integrated with them. In many cases, too, there already exist software building blocks or software tools that facilitate prototype construction but are not available in the prototyping language. To cut down the problems of embedding the prototypes, the application system and the tools used in the development process, it is imperative that the languages used in each case be "open".
  (*Tool language, prototyping language, programming language, project language*)
- The language should allow meta-programs to be written (for debugging and program analysis) and should provide compiler-compiler features.
  The construction process is speeded up considerably if it is possible for the programs written in a specific programming language to be themselves, in turn, the subject of other programs. This enables analyzers and generator programs to be written quickly, which is of particular benefit if similar technical problems frequently crop up.
  (*Tool language, prototyping language, programming language*)
- The language should provide powerful data types and generic I/O facilities.
  During the design and construction of software tools and prototypes, we frequently encounter data types that cannot be simply represented as integers or arrays. Languages providing universal and powerful data types such as terms (in Prolog) or lists (in Lisp) facilitate development work. For rapid construction and testing, then, it is useful to have generic I/O operations at one's disposal.
  (*Tool language, prototyping language*)
- The language should facilitate the implementation of rule-based techniques and contain logical constructs.
  The activities in the software development process cannot be formalized en bloc. However, certain standard procedures and heuristics can be defined. This applies to such seemingly simple things as the formatting of programs and other documents, but is also true of work agreements and the way results of work are used. Activities of this sort should be supported by a programming environment. In this case, however, the relevant languages must provide means of expression enabling the developer to formulate sets of rules, heuristics and logical dependencies.
  (*Design language, tool language, project language*)
- The language should allow a system's functional and interactive components to be represented easily but separatetly from one another. Window systems should be available in the programming environment; they should match the programming model of the languages and not be devised as mere "appendages".

The intelligibility of prototypes and application systems is considerably improved if the functional and interactive components can each be formulated separately in a language (and language style) of their own (cf. Sec. 6.1.4).
(*Design language, prototyping language, programming language*)

- The language should support units for software development in teams.
Professional software development is mostly teamwork. Software systems must therefore be broken down into units, each presenting the individual developer with a work object that is as "self-contained" and as independent as possible from the other parts. This corresponds to the module concept in software engineering. On the other hand, prototypes are mostly developed in VHLLs that offer only scant support to traditional module concepts. We are therefore faced with the question of which "units" prototypes should be developed in, and how they can be subsequently integrated into modular application systems.
(*Programming language*)
- The language should provide a variety of user support facilities (help, tutorials, online documentation, protocols).
This requirement – desirable for any form of software development – applies particularly to prototyping, since special importance is attached here to communication between users and developers.
(*Tool language, document language*)
- The language should allow stand-alone applications.
This is of importance for all development systems using "interpreted" languages (e.g., Lisp, Prolog, Smalltalk), for it is by no means normal for applications to be usable without the whole programming environment being available at the same time. Here, again, the relationship between prototype and application system is of particular significance. If prototypes are implemented in a VHLL and the application system in a conventional language, this requirement is generally easy to meet for the programming language of the application system. But we are then confronted with the problem of the transition from the prototype to the application system and how this transition can be supported by a programming environment. If the prototype and application system are both implemented in one (and the same) VHLL, the transition problems may be less serious, but in many cases the application system will then be based on elements such as window management and forms of interaction that are an integral part of the programming environment.
(*Programming language*)
- The language should allow experimentation without permanent sideeffects.
Testing and evaluation of models frequently gives rise to sideeffects in the active application and in the programming environment. This is particularly true of the experimental use of prototypes. There must be facilities for undoing sideeffects, for example, by means of a workspace concept providing for separation of the system parts stored in files from the workspace of the programming environment, or for configuration management.
(*Prototyping language, design language, project language*)

- The language should contain object-oriented components.
  The object-oriented paradigm is particularly well-suited for building interactive prototypes and modelling the development process. Interactive components such as a window management system can only be implemented quickly on an object-oriented basis. But *inside* a programming environment, too, the various development entities must exist as objects changing in time, this corresponding to the way the developers see their "working material" (cf. Sec. 6.1.1).
  (*Design language, prototyping language*)
- The language should allow swift development cycles.
  To support prototyping, a swift and easy run-through of the development cycles – alternating between specification, construction and evaluation – must be possible. The integration of editors and incremental compilers/interpreters enables the editing, loading, executing, testing and debugging operations to be performed in swift succession.
  (*Prototyping language, design language, tool language*)

It is obvious from the above list that these requirements have their origins in different areas of software development and represent different perspectives. Some are derived from software engineering principles, such as information hiding and modular design; others are drawn from the sphere of communication between users and developers, such as user support and safe experimentation (i.e., without harmful sideeffects). Further requirements are derived from the basic concerns of team-oriented software development (e.g., compact and easily modifiable programs, object-oriented construction). Here, it becomes obvious that certain criteria are contradictory (e.g., demands for both strict typing and no typing at all). This reflects the different interests and views held in a development project. Compromises must be found here.

## 11.4 Building Prototypes

In our discussion of the desirable features of programming environments, we recognized the need for different (types of) languages. We are nevertheless troubled by the evident diversity here, for different languages generally mean different "programming models" and language constructs. Practitioners are thus faced with the question of whether individual languages can be combined. For example:

- *Design language = prototyping language*
  This is the approach pursued when working with executable specifications. It represents a special variant of prototype construction focussing on the functionality of the application system.
- *Prototyping language = programming language*
  The equation of these two languages types is common when using database-oriented tools, as described in Chapter 9. In some application fields, the

availability of high-performance computers enables the last prototype written in a VHLL to be used as the application system (taking into account software engineering standards of quality). This does away with many of the technical problems caused by the transition from prototype to application system.

- *Tool language = prototyping language = programming language*
  This variant is chosen when constructing most programming environments. If these languages are mapped on to each other, a programming environment can be further developed on a self-contained basis. Another consequence is that parts of the programming environment are incorporated into the application system. This has the advantage of enabling prototypes to be built efficiently, but it makes it difficult to develop environment-independent ("standalone") systems.
- *Design language = prototyping language = programming language = tool language*
  When developing the programming environment *ProLab*[51] for the logical VHLL Prolog, we opted for this particular solution because it offered advantages for the prototyping process as well as facilitating further development of the programming environment itself. It should be evident that, in this case, a VHLL is the only suitable language type.

We assume that the prototypes and the application system are largely compatible as regards their architecture. This is a prerequisite if the results of prototyping are to be transferred to development of the application system without major problems. It applies on two levels:

- to the conformity of user requirements with the software product, and
- to the technical design of the system.

It is therefore important to be able to revise, in the programming environment, not only the actual software itself, but also the description of the system's architecture.

## 11.5 An Example of a Programming Environment

In this section, we present our ideas on a programming environment to support prototyping. We do so by reference to the programming environment *ProLab*. *ProLab* supports programming in Prolog and is a programming environment implemented in Prolog. When developing *ProLab*, we were guided by the principles of evolutionary system development and prototyping. In other words, the programming environment was not only designed to support prototype construction; when building it, we also examined and gave concrete form to our own ideas on software development.

---

[51] *ProLab* is an acronym standing for both *Prolog Laboratory* and *Prototyping Laboratory*. See [BaeBudKuhlSylZue88].

We have selected this particular example because it allows us, by drawing on our own experience, to outline what we consider to be an "ideal" programming environment, exhibiting for our purposes several features of general significance:

- A programming environment supporting prototype construction should be based on a powerful VHLL.
- In order to be machine-independent, a programming environment should be based on Unix. Unix is the first widely-used machine-independent operating system, and it has acquired importance far beyond the confines of R & D laboratories.
- In order to provide an appropriate user interface and handling facilities, a programming environment should be implemented on a workstation.

## 11.6 Tools in a Programming Environment

This section describes a set of tools designed to illustrate our idea of how a programming environment might look. As in the previous sections, we focus on the aspect of prototyping.

### Procedure Manager

The user-favoured editor is linked to the programming environment. Termination of an editing operation causes the processed file to be reloaded into the system or compiled incrementally. The operations or procedures are automatically checked by the **procedure manager** for possible name conflicts and violations of declarations. Editing can be easily initiated from the active programming environment via file or procedure names. Data from the editor can be transferred to the programming environment's tools and processed by them (e.g., syntax errors checks, connection of analyzers, formatters and type checkers). The result of this processing is returned to the editor. This enables software engineering requirements to be taken into account step by step during prototyping. For example, if, to begin with, only syntactical error messages and name and programming convention violations are displayed, type checks may be subsequently added if desired.

In our view, the combination of external files and programming environment workspace has proved useful, and this is not only true of Prolog. This means that program sources are generated and updated in external files only. The environment may exist in different configurations, which can then be saved in appropriate workspaces.

### Environment Manager

The **environment manager** is a tool facilitating general use of the programming environment. It controls system adaptation to user needs. While working with the programming environment, users can permanently adapt the display formats and system component parameters (menus, prompts, etc.) to their needs. This is important in order to present the users with their individually preferred working environment when evaluating prototypes.

### Program Checker

The **program checker** is an analyzer similar to *lint* for C. It checks names and programming conventions. The **program checker** uses heuristics to detect error-prone code. Thus, a message is issued if a variable occurs only once within a procedure, i.e., if it is not used for the data flow. The **program checker** has interfaces to numerous smaller analyzers which process the call hierarchy of a program, for example. The **program checker** can also be addressed from the editor. In our discussion of the **procedure manager**, we have already pointed out the importance of such optional analyzers; they increase reliability when developing prototypes without calling for complete programs or the observance of all conventions throughout.

### Call-Tree Analyzer

This analyzer searches for undefined procedures and allows specification of minimal systems in order to make them available as independent prototypes or application systems (standalone systems).

### Type-Checker

This analyzer offers a type-checking facility for untyped languages (such as Prolog). The check is a static one (i.e., without runtime tests) and is performed either at the time of loading or at any other time. This form of type-checking is highly conducive to prototyping.

### Pretty Printer

The **pretty printer** formats both texts for window display and source code for uniform representation in files. Compression and zooming techniques are used to ensure good readability of procedure displays in windows. The **pretty printer** is also used as a subsystem of other components (the editor or **call-tree analyzer**, for example). By being easily adaptable to different programming "styles", the **pretty printer** supports the development of different prototypes or system versions on a team basis.

### Source and Document Processor

One of the main problems in software development is the separation of program construction and documentation. Particularly when constructing prototypes, it is necessary to reconcile the demand for rapid construction with the call for early documentation of development decisions. Donald Knuth has suggested combining programming and documentation to form a single work step (see [Knuth84]). We have implemented Knuth's concept experimentally for Prolog. Accordingly, both the Prolog programs and the accompanying program documentation are developed in one and the same file. Here, macros can be used and expanded in the programs. It is also possible to mix program and documentation texts. From this common file, Prolog programs or the program documentation can be generated, as the case requires. The drawback with files of this sort is that they tend to be complex. This is particularly true where program structures change, necessitating extensive changes in the arrangement of texts. However, since this model comes very close to the concept behind hypermedia, the use of hypermedia systems might offer an alternative for this sort of tool.

### Compiler-Compiler Tool

Prototype construction and the development of application systems can be seen as analogous to compiler construction:

- In the application area, there exists a special technical language in which the users formulate the commands and queries they wish to address to the software system.
- The system's interactive components convert these commands into an internal representation, which we may visualize as an abstract syntax tree.
- The functional component interprets this abstract syntax tree, i.e., it defines the semantics for the commands.

If we accept this analogy, programming can be viewed in general terms as language development. This is why it is useful to employ for prototyping tools that have proved successful in compiler construction. Instances of **compiler-compiler tool** components are *parsers* and *tokenizers*.

### Window Manager

The **window manager** is, today, an integral part of every programming environment. It is addressable from the programming language being used and provides window operations and interactive types. This makes it an essential tool for the construction of interactive prototypes. Systems supporting toolkits like *X Windows*, for example, are particularly suitable as a basis for a **window manager**.

### Session Logbook

The **session logbook** records for subsequent replay command sequences directly at the level at which they are written. A cut-&-paste editor is available in the active system, enabling calls and results to be modified and used repeatedly. Commands which have been previously executed can be selected via names and patterns and executed repeatedly.

The **session logbook** also provides facilities for recording and replaying construction and evaluation steps by means of a logging device and history files. These enable reusable parts of a testing and evaluation session to be stored and replayed for subsequent prototypes or for the application system.

### Module Manager

This tool stores relations between development objects (files and procedures, documents). It thus constitutes an important prerequisite for systematic prototyping by ensuring transparency of the development process. Procedures (rules) contained in the database are linked to the files in which they are defined via a **contains** relation. The link to the online documentation is established via the **explains** relation. The procedures have annotations characterizing the visibility, the changeability and the type of the procedure in terms of attributes. The attributes are evaluated by the **debugger**, for example.

### Configuration Manager

One of the major organizational problems associated with prototyping is configuration, version and variant management. The knowledge as to how the various components must be selected and combined to suit different computers must be stored in the system itself. Configuration managers such as *make* in Unix help here, but they are not sufficient to meet the needs existing in a programming environment.

Dependencies between programming environment components, such as files, procedures, documentation, versions and variants of components, are recorded in the **data dictionary** of the configuration manager for use in project administration.

### Test Driver

The **test driver** allows stored tests to be carried out. It checks the results of computations, the assertions added by the developers and the test coverage of a procedure. The **test driver** offers facilities for writing and updating tests along with the source code and for extracting these when required for test purposes. Thus, a test, once written, can be used for several prototypes.

### Debugger

For the developers, debuggers constitute a major component of the programming environment. Their structure and functionality are closely tied to the particular VHLL being used. We distinguish between low-level and high-level debugging.

Low-level debugging is based on stepwise execution of a program (tracing). It follows the operational semantics of the language and is easy to keep track of. The flood of data generated by a stepwise debugger proves to be something of a problem. It can be checked with the help of parameterization, by setting spy points, by excluding procedures from debugging and by executing program parts outside the debugger.

High-level debugging allows the whole test run to be viewed as the object under investigation. The typical sort of questions asked in high-level debugging are: Does that other call always occur before this sort of procedure call? Which procedures has this data object flowed through? At which points was it modified? In Prolog, three basic techniques exist for high-level debugging: retrospective zooming (see [Eisen85]), algorithmic program debugging (see [Shapiro82]) and rational debugging (see [Pereira86]).

The technique employed is to store the execution sequence of the program under examination in the database. These stored program steps can be subsequently (retrospectively) examined with the help of various diagnostic tools. An essential prerequisite for the usability of this concept is, in our opinion, the definition of suitable views on the stored program steps, enabling the developer to evaluate the vast quantity of data. A **high-level debugger** based on this concept offers a number of advantages. First of all, low-level debugging can be easily implemented as a view. This helps avoid the problems encountered when debugging interactive applications (mutual interference between debugger and program outputs, changed user interface behaviour, etc.).

### Tutor

The **tutor** links system and user documentation by means of the online help system. The **tutor** facilitates the search for explanations by taking into account the context, etc. This tool also provides demos of prototypes and guidelines for evaluating and comparing different prototypes.

### Newsboard and Document Manager

These tools manage news messages addressed to the users of the programming environment and keep a check on the status of documents.

The **newsboard** provides news about the system and manages a message system for the use of developers and users. For example, during testing of a prototype, feedback messages can be left for individual developers. Finally, the **newsboard** supplies the files with memos (containing, for example, information about new procedures of a prototype).

The **document manager** keeps track of the status of the development documents. It issues warnings, for example, if prototype development is continued without the accompanying documentation. It draws the attention of the project team to deadlines and agreements, but it does not implement a predefined life cycle plan. This means that the advice and guidelines offered by the **document manager** can also be ignored by individual team members. To avoid undermining the free exchange of information and ideas between users and developers, there should be no "hidden" control mechanisms implemented in the **document manager**.

## 11.7 Our Assessment

So far, the use of integrated software engineering environments has been confined almost exclusively to universities and R & D laboratories. Only a few specialized software engineering environments such as SDS (see [AlfoDavis80]) have found their way into commercial applications. And the situation is similar with regard to programming environments. The only ones to have been adopted on a wide scale are language environments such as CommonLisp and – if it may be considered a programming environment on the grounds of its toolbox nature – the Unix system.

There is a marked trend towards the use of programming environments on workstations and high-capacity PCs for specific programming languages such as C++ and Smalltalk, for example. These systems exhibit many of the above-mentioned features of programming environments and are in widespread use. Application generation systems (cf. Chap. 9) can also be classed along with these. However, systems of this sort are not designed chiefly for prototype construction.

Thus, we feel it is useful to consider once again the advantages and disadvantages of programming environments for prototyping:

- The various documents produced during system development and the different models of the application system are accessible within a single uniform environment. Many of the tools provided by a programming environment support search, display and change operations on these documents. Since prototyping and evolutionary system development dispense with the rigid sequencing of work on system models and documents, technical support is required to ensure easy access to, and swift alternation between, different work objects. And this is where the programming environments come in, providing as they do uniform interfaces to the documents and tools that exhibit the same behaviour, without which a swift alternation of this sort would not be possible.
- The special importance of "operational" system models has already been discussed in detail. By this, we do not only mean the use of prototypes. In order to be able to evaluate prototypes properly, it is essential that other development documents such as user needs analyses, design decisions or user guides are accessible easily and in a suitable representation. Although there are few existing programming environments that totally meet this requirement, those available do, nevertheless, offer important advantages in this area. Prefabricated building blocks for designing the interactive components of a prototype and an interface to a general window system are, today, standard features of programming environments. Document browsers, sophisticated search operations and the integration of hypermedia models (as in the Lisp machine, for example) facilitate work with all sorts of documents.
- In the development process, there is an alternation between different perspectives. These perspectives may be adopted by individuals or groups of people. We have so far distinguished between three fundamental activities in software development, for each of which there is a corresponding perspective:

- the declarative perspective during specification,
- the procedural perspective during implementation,
- the experimental perspective during evaluation.

All three perspectives (along with others, too) must be derivable from the documentation. This interplay between a VHLL and the tools of a programming environment is what constitutes the latter's particular strength.

- Professional system developers must be able to handle large software systems. If the strategy pursued here is to develop the overall system in a number of increments of manageable size, then the corresponding prototypes will also be of a "handy" size. It is practically impossible, though, to process the necessary components and put them together easily without the help of a programming environment.
- Software development is teamwork. Prototyping, too, mostly involves teamwork, even though the prototypes themselves are often constructed by one individual developer. Programming environments can support teamwork by providing tools for cooperation and communication. It is gratifying to note that tools for supporting cooperation and coordination are at present a highly topical subject of discussion in R & D circles, where they are known as *groupware*. There are, then, likely to be rapid advances in this field in the near future.
- When using a programming environment for prototyping, it is often useful to be able to utilize already existing systems and tools belonging to the programming environment as parts of a prototype. In most programming environments, suitable support is available here. A more difficult problem is integrating a prototype into the application system if different languages are used in each case. There is little technical support for this transition process. A further problem already touched on is the prototypes' lack of "self-reliance", being as they are generally incapable of execution without major parts of their programming environment.

By way of conclusion, it may be said that, so far, there have been few programming environments specifically designed for prototype construction. Nevertheless, some of the available systems go a long way towards meeting prototyping requirements. In development projects where the application situation suggests the use of a VHLL anyway, the use of such programming environments is highly advantageous. As workstations and application generation systems become increasingly popular, programming environments, too, are likely to become more attractive and be more widely adopted.

# 12
# Prototyping in Practice

In this chapter we look at the role already being played by prototyping in industrial software practice. This involves going beyond the examples considered in Section 4.5 and combining discussion of the concepts examined so far and our own assessment of the relevant tools with practical experience in this field. The purpose of this chapter is to provide a sort of guide to the typical approaches and problems associated with prototyping. To this end, we draw not only on first-hand reports from the literature, but also on our own experience with the construction of large software systems as well as with teaching groups of students (see [BaeBudKuhlSylZue88, GrycKaut90]). Another important source was our analysis of a number of industrial software projects which we conducted in the context of a GI working group.[52]

In Part I of this book, we discussed various system development models and underlined the importance of prototyping for these models. We now set out to classify prototyping strategies that are frequently encountered in practice in terms of these models. We begin by looking at approaches that integrate prototyping into conventional life cycle plans and then go on to consider approaches that we would subsume under the heading evolutionary system development.

The differences in the degree to which prototyping concepts are integrated into the development process are rooted in uncertainties on the part of many organizations as to just how sound these concepts are for commercial software development. An objection still frequently encountered is that prototyping is not suitable for large or highly complex software projects, to which the following sorts of systems are considered to belong:

- systems requiring extensive data protection and recovery facilities,
- systems with very large numbers of transactions,
- systems that are subject to auditing,
- systems requiring professional maintenance, or
- systems that are highly resource-intensive in operation.

In the previous chapters, we have discussed at length that it is not the application area or specific technical requirements for a system that make it suitable or unsuitable for prototyping. It is rather the degree of uncertainty affecting a particular development project. If there is a very high degree of uncertainty, adoption of a prototyping strategy is advisable precisely for the sort of systems listed above. In the following sections, we set out to show the sort of situations in which prototyping can provide a solution to important problems encountered in software development.

[52] Cf. [KieLicSchZue91]. GI stands for Gesellschaft für Informatik (German Computer Association).

## 12.1 Prototyping and Conventional Development Models

Despite the fact that we consider prototyping the most appropriate approach when pursuing an evolutionary system development strategy, there is no denying the practical significance of other approaches. We therefore take a look now at situations in which prototyping can be profitably employed as part of classical life cycle plans.

### 12.1.1 Specification of Requirements

Many organizations have long been using computers for largely well-known applications. There has also been a switch from mainframes to workstations. The applications themselves, though, are basically fixed in terms of their functionality. User wishes do not therefore relate to completely new application areas, but rather result from the constant necessity of adapting a software system to the work environment. Such adaptations must, however, be carried out in compliance with high software engineering standards. Situations of this kind are encountered predominantly in transaction-oriented applications or in process control systems. In such cases, it can make good sense to integrate prototyping into a conventional life cycle plan. It is above all the so-called early phases that prototypes support here. A typical project strategy might take the following form:

- The activities of requirements analysis and the feasibility study are carried out along conventional lines. This helps ensure careful analysis of the information system.
- Prototyping is used chiefly to support modelling of the software system requiring modification. In addition to a functional prototype modelling the desired changes, a written system specification is produced.
- On conclusion of the prototyping phase, the model of the software system is fixed and the target sytstem then developed. Here, building blocks from the prototype are utilized as far as possible. Whether the prototype is to merely serve as the specification or is to be used as a pilot system is a question that cannot be answered on a general basis, but only from case to case.
- Implementation of the target system is carried out along traditional lines, apart from the utilization of the prototype building blocks and the use of suitable prototyping tools.

An approach of this sort is only advisable in cases where the functionality of the target system is largely fixed and the class of application problems well-known. Otherwise, building prototypes may help in determining current user requirements, but the freezing of the system model with the conclusion of this prototyping phase entails a number of risks for the further course of the system development, as we have already seen in Section 3.4.

### 12.1.2 Requirements Analysis and Project Acquisition

A similar approach is encountered where prototyping is used exclusively for clarifying user requirements. A typical case would be where a client is not certain whether and to what extent a software system can be meaningfully employed to tackle technical or organizational problems arising within his particular organization. Since, in a case of this sort, the major problems are those relating to user requirements and the basic functionality – there being no necessity for prototypes to be suitable for stepwise integration into a target system –, such prototypes are built fairly quickly and written in a language that is as problem-oriented as possible. The use of modern workstations with development environments such as Smalltalk with a powerful graphic user interface is of particular importance here.

An interesting variant on the integration of prototyping in a conventional strategy is the initial use of prototyping by some software manufacturers for the purposes of project acquisition only. This involves already building and demonstrating small prototypes to potential clients during preliminary talks or contractual negotiations with them. Such prototypes are frequently mere mockups demonstrating the surface only without incorporating any aspects of functionality, or they merely illustrate basic handling characteristics of the system without, at this stage, modelling the concrete application area. The benefits of using such prototypes should not be underestimated. Reports from experts in the field of commercial software development indicate that the demonstration of such *unsolicited* prototypes is frequently what clinches important project deals.

### 12.1.3 Our Assessment

These advantages offered by the integration of prototypes into conventional life cycle plans should not, however, make us blind to the disadvantages it also entails. First of all, we have the break between the dynamics of prototyping and the rigidity of the subsequent conventional activities: while prototyping still provides for the sort of feedback we advocate between design and evaluation activities, this is abandoned again in the subsequent classical phases as a result of efforts to separate these activities. Nor should we overlook the fact that the increases in productivity frequently expected from prototyping within a development project are unable to become properly effective if, despite the use of prototyping, project organization continues along conventional lines. This is also true in cases where application generators or VHLLs are used in the actual implementation phase. Experience here has shown that the amount of effort required for producing the various documents in the different phases remains as great as in conventional projects and that the only time-saving is in programming itself.

Another drawback of this *mixed* approach is that the expectations of user management and the end users are directed along the wrong lines. We frequently hear that the general view of such groups is that, once prototyping has been used to support requirements analysis, it will only be a few days before the finished application system is available. In such a situation it is difficult to convey the fact that there will be no more *tangible* results for a long time during the following conventional phases of the project.

To summarize our assessment of the use of this type of prototyping as part of a conventional strategy: the more knowledge there is available about an application area and the more precisely the solution can be specified in advance, the more successful traditional life cycle plans making selective use of prototyping are likely to be. Where this situation is not given and a system requires substantial adaptation to the work environment, the desired results can only be obtained by evolutionary strategies.

## 12.2 Prototyping and "Surface-Down" Development

The prototyping strategy described in this section may also be considered as belonging rather to the traditional concepts. The point of departure is similar to the one in the previous section. We look, by way of an example, at a situation in which a new application is to be realized for an existing database system. A characteristic feature here, however, is that prototyping is integrated more strongly in the application development by the use of a suitable tool, e.g., a database-oriented development system or a VHLL. The system is built from the surface "downwards".

Starting from the screen layout, dialog sequences are modelled. These program skeletons are extended into complete prototypes either by suitable parameterization of generators or by the integration of functional modules. Such prototypes can frequently be employed as pilot systems. Where standard applications are to be provided with an adapted surface, a ready-made functional core is available anyway. In the case of performance problems, when generators are used for the functional core, it may be helpful to rewrite modules in a conventional programming language. Any generator used for prototyping should allow this.

Let us take a closer look at this approach:

- In the early phase of requirements analysis as part of information system modelling, a prototype is generated from the series of screen layouts that are integrated into a program skeleton. This skeleton simulates the behaviour of the application system. The rudimentary prototype is discussed jointly by developers and users, the most important questions posed here relating to the information required for a particular work step and the way such information is to be represented on the screen.
- In technical terms, this means identifying the data needed by the new system. The developer seeks to attain a balance between the information needed by the user for working with existing forms and documents in his or her particular user department and the data types to be defined in the system. At this point, it is already possible to define specific checks to be carried out on the data types and to explain relations between data types.

- A data dictionary is used for the definition of data types. This contains details of all the programs developed by the users. The developers are expected to use existing definitions from other applications for their own purposes. This speeds up the definition of data types and promotes the mutual adjustment of the types used.
- Starting from the program skeleton, either programs or further screen layouts are called. Queries can be made to the database, provided this is already available; otherwise, the developer creates temporary files. The individual parts of the program skeleton are now filled in with functional modules. These prototype extensions are again discussed jointly by users and developers. Here, many desired changes are made on an ad hoc basis with the help of an interpretive language. More elaborate changes are made in the course of the next few days.
- Several prototyping cycles are run through in this way until the user requirements become stable. The final prototype forms the basis of the target system.
- The next step is the development of the target system. Here, the prototype's architecture and, as far as possible, its program code are used.
  In the case of single-user or infrequently used application systems, the last prototype can often be used as the target system, the implementations being efficient enough for this purpose.
  If the prototype does not meet the necessary software engineering standards for direct use as the target system, it is necessary to look into the question of to what extent modules written for the prototype (maybe in a specialized language) can still be used efficiently in the target system or where, for reasons of efficiency, a rewrite in a "lower-level" language is appropriate. Accordingly, individual prototype parts are replaced by machine-oriented modules, or supplementary parts are added for lower system layers.

### 12.2.1 Our Assessment

This approach is commonly used in many organizations working with application generators and database applications. Provided the appropriate tools are available, it ensures good integration of prototyping into a conventional strategy. Development can still be described using a conventional life cycle plan, with project documentation covering the different phases from requirements analysis to acceptance testing, but extensive use is made of prototypes within the individual phases. Another characteristic feature of this approach is the *surface-down* development of the application system.

The use of tools plays an important part here. Poor integration of the various tools used often results in breaks between the different prototypes. This is the case, for instance, when only one form generator is available and there are difficulties fitting its form definitions into a so-called dialog manager. Or if the generated program skeleton does not allow selection of dialog paths in accordance with user inputs, requiring these to be controlled explicitly via function keys. In such cases, it is impossible to ensure that the development of the successive prototypes proceeds without breaks.

An important aspect of this approach is its effectiveness. Developers appear to agree on the fact that software projects of this sort have become shorter. This applies both to their temporal duration and to the scope of the application systems produced. We occasionally hear of prototyping projects being completed in a third of the time needed by traditional COBOL projects. Here, though, it is worth while looking more closely at the reasons for claims of this sort.

There is, first of all, clear evidence of time-saving in terms of pure programming. Programming and testing are facilitated and speeded up by the use of an interpretive language and the ability to execute still incomplete programs. Also, it is often possible to greatly reduce the effort required for milestone documents as compared with traditional projects since management interest focusses on production of an operational prototype. In some cases, this may even lead to situations in which – notwithstanding our recommendations concerning the complementarity of documentation and prototypes – there is no call for any sort of system documentation to accompany the prototype.

There is also evidence that the continuous further development of application systems is – in line with our reflections in Section 5.3.4 – becoming a common strategy. Here, changes to systems developed using prototyping and written in a high-level language prove to be less resource-intensive than, say, the maintenance of COBOL systems. This presupposes, of course, that use is made of the facilities for ensuring soundness of design from the software engineering point of view.[53] We frequently hear that prototyping concepts can be coupled with development and product guidelines without any major problems. Irrespective of the way prototyping is integrated into the development process, our impression is rather that, here, the compliance with such guidelines and product standards is less of a problem because it is easier to see their necessity. Also, communication between users and developers is improved such as to give both sides more concrete ideas about what can meaningfully be included in development and system documentation.

One problem we do see is that coupling prototyping with traditional life cycle plans and developing horizontal prototypes may involve a number of snags. First of all, there is the question of when to *freeze* the prototypes – as a result of the lack or poor integration of tools or procedures – and proceed with development of the target system along conventional lines. A more fundamental question here, though, is that concerning the validity of a collection of screen forms in an otherwise functionless program skeleton. We know of projects in which, to begin with, several hundred screen forms were designed and endorsed by the users without any other functional components being available in the prototype. And yet our analysis of student projects has shown that the screen layout can only be properly evaluated once it is possible to discuss the functions and interaction forms needed for a particular work context. It only then becomes apparent whether specific data must be kept simultaneously *in view* or

[53] Cf. our remarks in Sec. 6.1.

whether new forms of interaction, such as the use of the mouse, result in important changes to existing work procedures. First-hand reports here confirm that these problems are closely tied up with the *surface-down* development strategy selected. The problems are less evident in cases where a set of application programs provided by a well-known database system are supplemented by a further tailor-made application – offering, for example, a new view on existing data.

## 12.3 Prototyping and Evolutionary Strategies

What practical form does prototyping take in an evolutionary development strategy? To illustrate this, we have taken an example *adapted* from a real project and use it to point out a number of characteristic features:

- Parallel to discussions on introduction of a new application system, a demonstration prototype is built in order to show management and users what a system of this sort basically looks like on a new type of workstation, for instance. Depending on the tool support available, use is frequently made here of an application generator capable of realizing both a rudimentary functionality and a standardized surface with a minimal amount of effort. In most cases, though, it is sufficient to demonstrate the handling characteristics and typical forms of representation of, say, a CAD program from another application area.
- The groups involved reach agreement on the general requirements and the scope of the future system. This form of specification constitutes the *overall framework* within which system development takes place. The parties involved are aware that changes in the organizational situation or experience gained in the course of the development process may make it necessary to modify this overall framework.
- Starting from the initial prototype and this overall framework, the developers build the next prototype, which serves as the technical core of the development. This prototype generally models both major aspects of the interaction with the system and certain selected functional components.
- This *core* prototype is further developed iteratively until it attains the quality of a pilot system ready for testing at individual workplaces. During this pilot phase, the users are responsible for producing the sytem's user documentation based on a system specification provided by the developers.
- In the course of development from the initial prototype to the accepted application system, the developers build a series of smaller prototypes – breadboards for their *own needs* – serving to help clarify specific technical problems arising during the development process. Resources are earmarked for these breadboards during project planning.
- On the basis of experience gained with the pilot system, further system versions are built and made available to an increasingly large group of users. In these later versions, provisional system components are either replaced by what are, in software engineering terms, more elaborate ones or other functional components are added. Further breadboards are developed for

technical implementation purposes and to support discussion of design alternatives. Thus, there is no longer a clear distinction between new and further development of an application system.

In this approach, the different forms of prototyping are used as the situation demands. If a new software project is to be set up – along with the contracts this may entail – a *demonstration prototype* is a good help to begin with. It not only helps in initiating the project or concluding the necessary contracts, it also serves to direct users' and management's expectations into the right channels.

The actual project work then proceeds on two different levels. Together with the users and the application management, a number of different prototype versions are developed and experimented with. Even the early prototypes demonstrate aspects of both handling and functionality. What is implemented in each prototype version depends primarily on the priorities set by the users. These requirements are assessed by the developers in terms of what is technically feasible in each case. We know of software projects in which, from a certain version onwards, every prototype could have formed the basis for a usable application system, implementing as it did a further requirement with regard to functionality. Parallel to these prototypes, the developers also build a series of breadboards to help solve specific design and implementation problems.

A crucial juncture in any development project is the transition from the various prototypes to the pilot system that is tested by selected users under real working conditions. This juncture is usually marked by an explicit decision on the part of the groups involved. From this point onwards, special documentation and user training activities become necessary. The users' daily work with the pilot system brings to light all the snags and hitches that were overlooked during experimental testing. This relates to both individual functions and system handling as a whole, it becoming apparent, for example, that important features are missing or that certain user actions are felt to be monotonous or awkward. Equally important, though, are problems connected with the integration of the new application system into the existing information system infrastructure, for instance where interfaces to other systems become necessary.

The transition from the pilot system to the application system *proper* is often a fluid one. Depending on the application context, system versions are presented to an increasingly large group of users, this being accompanied by the integration of necessary and desired changes in functionality and handling. Such changes are initiated by the users and are perceivable at the system's surface. Further changes are made to system components which are reimplemented for reasons of efficiency or to enhance the quality of their software. Generally speaking, such changes are only detectable in the system's performance. The hardware and software used today in prototyping seldom necessitate complete reimplementation of an application system based on a sound pilot system.

### 12.3.1 Our Assessment

An interesting feature of these examples is the role played by the different sorts of prototypes.

The significance of demonstration prototypes has so far been generally underestimated in the literature. In practice, though, it is important that all the parties involved become clear, early on in the development process, as to what a prototype can and, above all, cannot accomplish. Since, in most cases, a demonstration prototype differs perceptibly from the desired application system, it is easy to convey the special role played by prototypes in the development process. One developer told us that he used a mockup of a cake – comparing this to a prototype – to put across to those participating in a prototyping demonstration the particular role of the prototype here.

Breadboards are generally seen as merely serving to demonstrate aspects relating to the feasibility of a specific software system. And yet their importance as a *motor for ideas* should not be underestimated, for their development allows the testing of aspects and functions not yet specified as requirements. We repeatedly hear cases of breadboards' giving rise to important ideas for subsequent versions of an application system. Their function as a *motor for ideas* is also significant because there are rarely any *innovative* suggestions from the users during this phase of prototyping. There is a greater likelihood of well-founded criticism of existing functions and handling characteristics coming from this quarter. At this point, the users generally lack the necessary experience and know-how to come up with new ideas – particularly when dealing with a new application.

Finally, this approach also throws a new light on the problem of transition from the prototype to the finished application system. Where VHLLs or database-oriented development systens are used, the corresponding workstations are generally so powerful that there is rarely any call for a complete reimplementation of the whole system in a traditional programming language. We know of cases where, for example, rule-based system components written in Lisp or Prolog were integrated into a conventional system environment. Considering the low cost of high-performance workstations and advances in networking different sorts of computers and operating systems, the combination of various system components is, in future, likely to be the most practicable approach to the evolutionary (further) development of application systems.

## 12.4 Prototyping and User Development

We conclude our examination of practical prototyping strategies by looking at a controversial issue: the development of application systems by the users themselves. Some see in this the future solution to all the problems associated with software development; others fear the outbreak of chaos in the field of data processing. We choose to take a more discerning view of this question, for the development of prototypes by their users can – under certain circumstances – be an important element in the move towards evolutionary system development.

In the field of office applications, reports are often needed to meet current requirements. The databases accessed here are read only and not modified. The required program is relatively short and is used once or a few times only. The user requirement for immediate availability of such data is frequently at variance with the considerable effort involved in making the necessary official request for them and the large backlog waiting to be processed in the DP departments.

In the face of these problems, it has proved the best policy to let the users themselves develop such applications. Prototyping is the only suitable approach here as far as the users are concerned, because they are only able to develop software on an experimental basis, and not along traditional lines calling for a separation of specification and implementation. Use is generally made here of application generators or application-oriented language interfaces to relational databases. Of particular importance, too, are application systems such as are available on modern workstations for word-processing, desktop publishing, simple data storage and spreadsheet analysis. These systems, which are based on the so-called desktop metaphor, are not confined to one particular application and can be modified by their users to suit different purposes. Since specialized command languages are used here, the boundaries between application and programming are frequently blurred.

So far, we have looked at the development of software by users to meet their own needs, and here chiefly for one-shot applications. However, we frequently encounter situations in which prototypes are utilized by users for other purposes. Initially, they are part of their creator's work environment; but then they are adopted by other colleagues. A useful rule of thumb here is: only allow others to use the system if it meets accepted standards of quality. In practical terms, though, this means that such prototypes must be further developed in order to comply with software engineering standards for application systems. That is a job for computer specialists, who will be dealing in particular with aspects that are largely inaccessible to the user, e.g., program restart or robustness. And, again, it is only computer specialists equipped with the necessary expert knowledge who will, for instance, be in a position to choose between several functionally equivalent database queries on the basis of operational efficiency and reliability.

The continuous further development of an information system is not, however, the only area in which we find this interaction between computer specialists and users acting in the role of developers; such an interaction is occasionally encountered, too, as an explicit strategy in independently established software projects. Given the proper technical environment and the appropriate skills on the part of the users, the latter may assume responsibility for the construction of the initial prototypes, the computer specialists offering support in an advisory capacity. At some point, the users decide that they are no longer able to improve those aspects of the prototype that are of particular relevance to them, and they then leave its further development to the computer specialists. The resulting prototype combines both problem-oriented and computer-oriented knowledge and serves as a basis for discussion between users and computer specialists.

### 12.4.1 Our Assessment

In certain application areas, the development of prototypes by the users may be a key concept offering advantages over the approaches previously discussed.

Such areas include office applications with suitable technical support on workstations as well as applications in technical fields such as mechanical and electrical engineering in which the users are already professionally trained in the formalization of application problems. For programming requires of users the ability to formulate a problem solution in precise terms. Such a program, written in an application-oriented programming language, is not necessarily the final solution to the problem — it may, for example, be too inefficient or not sufficiently integrated into the working procedures. But such a prototype does provide the executable specification for the subsequent work of the computer specialists. They are thus cast in the role of consultants, assuming the job of developing the so-called *lower layers* as well as that of quality control.

This marks a change in the part played by prototypes in the development process. The prototype is no longer a mere operational model used by the developers to demonstrate solutions to the users. The users have become the computer specialists' partners and peers, using prototypes, for their part, to illustrate to the computer experts their ideas for a technical solution. In the development process, prototypes become the common work object of two groups of developers belonging to different worlds – the world of the application and the world of the computer.

We realize that there are clear limits to programming by users: there is little sense in trying to develop in this way complex or wide-range applications. This applies particularly to networked systems or those requiring sophisticated software. After all, it cannot be the goal – especially not of evolutionary system development – to have users devoting more and more of their time and effort to software engineering problems instead of getting on with their own work. But even in the case of application-oriented prototypes, restrictions must be made. For instance, in cases requiring the modification of operational data, it is imperative that users only be allowed to test their prototypes on copies of the operational data.

Despite these restrictions and reservations, the importance of expert knowledge for developing good application programs should not be underestimated. Combining the efforts of competent users and computer specialists is a useful approach for the sort of applications outlined above. It should not be forgotten that active user participation in the development process can help to both reduce inhibitions on the part of the users and to replace unrealistic expectations with regard to the computer by a more realistic view — and this, in turn, frequently leads to a greater sense of commitment on the users' part and increased motivation to cooperate with the developers.

## 12.5 Prototyping and Documentation

An assessment of the different approaches used in prototyping would be incomplete without a look at the importance of *documentation of the development process and the application system*. Documentation remains the Cinderella of software development. And prototyping has done nothing to alter this fact. Why is this so?

We are only just beginning to understand how to deal technically with the constant changes in a system like software that is basically seen as being static. And even more complex and subject to change are the texts designed to describe such systems. These changes are unavoidable, both during the actual development process and once the system is in use. This is, after all, what prototyping is all about. On the other hand, nobody really enjoys the job of documenting, especially as computer support is weak here. All attempts to move beyond the realm of traditional text production have either failed to carry conviction or are not yet practicable.

But not even prototyping can dispense with documentation. Even though prototyping would appear, at first sight, to make written documents superfluous – the prototype replacing the specification as an operative model – the effects of inadequate documentation soon make themselves felt in practice. First of all, there are the indispensable user reference documents. Here, there is a tendency among developers to take their prior technical understanding of the problem as an implicit basis when documenting a system. Besides the user documentation, the documentation of the development process is also of crucial importance, particularly for the further development of the system. This includes both descriptions of the system architecture and the documentation of design decisions without which it is practically impossible to define the relations between technical components and user requirements.

As far as the actual user documentation is concerned, it has proved helpful to allow the users to assume responsibility for its production because they take a technically *unbiased* view of the system. And this is considered a positive factor by all the parties involved. It is also a job that can be handled well by user representatives who are integral members of a developer team. There is thus a tendency for documentation to become an independent task, as is already the case with software manufacturers developing application packages for PCs and workstations. Here, we find specialized teams not only with the required technical expertise, but also equipped with the necessary didactic and layout skills.

Once the users themselves start programming, reference manuals for prototype construction are of crucial importance. The effort required for updating such manuals and supervising their use is underestimated to the same extent as the benefits they bring. A manual describing the quality requirements for prototypes should never be normative in character. It must contain examples of good structuring and documentation and persuade the reader of the benefit of these by reasoning. A high degree of formalization is pointless.

### 12.5.1 Our Assessment

There have been some promising advances in the area of documentation, but they still constitute fairly new ground. This applies to documentation of both the development process and the software itself. We nevertheless see the development of hypermedia systems as offering good prospects for finding an alternative to the separation of software construction and documentation activities. With their help, it might be possible to adopt different views on an application system, allowing us to consider, say, its development history or its software architecture.

# 13 The Groups Involved in Prototyping

In the course of this book, it should have become clear that, whatever form it takes, prototyping invariably means a departure from traditional ways of thinking and working in software development. And this has – as we have repeatedly seen in the previous chapter – repercussions for the groups involved. Following the division adopted so far, we now go on to consider what the effects are on the three main groups involved in the design of prototyping processes:

- the developers,
- the users, and
- the management (a distinction being made in specific cases between user management and DP management).

## 13.1 The Developers

Changes in the working situation brought about by prototyping are felt most acutely by the developers, for they are affected in a number of different ways:

- Prototyping almost invariably involves the increased use of tools, with new languages frequently being used on new types of computers. This means a break with the accustomed technical environment.
- Prototyping involves experimenting with programs and getting the users to evaluate them. For the developers, this means increased discussions with the users and the need to revise their own work results in the light of the users' criticism.
- This revision of prototypes in the light of user criticism seldom results in detailed written specifications but mostly in supplementary documents only. Detailed programming instructions in the form of decision tables or even pseudocode are no longer used. This does away with many of the usual documents produced in the course of a traditional life cycle plan, documents which, as we have seen, merely offer a sense of security in the development process, but which are nevertheless – and perhaps for this very reason – seen by many developers as being indispensable.

The effects of these changes become evident in various ways. First of all, there is the problem of skills; then there are changes in the project work; and finally there are changes, too, in the technical environment. We take a closer look at these changes in the following sections.

### 13.1.1 Opposition from the Developers

We have looked earlier on at the *generation problem* among developers (cf. Sec. 5.3.3). There are indications of a growing dilemma here between the *young* professionally trained developers, on the one hand, and the *established* programmers with their on-the-job experience, on the other. Whereas the latter group is often reluctant to use application generators or VHLLs, but is accustomed to working with programming instructions and milestone documents, there is little inclination on the part of developers experienced in the use of these new programming tools to adhere to traditional development concepts.

And the situation is a similar one as regards the relationship between the developers and the users. *Conservative* developers in traditional DP departments frequently consider communication with users to be unproductive and a waste of time generally. They prefer working according to fixed instructions rather than *chasing after* user wishes. This *closed shop* mentality – accompanied as it is by the not ungrounded fear of a possible loss of professional prestige – is at variance with the idea of prototyping. In practice, this problem is exacerbated by the fact that developers are often assigned to several parallel projects, resulting in the feeling that their work load is too great and their work itself unproductive. In such cases, the communication barriers between developers and users are particularly high.

### 13.1.2 New Forms of Project Work

Let us now go on to consider what we have said in the previous section in terms of the new requirements facing developers in their project work as a result of prototyping. One obvious fact here is that the use of suitable tools and aids to support prototyping makes greater demands on the developers' analytical and constructive design skills. Since in prototype construction there are seldom any detailed programming instructions, more design decisions have to be taken than when programming in a conventional style. Also new are dealings with the users, which now become an integral part of the developers' work.

There is a considerable change in the skill profile of developers working in prototyping projects:

- The requirements and system analysis carried out as part of information system modelling acquires a much greater importance than coding.
- Also of growing importance are the motivation and ability to talk to the users and prepare their material in such a way as to make it intelligible to them.
- Programming in a traditional language like COBOL becomes less important. Instead, the developers' work will involve increasing familiarity with a number of different database-oriented development systems, development environments and VHLLs.
- The growing importance of interactive systems makes high demands on technical system design and implementation. Many developers are just as unfa-

miliar with the idea of separating interaction and functionality as they are with using window and graphics systems on workstations.

In addition, software projects are beginning to follow a new *pattern*. The individual application is becoming smaller; project size and run time are on the decrease. And there is a general tendency towards interactive applications. Here, the application systems are designed on a modular basis and developed in *versions* starting from a core which is considered to be particularly relevant. There is thus a change, too, in the developers' work object.

### 13.1.3 New Technical Environment

The use of prototyping as part of a development strategy does, however, also affect the developers' work situation above and beyond the confines of the individual development project. In Section 5.3.4, we pointed out that the particular importance of prototyping is due to the fact that, today, the use of computers is on the increase in all areas of work and, at the same time, that there is a growing need for swift adaptation of the information system infrastructure to new technical and organizational requirements. In practice, though, we may observe a contrary tendency on the part of developers in DP departments – but also of users – to quickly become blind to the real problems facing an organization. Their work load compels them to confine their attention to their own *specific* tasks. They lose sight of what is going on around their own narrow work area and thus fail to keep up with technological developments. There is as little likelihood of the user working with an application generator in an accounting department being able to keep track of all the new advances in the computer field as there is of the developer, responsible for the programming of this generator, being able to produce a study examining the suitability of different application generators for accounting applications.

It is evident here that prototyping and evolutionary system development call for a more comprehensive technical environment involving additional tasks for the developers. It is already current practice in a number of large organizations to assign responsibility for technology transfer to the developers. It is their job to draw up a framework for the subsequent work of the users groups – the programmers and the end users. We consider the following areas to be of particular importance here:

- word-processing, integration of text and graphics, desktop publishing;
- database-oriented development systems and other database applications;
- configuration and installation of different types of devices such as mass storage units, scanners, displays and printers;
- networking of workstations and mainframes.

These areas are of major importance for two reasons: firstly, the use of application systems is part of everyday practice in many organizations. Particularly in the area of office work, there are a great many such systems available. An essential part of the work of developers and users is trying out and getting acquainted with new systems in order to facilitate their evaluation and initial training on them. Here, they need professional, systematic support. The diversity in the computer landscape of a large organization makes the integration of widely varying systems into a uniform DP concept a separate and demanding task. One way of accomplishing these two tasks is to divide up the developers into separate groups with different jobs.

Consulting and training groups are responsible for supporting the users, for example, in word-processing activities and the use of application packages on workstations and mainframes. Here, depending on the specific work context, they recommend the use of different applications and enforce inhouse standards. It is the computer specialists' job to offer their services as consultants and, drawing on their professional knowledge, to actually help in finding solutions to application problems. The main job of these consultants, however, is not to program applications. A crucial part of their work is training – drawing up ideas and presenting them to developers and users so as to constantly encourage them to examine the effectiveness of their own work.

Other groups are responsible for the system integration. They are concerned with developing interfaces between the workstations and mainframes, improving menu interfaces for mainframe applications and application packages and evaluating commercial software products. This integration and networking of the various systems is a specialist job requiring coordination. This group of specialists should also have a big say in system selection and acquisition.

The importance of such groups in terms of increased productivity is difficult to gauge, but it should not be underestimated. For organizations subject to swift changes in their technical and organizational environment, such specialists are practically indispensable. Didactic abilities play a major role in selecting skilled consultants. This sort of work calls for highly motivated computer specialists. Prototyping and evolutionary system development have become the main development strategy employed here.

### 13.1.4 The Users

That prototyping brings about a fundamental change in the role of the users in the software development process is a fact that we have repeatedly drawn attention to in the course of this book. This section takes an explicit look at the additional work this involves for the users.

Whatever form prototyping may take in the specific development situation, one thing is clear: prototyping and evolutionary system development call for a high degree of user participation. Some organizations make it a precondition for initiation of a prototyping project that the users specify the personnel resources they are prepared to invest in the project. In other cases, it is assumed that a user representative will be a full-time member of the project team. But this necessary user participation is not without its problems. On the one hand, there are the sort of programmers described above who would rather get on with the job of programming instead of having to spend their time dealing with the users.

And on the other, there are a great many users who consider themselves too busy to deal with the problems of software development.

User participation in the development of prototypes greatly extends the DP knowledge base within an organization. This also has a positive effect on all other application programs; it helps to reduce user problems, even when dealing with older software. And it also helps to bring about a change in attitude towards the development process. Since the users are soon presented with tangible results, their requirements relate to a system that reflects current needs. At the same time, the users are given a realistic picture of the scope offered by the use of computers. This helps to avoid unrealistic requirements. And it contrasts with the conventional idea of the users setting down absolutely every conceivable requirement in the contract data requirements list in the expectation of getting a finished system only in the long term anyway, and then having little scope for changing it.

We often hear talk, in this connection, of a new sense of identity among organizations or of a new project culture for solving such problems. We see these concepts as making sense where they are discussed in relation to enhancing user skills. In many sectors, the competitiveness and economic stability of industrial organizations are, we feel, dependent today on the quality of the work performed by those employed in these organizations. And this is why we see the need to provide users with the necessary skills for working with computers. This goes beyond the traditional notion of user participation, for user participation – as we understand it – already presupposes computer-related skills, that must first be acquired by suitable training measures, and the willingness on the part of the users to obtain the required know-how. This is by no means a utopian demand, as a look at the everyday practice of many organizations shows. Here, there have already been changes in the demands made on many users with respect to their knowledge of how to use computers:

- They need a basic knowledge of computers in order to be able to understand the effects of computer use on their own work activities.
- They require the necessary skills enabling them to give an abstract representation of their own work activities as part of requirements analysis.
- They need additional knowledge in order to be able to use problem-oriented languages (e.g., as part of an application generator) to support their own work with self-programmed applications.

Many application systems running on workstations and PCs have already set new standards here. They provide language constructs and a variety of parameterization facilities that help to break down the boundaries between application and programming. Such were our findings at courses we attended on HyperCard. Brooks points out that the availability of word-processing, data storage and spreadsheet systems constitutes a decisive step towards a new era in the use of computers (see [Brooks87]). We know of firms in which every single member of staff is equipped with a workstation and has the option of attending courses on standard application systems.

## 13.2 Management

The use of prototyping must also be accepted at management level and supported by suitable strategic measures. This applies to both user and DP management, and it poses a number of questions. After taking the basic decision to use prototyping, the DP management has to work out the changes required in the organizational and technical infrastructure if it is to support an approach of this kind. Prototyping projects involving external partners call for new forms of contractual arrangements. Finally, personnel management in the DP and user departments is also affected. We look at each of these issues in detail in the following sections.

### 13.2.1 The Break with Conventional Methods

Many organizations have just completed the laborious task of putting software development in their DP departments on a sound engineering basis – a move, say, away from *freehand* towards structured programming. It will be difficult to get such firms – with their comparatively low level of software technology – to adopt an even more sophisticated development concept, because

- swift production cycles in prototyping call for the increased use of tools, and
- prototyping requires better control and understanding of programming methodology than many traditional development strategies.

The initial question facing the DP management is whether such a change in strategy can actually be accomplished using existing developer resources. It results in changed requirements with respect to the developers' knowledge and willingness to learn, and these are not easy to meet given the personnel situation in many DP departments.

Many top-level managers – with both user organizations and software manufacturers – are, for other reasons too, reluctant to abandon traditional development strategies with their fixed documents and milestone principles in favour of an evolutionary approach. They are no longer involved in the everyday development work, and so milestones and other scheduled documents provide them with a means of formal control of the development process. That is why many DP managers still cling to the proven techniques of programming using methods like HIPO. They fail to see that this is not the way to ensure the quality of software.

Evidently, prototyping calls for some degree of willingness on the part of management to take risks. A fact which should not be overlooked, though, is that many organizations with a conventional information system infrastructure are scarcely able to master the problems of system construction and maintenance and are therefore compelled to seek for *new options.* And many organizations appear to realize that their hopes lie not in bigger and faster computers or in some new CASE tool, but in a change in attitude towards system development, i.e., what we have called evolutionary system development.

### 13.2.2 New Forms of Project Organization

In our examination of the effects of prototyping on the group of the developers, we have already pointed to the need for a redefinition of tasks and a reallocation of responsibilities. The most obvious change here is the organization of prototyping projects in small teams. But other factors are of importance, too: management frequently underestimates the extent to which productivity is adversely affected by developers' simultaneous involvement in a number of different projects. And yet experience in this area has shown that grouping together highly motivated users and developers in a small team with little organizational ballast and with their efforts focussed on one specific goal – occupying the whole, and not only 30%, of their time – has much greater prospects of success. To enable project members to coordinate their activities at all times, it is extremely important that they work together at one and the same location. However, the current excessive work load of many DP departments only permits this form of organization in cases where the projects are assigned developers from external software manufacturers.

### 13.2.3 New Technical Infrastructure

Management is often unclear as to what form a flexible DP infrastructure should take if it is to meet the work requirements on the user side and, at the same time, facilitate evolutionary further development of the information system. There are, then, in our view – irrespective of the size of an organization and the level of existing computer support – two basic principles that must govern considerations in each individual case.

#### Further Development of the Existing Infrastructure

Let us take a look, first of all, at large organizations that already have an elaborate DP infrastructure. Here, we meet with a familiar picture. Management of the relevant organizational data is carried out on mainframes using traditional application systems. But, in addition, the various user departments are equipped with PCs and workstations operated by the users themselves and adapted to meet individual needs. Typical applications here are spreadsheets, graphics and word-processing. Networking between mainframe and PCs is weak. Data are frequently transported via homemade interfaces. Given this situation, DP management fears increasing chaos as a result of the use of additional nonintegrated workstations and attempts to use its centralized authority to ensure a process of standardization and secure its old position of power. User management is reluctant to accept a uniform mainframe solution because in spite of all the technical problems involved – particularly with regard to the compatibility of data and applications – the installation of a number of different workstations or PCs has proved a suitable solution to many application problems.

In Section 5.3.4, we have shown that prototyping and an evolutionary further development of the information system infrastructure go hand in hand. The technical know-how for networking nonuniform computers is already available today.

Local area networks allow both the various types of workstations and PCs and mainframes to be linked together and to other peripheral devices without any major difficulties. This means that the respective computers can be employed in those areas to which they are best suited – either as graphics or desktop publishing computers at the individual workplace or as high-performance servers in the background. Prototyping facilitates such steps and also helps in the choice of suitable application systems. Experience has been positive where new applications in this area have been conceived as *learning projects* in which the emphasis is on all the parties involved getting acquainted with new procedures and techniques instead of the usual pressure to meet deadlines and produce results. All in all, we see this approach as currently representing what has been called the *major solution* to the problem of further developing the technical infrastructure.

### Establishing an Infrastructure

There are, however, a large number of other, smaller organizations in which management is still contemplating the introduction of computer technology. The major question here is whether to use this opportunity to establish a comprehensive, uniform solution incorporating an application system tailored to local needs. Software manufacturers often recommend solutions of this sort, and these may in some cases be useful. As a rule, though, such recommendations tend to reflect personal commercial interests. Another approach would appear to be more promising here. It is precisely in situations of this sort that evolutionary system development comes into its own: users and user management should be in a position to gain experience with the use of computers on an experimental and exploratory basis. This, however, means that decisions that have already been taken but are subsequently felt to be wrong can be reversed again without major sideeffects. Accordingly, it is advisable to begin by installing small workstations with standard ready-to-use application packages for use as pilot systems. For, normally, 90% of the required applications can be tested experimentally in the initial phase by using standard system packages. The real difficulties lie, initially, in the organizational integration of the application systems into the accustomed working routines. Not until it becomes clear which activities can and should be supported by which sort of application systems is the time ripe for more comprehensive software solutions. Such an approach enables all the groups involved to gain extensive experience with the use of computers without investments in hardware and specialized software reaching such a level as to rule out the possibility of testing other options. And it also helps avoid premature commitment to a specific hardware or software manufacturer.

## 13.2.4 New Contracts

When reflecting on the pros and cons of prototyping, management are soon confronted with the question of the form contracts with external partners might take. We have already gone into the problems associated with traditional milestone documents for monitoring and controlling the progress of development projects (cf. Sec. 3.4). And in prototyping projects, too, contractual arrangements often follow the pattern of conventional life cycle plans. There are two main types of contract here: contracts in which prototypes are either not mentioned at all or treated like traditional milestone documents; and contracts which do actually provide for the construction of prototypes, but which calculate the costs involved on a flat-rate basis. Neither of these two types is really suitable for securing the advantages promised by prototyping in contractual terms, too.

If conventional milestones are laid down in the terms of the contract, it is usual for documents to be produced exclusively for the purposes of fulfilling the contract and for the benefit of project management. If prototypes are treated as milestone documents, the project resources are usually lacking for a thorough revision of these prototypes – subsequent to their evaluation by the groups involved – with a view to their use as a technical basis for the further development. And the effects are similar, too, if budgeting for the project as a whole is carried out on a flat-rate basis. This means that necessary and inevitable requests for changes are either neglected, or that the financial onus for these falls on one of the contracting parties – frequently the software manufacturer. Many organizations experienced in prototyping have therefore taken to gearing several consecutive contracts to the activities and results of an evolutionary development process. Accordingly, these contracts contain requirement analyses, descriptions of the whole development context, a glossary of the terminology in use in the application area, demonstration prototypes or pilot system installations as units for evaluative and calculative purposes.

One objection raised against these new forms of stepwise contractual arrangements is that some software manufacturers have had negative experience with prototypes that were adopted by clients without follow-up contracts, for further development within their own organization. Unquestionably, there are still loopholes today in software copyright regulations. It is possible, though, by making suitable contractual arrangements, to guard against the improper use of prototypes. One feature of the redefinition of roles between developers, user organizations and end users is the fact that prototyping presents the user management with greater scope for abandoning a development project at a designated point in time or handing it over to another software manufacturer.

### 13.2.5 New Forms of Personnel Management

A pressing issue for the management of an organization in which both user and DP departments exist side by side is the need to break through the closed-shop mentality of the centralized DP departments and help the developers employed in them to evolve a new professional profile. There is no longer any call for the dominant, omniscient authority with all the reins in his hand; what is needed is the consultant who takes into consideration the wishes and needs of the users and proposes a number of different options. Resistance may be expected, however, where positions of power and professional prestige are tied up with the size of projects and personnel resources. The organization of development projects in small, decentralized teams calls for new ways of motivating project members and measuring their achievements.

An objection sometimes raised against this form of organization is that the small teams in a prototyping project are more susceptible to changes in personnel. For, apart from the obvious unrest caused by a fluctuation of personnel in a small project, an additional factor here is the greater *perseverance* shown by COBOL programmers in a particular job as compared with developers using new systems and languages. This factor should be taken into account; but it should also be borne in mind that modern management sets greater store by highly skilled and motivated personnel than it does by members of staff who are content to get on with traditional routine tasks.

But this does not only apply to the developers. We have pointed out just how important user participation is for prototyping. There are two sides to this: on the one hand, there must be a willingness to participate on the part of the users, and on the other, they must be given the opportunity to do so. It is up to management to take the necessary steps to secure this participation. A basic precondition for user commitment to participation is an open information policy with respect to the goals and expected implications of system development. Next, user management must ensure – by an appropriate division of labour and assignment of duties – that substantial participation in prototyping projects by the users is actually feasible within the time available. A final factor is their assessment of the users' willingness to participate; the users' willingness or reluctance to participate has proved a good indicator of the overall success or failure of a development project. Where there is a lack of willingness on their part, none of the technical methods available is going to help produce a usable system.

A fact frequently overlooked is that evolutionary system development is primarily a learning process for users and developers. Just as users must learn to handle the computer in their everyday work, so must developers acquire growing insight into the tasks and problems associated with the different application areas. This does not happen on its own; it must be supported by management and secured by suitable forms of organization.

To this extent, planning and control of the development of an information system infrastructure must be seen from a new perspective.[54] Success can no longer be measured in terms of lines of code, but rather by the usability of an application system and its acceptance by the users. This means that both user and DP management must join in the discussion on application systems and prototypes as well as in their evaluation.

[54] Cf. also our discussion in Sec. 3.4

# 14 Summary

This final chapter summarizes the main points made in the previous chapters. It thus recapitulates, for the benefit of the reader, on the ideas and arguments put forward by us and the approaches we have chosen to adopt in our work. In addition, it provides a series of cross-references and may thus serve the reader as a sort of detailed index to the topics treated in the book.

We have defined prototyping (see p.6 and 34) as an approach to software development incorporating the following features:

- Operative versions are produced at an early stage.
- Relevant problems are clarified by experimentation.
- Prototypes provide a common basis for discussion between developers, users and other groups.

Prototyping has grown out of the realization that

- requirements frequently do not become apparent until a system is in use
- specifications cannot be completed until during the construction process
- users and developers must learn from each other
- computer specialists are being increasingly assigned to work in user departments.

Looking at software development generally, we find two essential forms of feedback in the development process (see p.13):

- Verification:
  - Checking the consistency and completeness of a model in relation to itself and the preceding model.
- Validation:
  - Evaluation of a model with respect to its usability.
  - The evaluation is based on measurements and human judgement.

These forms of feedback govern the whole development process. But since the traditional principle for dividing up software development activities is "First specify as completely as possible, then implement as linearly as possible", we constantly encounter feedback problems in practice:

- The problems encountered in software development usually occur during requirements specification; and it is there that elaborate feedback cycles are needed most, though they are not normally provided for.
- As a consequence, development concepts that do not include prototyping make no provision for evaluation of so-called early activities until late on in the development process.

- Software construction proper confines feedback to testing and verification cycles in which only the software developers are involved.

There are a variety of problems associated with poor communication and feedback during system development, and these, taken together, constitute what is known today as the "software crisis" (see p.28):

- A complete and permanently correct description of information systems is not possible.
- Specification and implementation of a software system cannot be performed as separate work steps in time.
- Formal, nonexecutable specifications are largely unintelligible to users and developers.
- Traditional development strategies exclude the users from crucial activities.
- The label "maintenance" conceals vital aspects of development work concerned with adapting a system to the application context.
- Life cycle plans are unsuitable for controlling software projects. Milestone documents are produced for the benefit of management only.

Prototyping is used to eliminate these system development problems. The prototyping process itself and the products of this process, the prototypes, may assume a variety of different forms. We therefore distinguish first of all between the following kinds of prototypes (see p.35):

- We use the term prototype proper to describe a provisional operational software system. A prototype of this sort is generally designed to illustrate specific aspects of the user interface or part of the functionality and thus helps to clarify the problem in hand.
- We call a prototype that is designed chiefly to help clarify construction-related questions facing the developer team a breadboard. This kind of prototype is also encountered in traditional software projects, though the experimental approach associated with it is seldom given explicit recognition as such. Users are generally excluded from the evaluation of breadboards. To this extent, the use of breadboards is a restricted form of prototyping.
- If a prototype is used not only for experimental testing of an idea or for "illustrative purposes", but is actually employed in the application area itself as the core of the application system, it is known as a pilot system . In such cases, there ceases to be any strict distinction between the prototype and the application system. After reaching a certain degree of "sophistication", the prototype is practically implemented in the form of a pilot system and incremented in cycles.

Looking at prototyping in conjunction with the system development process as a whole, we are able to distinguish the following kinds of prototyping (see p.38):

- Exploratory Prototyping. This is used where the problem in hand is unclear. Initial ideas are used as a basis for clarifying user and management requirements with respect to the future system.

- Experimental Prototyping. This form of prototyping focusses on the technical implementation of a development goal. By means of experimentation, the users are able to further specify their ideas about the type of computer support required. The developers, for their part, are provided with a basis for appraisal of the suitability and feasibility of a particular application system.
- Evolutionary Prototyping. Here, prototyping is not merely used as a tool in the context of a single development project; it is rather a continuous process for adapting an application system to rapidly changing organizational constraints.

If we view software development as the design and implementation of a number of layers, ranging from the user interface to the base layer, the subdivision into horizontal and vertical prototyping becomes meaningful (see p.39):

- In horizontal prototyping, only specific layers of the the system are built, e.g., the user interface layer along with its forms and menus, or functional core layers such as database transactions.
- In vertical prototyping, a selected part of the target system is implemented completely.

A further criterion for classifying prototypes is the relationship between the prototype and the application system (see p.40):

- Prototypes are incremented to produce the application. system
- A prototype is part of the application system. specification
- Prototypes serve to clarify problems only.

Prototyping can be embedded in a number of different approaches. We feel that the best way of tackling the problems currently facing software development is by adopting an evolutionary system development strategy. The special perspective of evolutionary system development involves posing the fundamental question as to the form meaningful support of the software development process should take (see p.49):

- Communication between developers and users takes place throughout project run time and is not confined to the phases of user needs analysis and system installation.
- System development is a mutual learning process for all parties concerned, and not merely the process of transforming a specification into a target system.
- A system is built in a number of small work steps and parts of manageable size. This makes it possible to redefine or correct, step by step, the direction development is taking.
- Specification and implementation are connected, complementary activities. They cannot be divided up into consecutive phases.
- The development models are complemented as far as possible by operational software versions in order to allow and facilitate evaluation of the models early on in the development process.

Evolutionary system development is possible and necessary because (see p.60):

- Small, high-capacity computers are available at a reasonable price.
- High-performance languages and development tools are available.
- Interactive application systems are "standard" software on workstations.
- Users have become more demanding in their requirements.
- Influential users groups have begun to voice their demands.
- There is a clear trend towards interactive programming.
- A new professional profile is being created by a new generation of software engineers.

Evolutionary system development makes sense because:

- Software systems evolve and are no longer constructed from scratch.
- Restoration instead of demolition is in keeping with the spirit of the times.
- We are faced with the co-existence of different technologies.
- Experimentation enables us to construct interfaces between systems built using different technologies. There is no other remedy to the problem.

The idea of prototyping has long since ceased to be confined to the research laboratory. If we look at software development in the commercial, technical and scientific sectors, we find that prototypes are already widely used today, either as part of a development strategy, or because of the urgent need to clarify the requirements for a particular software system.

There are scarcely any instances of prototype construction without special tools or toolkits. The tools and toolkits currently in use can be divided up into four classes: screen generators, database-oriented tools, Very High Level Languages and programming environments (see p.80 and the corresponding chapters).

In commercial data processing, screen generators provide suitable support for the design and generation of the "classical" standard screen maps needed there. They are traditionally looked on as quite effective and helpful tools, despite the fact that they fail to support more recent interaction techniques such as window systems. We nevertheless feel that they should be submitted to a somewhat more critical appraisal:

- Compared with classical programming languages, screen maps allow simpler and quicker description of the screen layout for screen map representation. They can be easily generated and demonstrated for use as prototypes where the main concern is with requirements analysis and the specification of user interfaces.
- The simulation components available allow only static linking of maps to be carried out easily. Where the focus is on alternative solutions for human-computer interaction or on the dynamic behaviour of the application system, the benefits of such prototypes are limited.

- On construction of the target systems, screen generators take over a large portion of the standard tasks involved in implementation of the user interfaces. Many screen generators, however, impose restrictions through the interfaces to the classical programming languages available – which means that knowledge of these languages is a prerequisite for using the tools.

To sum up, it may be said that the use of classical screen generators offers a number of advantages for the construction of both horizontal and vertical prototypes in traditional data processing. However, we feel that both the use of these tools "in isolation" and their close coupling with classical programming languages limit their benefits with respect to prototyping.

As a basic principle, database-oriented development systems support prototyping strategies. They offer support in clarifying a wide variety of problems ranging from the specification of requirements to the modelling of interactive and functional components of the application systems under development. Database-oriented development systems and the programs generated with them meet some of the essential requirements for prototyping:

- They are more problem-oriented than traditional commercial programming languages.
- Their powerful nonprocedural language elements make the programs compact and easier to understand.
- The construction of application programs is highly efficient. Simple and complex prototypes can be "built" by combining powerful operations with simple screen maps. The interactive, integrated system components allow rapid design, construction and evaluation cycles.
- At the user interfaces, most development systems provide strictly hierarchical menus for selecting system components. These offer useful support to the users in familiarizing themselves with a system of this sort. With growing experience, though, they are more of a hindrance than an aid.
- Many development systems provide only a limited number of interaction forms for developing application systems. They are, therefore, of only limited suitability for the development of prototypes with individual user interfaces.
- Substantial differences are also found in the user interfaces of the various system components. These range from simple text editors to table-oriented and graphic tools.
- The language constructs integrated as system components support programming in the small and the reusability of algorithms. Since the available constructs are, however, highly restricted in their syntactic forms, problems can arise.
- For programming in the large, only transaction, procedure and file concepts are normally available.
- If a prototype is to be extended into an application system using only the system components provided by the development system being used, frequently the entire development system is needed to execute the application system.

- Generally, a combination of the development system's and a classical programming language can be used to adapt and extend parts of a prototype into an application system
- Some database-oriented development systems strictly prescribe the adoption of a uniform approach throughout the development process, especially during the design and modification of user interfaces, data models and dialog sequences, which frequently causes problems. Prescriptive strategies of this sort also interfere with methods for carrying out the necessary revision cycles.
- In addition, the various implemented concepts for checking the logical schemata and the specifications of the objects' screen representation prevent the construction of an incomplete or inconsistent data model. In some cases, this means that it is impossible to store incomplete and temporarily inconsistent schemata and screen specifications in order to interrupt one's work at some desired point, which is usually extremely annoying.

Going on to consider Very High Level Languages, we conclude that these are of interest for the purposes of both specification and implementation. We emphasize one of these two aspects when we call a VHLL an executable specification language or a problem-oriented implementation language. Both aspects highlight the benefits VHLLs offer for prototype construction.

- The chief criterion in selecting a VHLL is the particular problem in hand. VHLLs are tailored to specific applications and tend to be clumsy when used in other contexts.
- Nearly all the VHLLs mentioned in this book have reached a considerable level of technical perfection. In the research and development sector, recent years have seen an increase in the importance of logical, functional and algebraic VHLLs in particular, while object-oriented languages are currently considered promising in both commercial and research environments.
- Most VHLLs lack the libraries, along with their prefabricated building blocks, that are needed for the prototypical construction of interactive components.
- The VHLLs generally available today are particularly well-suited for implementing prototypes and applications for single-user systems. VHLLs are unsuitable for constructing applications for multi-user systems offering simultaneous access to a common database or for large databases with high transaction requirements.

So far, the use of integrated software engineering environments has been confined almost exclusively to universities and R & D laboratories. There is, however, a marked trend towards the use of programming environments on workstations and high-capacity PCs for specific programming languages such as C++ and Smalltalk. As these environments are not designed chiefly for prototype construction, it is useful to consider the advantages and disadvantages of programming environments for prototyping:

- The various documents produced during system development and the different models of the application system are accessible within a single uniform environment.
- Prefabricated building blocks for designing the interactive components of a prototype and an interface to a general window system are, today, standard features of programming environments.
- The interplay between a VHLL and the tools of a programming environment is what constitutes the latter's particular strength.
- Current programming environments rarely support teamwork by providing tools for cooperation and communication.
- A difficult problem is integrating a prototype into the application system if different languages used in each case. There is little technical support for this transition process. In addition, prototypes are generally incapable of execution without major parts of their programming environment.

Next, we look at the role already being played by prototyping in industrial software practice (see p.160):

- There is no denying that prototyping can be profitably employed as part of classical life cycle plans. The more knowledge there is available about an application area and the more precisely the solution can be specified in advance, the more successful traditional life cycle plans making selective use of prototyping are likely to be. Where this situation is not given and a system requires substantial adaptation to the work environment, the desired results can only be obtained by evolutionary strategies (see p.161).
- A different approach is commonly used in many organizations working with application development systems and database applications. Development can still be described using a conventional life cycle plan, with project documentation covering the different phases, but extensive use is made of prototypes within the individual phases. An important aspect of this approach is its effectiveness. There is also evidence that the continuous further development of application systems is becoming a common strategy. However, coupling prototyping with traditional life cycle plans and developing horizontal prototypes can cause various problems (see p.163).
- In an evolutionary development strategy, the different forms of prototyping are used as the situation demands. If we are dealing with the new development of an application system, a "demonstration prototype" is a good help to begin with. Then, a series of prototypes are developed iteratively until a prototype attains the quality of a pilot system ready for testing at individual workplaces. The transition from the pilot system to the application system is often a fluid one. The hardware and software used today in prototyping seldom necessitate complete reimplementation of an application system based on a sound pilot system (see p.166).
- In certain application areas like office work or engineering, the development of prototypes by the users may be a key concept offering advantages over the approaches previously discussed. In the development process, prototypes become the common work object of two groups of developers belonging to the

world of the application and the world of the computer, respectively. There are, however, clear limits to programming by users: there is little sense in trying to develop in this way complex or wide-range applications. Despite these reservations, the importance of combining the efforts of competent users, and computer specialists, expert knowledge for developing good application programs should not be underestimated (see p.168).

- Documentation remains the weak point of software development. And prototyping has done nothing to alter this fact. A prototype can never be a substitute for target system documentation (see p.170).

Prototyping invariably means a departure from traditional ways of thinking and working in software development. And this has repercussions for the groups involved (see p.173):

- Prototyping almost invariably involves the increased use of tools. This means, for the developers, a break with the accustomed technical environment.
- Prototyping involves experimenting with programs and getting the users to evaluate them. For the developers, this means increased discussions with the users and the need to revise their own work results in the light of the users' criticism.
- This revision of prototypes in the light of user criticism seldom results in detailed written specifications. This does away with many of the usual documents produced in the course of a traditional life cycle plan, which are nevertheless indispensable.
- Prototyping brings about a fundamental change in the role of the users in the software development process. Whatever form prototyping may take in the specific development situation, one thing is clear: prototyping and evolutionary system development call for a high degree of user participation. But there are many users who consider themselves too busy to deal with the problems of software development.
- User participation presupposes computer-related skills, that must first be acquired by suitable training measures and the willingness on the part of the users to obtain the required know-how. We see the need to provide users with the necessary skills for working with computers as well as the ability to talk about this work.
- The use of prototyping must also be accepted at management level and supported by suitable strategic measures. This applies to both user and DP management. After taking the basic decision to use prototyping, the DP management has to work out the changes required in the organizational and technical infrastructure. Prototyping projects involving external partners call for new forms of contractual arrangements. Finally, personnel management in the DP and user departments is also affected.
- Evolutionary system development is primarily a learning process for users and developers. Just as users must learn to handle the computer in their everyday work, so must developers acquire growing insight into the tasks and problems associated with the different application areas. This must be supported by management and secured by suitable forms of organization.

- Planning and control of the development of an information system infrastructure must be seen from a new perspective. Success can only be measured in terms of the usability of an application system and its acceptance by the users. This means that both user and DP management must join in the discussion on application systems and prototypes as well as in their evaluation.

The communicative, organizational and technical problems encountered during system development can only be solved in a practical, experimental manner. Prototyping within the context of evolutionary system development is a practical step towards ecological thinking in software development and computer science.

# References


[AlfoDavis80] M.W. Alford, C.G. Davis: *Experience with the Software Development System.* In: H. Hünke (ed.), Software Engineering Environments. North-Holland, Amsterdam, New York, 1980.

[BaeBudKuhlSylZue88] A. Bäcker, R. Budde, K. Kuhlenkamp, K.-H. Sylla, H. Züllighoven: *ProLab – A Prolog Programming Environment – User's Manual.* GMD-F2G2, St. Augustin, 1988.

[BaecBuxt87] R.M. Baecker, W.A.S. Buxton: *Readings in Human-Computer Interaction: A Multidisciplinary Approach.* Morgan Kaufmann Publishers, Los Altos, CA, 1987.

[Bahr83] Hans-Dieter Bahr: *Über den Umgang mit Maschinen.* Konkursbuchverlag, Tübingen, 1983.

[Bailey85] R. Bailey: *A HOPE Tutorial.* Byte, pp. 235-258, August 1985.

[BalGolWil82] R.M. Balzer, N.M. Goldman, D.S. Wile: *Operational Specification as the Basis for Rapid Prototyping.* ACM SEN Special Issue, Vol. 7, No. 5, pp. 3-16, December 1982.

[BalHopOppPesRohStr88] H. Balzert, H. U. Hoppe, R. Oppermann, H. Peschke, G. Rohr, N. Streitz (eds.): *Einführung in die Softwareergonomie.* W. de Gruyter, Berlin, New York, 1988.

[Balzer83] R. Balzer: *Evolution as a New Basis for Reusability.* In: Workshop on Reusability in Programming, pp. 80-82, September 1983.

[Balzert89] H. Balzert (ed.): *CASE : Systeme und Werkzeuge.* B. I. Wissenschaftsverlag, Mannheim, Wien, Zürich, 1989.

[Bauer84] M. Bauer: *Sprachen der 4. Generation.* Technical Report, GES, Allensbach, 1984.

[Bauer87a] M. Bauer: *Erfahrungen mit Sprachen der 4. Generation.* Online, Vol. 3, pp. 38-48, 1987.

[Bauer87b] M. Bauer: *Endbenutzer-Alltag schon individuell ?* Online, Vol. 5, pp. 45-47, 1987.

[Bauer87c] M. Bauer: *Einsatzspektrum von Endbenutzersystemen.* Online, Vol. 5, pp. 36-38, 1987.

[Bauer90] M. Bauer: *Sprachen der 4. Generation : Standortbestimmung.* Computer Magazin, Vol. 19, No. 1/2, pp. 52-56, 1990.

[Benington83] H.D. Benington: *Production of Large Computer Programs.* Annals of the History of Computing, Vol. 5, No. 4, pp. 350-361, 1983.

[BerWin85] D.M. Berry, J.M. Wing: *Specifying and Prototyping: Some Thoughts on Why They are Successful.* In: H. Ehrig, Ch. Floyd, M. Nivat, J. Thatcher (eds.), Formal Methods and Software Development, Vol.2, Lecture Notes in Computer Science 186, pp. 117-128. Springer-Verlag, Berlin, Heidelberg, New York, Tokyo, 1985.

[BiDaMyNy79] G.M. Birtwistle, O.-J. Dahl, B. Myhrhaug, K. Nygaard: *Simula Begin.* Van Nostrand Reinhold, New York, 1979.

[BjerEhnKyng87] G. Bjerknes, P. Ehn, M. Kyng (eds.): *Computers and Democracy – A Scandinavian Challenge.* Avebury, Aldershot, U.K., 1987.

[Bleimann89] Bleimann-Gather: *Vom Handwerk zur Fabrik.* Deckblatt, Vol. 2, pp. 62-66, February 1989.

[Blu87] B.I. Blum: *GAO Report FGMSD-80-4 Revisited.* ACM SEN, Vol. 12, No. 1, January 1987.

[Boar84] B.H. Boar: *Application Prototyping.* John Wiley & Sons, New York, Chichester, Brisbane, 1984.

[Boedker85] Susanne Boedker: *Utopia and the Design of User Interfaces.* In: Proceedings of the Aarhus Conference on Development and Use of Computer Based Systems and Tools, Aarhus University, Aarhus, August 1985.

[BoEhLyKaSu87] S. Boedker, P. Ehn, M. Kyng, J. Kammersgaard, Y. Sundblad: *A Utopian Experience.* In: G. Bjerknes, P. Ehn, M. Kyng (eds.), Computers and Democracy, pp. 251-278. Avebury, Aldershot, U.K., 1987.

[Boehm76] Barry W. Boehm: *Software engineering.* IEEE Transactions on Computers, Vol. C25, No. 12, pp. 1226-1241, 1976.

[Boehm79] Barry W. Boehm: *Guidelines for verifying and validating software requirements and design specifications.* In: P.A. Samet (ed.), EURO IFIP 79, pp. 711-719. North-Holland, Amsterdam, New York, 1979.

[Boehm88] Barry W. Boehm: *A Spiral Model of Software Development and Enhancement.* Computer, pp. 61-72, May 1988.

[Born86] Gary Born: *Controlling Software Quality.* Software Engineering Journal, January 1986.

[Bradford79] E.G. Bradford: *An Augmented Version of Make.* Bell Telephone Laboratories, 1979.

[Brooks87] Frederick P. Brooks: *No Silver Bullet.* Computer, pp. 10-19, April 1987.

[Brown85] P. Brown: *Managing Software Development.* Datamation, pp. 133-136, April 1985.

[BudKuhlMatZue84] R. Budde, K. Kuhlenkamp, L. Mathiassen, H. Züllighoven (eds.): *Approaches to Prototyping.* Springer-Verlag, Berlin, Heidelberg, New York, Tokyo, 1984.

[BudKuhlSylZue87] R. Budde, K.-H. Sylla, K. Kuhlenkamp, H. Züllighoven: *Programmentwicklung mit Smalltalk.* In: HJ. Hoffmann (ed.), Smalltalk verstehen und anwenden. Hanser-Verlag, München, 1987.

[BudKuhlSylZue88] R. Budde, K. Kuhlenkamp, K.-H. Sylla, H. Züllighoven: *Eine Übersicht über die Prolog-Programmierumgebung ProLab.* Jahresbericht 1987, GMD, St. Augustin, 1988.

[BudZue82] R. Budde, H. Züllighoven: *Some Considerations about Modeling Information Systems and an Interpretation of the PSC Model.* In: G. Goldkuhl, C.O. Kall (eds.), Report of the Fifth Scandinavian Research Seminar on Systemeering, Chalmers

University of Technology and University of Göteborg, Department of Information Processing, Göteborg, 1982.

[BudZue83a] R. Budde, H. Züllighoven: *An Investigation into System Modeling and Software Construction.* In: M.I. Nurminen, H.T. Gaupholm (eds.), Report of the Sixth Scandinavian Research Seminar on Systemeering. Institute for Information Science, University of Bergen, Bergen, 1983.

[BudZue83b] R. Budde, H. Züllighoven: *Socio-technical Problems of System Design Methods.* In: U. Briefs, C. Ciborra, L. Schneider (eds.), Systems Design for, with, and by the Users, IFIP Wg 9.1, North-Holland, Amsterdam, New York, Oxford, 1983.

[BudZue90] R. Budde, H. Züllighoven: *Software-Werkzeuge in einer Programmierwerkstatt.* Berichte der Gesellschaft für Mathematik und Datenverarbeitung; Nr. 182. Oldenbourg, München, Wien, 1990.

[BuKuSyZu89] R. Budde, K.-H. Sylla, K. Kuhlenkamp, H. Züllighoven: *Der Entwurf objektorientierter Systeme.* In: R. Budde, K.-H. Sylla (eds.), Objektorientierte Systementwicklung. Handbuch der Modernen Datenverarbeitung, Heft 145, Forkel-Verlag, Januar 1989.

[BulShaKor87] H. J. Bullinger, B. Shakel, K. Kornwachs (eds.): *Human-Computer Interaction – Interact '87.* North-Holland, Amsterdam, New York, 1987. Proceedings of the 2nd IFIP Conference on Human-Computer Interaction, Stuttgart, 1987.

[Canning81] B.C. McNurlin: *Developing Systems by Prototyping.* EDP Analyzer, Vol. 19, No. 9, September 1981.

[Canning84a] R.G. Canning: *Coping with End User Computing.* EDP Analyzer, Vol. 22, No. 2, February 1984.

[Canning84b] R.G. Canning: *Attacking the Backlog Problem.* EDP Analyzer, Vol. 22, No. 12, December 1984.

[Canning84c] R.G. Canning: *Tools to Rejuvenate Your Old System.* EDP Analyzer, Vol. 22, No. 4, April 1984.

[Canning85] R.G. Canning: *Speeding Up Application Development.* EDP Analyzer, Vol. 23, No. 4, April 1985.

[CaWe85] L. Cardelli, P. Wegner: *On Understanding Types, Data Abstraction and Polymorphism.* Computing Surveys, Vol. 17, No. 4, 1985.

[Charette86] Robert N. Charette: *Software Engineering Environments.* Intertext Publications, McGraw-Hill, New York, 1986.

[ClocMell84] W.F. Clocksin, C.S. Mellish: *Programming in Prolog.* Springer-Verlag, Berlin, Heidelberg, New York, Tokyo, second edition, 1984.

[Codd70] E. F. Codd: *A Relational Model of large shared Data Banks.* Communications of the ACM, Vol. 13, No. 6, pp. 377-387, June 1970.

[Codd71] E. F. Codd: *Normalized Data Base Structure : A brief Tutorial.* In: E. F. Codd, A. L. Dean (eds.), ACM SIG-FIDET Workshop on Data Desription, Access, and Control, San Diego, CA, USA, 1971.

[Colmerauer87] A. Colmerauer: *Opening the Prolog III Universe.* Byte, Vol. 12, No. 8, pp. 177-182, 1987.

[Conklin87] Jeff Conklin: *Hypertext: An Introduction and Survey.* Computer, pp. 17-41, September 1987.

[Cprolog] CAAD Studio, Department of Architecture, University of Edinburgh, Edinburgh, *C-Prolog User's Manual.*

[Darlington78] J. Darlington: *A Synthesis of Several Sorting Algorithms.* Acta Informatica, Vol. 11, No. 1, pp. 1-30, December 1978.

[Date77] C. J. Date: *An Introduction to Database Systems.* Addison-Wesley, Reading, MA, 1977.

[DECsystem-10-Prolog] Department of Artificial Intelligence: *DECsystem-10 Prolog User's Manual*, Department of Artificial Intelligence, University of Edinburgh, Edinburgh.

[Denert87] E. Denert: *Objekt-orientierte Kreativität statt Software-Bürokratie.* Computer Magazin, Vol. 9, 1987.

[DeSchoSchw82] R.B.K. Dewar, E. Schonberg, J.T. Schwartz (eds.): *High-Level Programming – An Introduction to the Programming Language SETL.* Courant Institute of Mathematical Sciences, New York, July 1982.

[DiaGilCocSha90] D. Diaper, D. Gilmore, G. Cockton, B. Shakel (eds.): *Human-Computer Interaction – Interact '90.* North-Holland, Amsterdam, New York, 1990. Proceedings of the IFIP TC 13 Third International Conference on Human-Computer Interaction, Cambridge, U.K., 1990.

[Dijkstra72] E.W. Dijkstra: *Notes on Structured Programming.* In: O.-J. Dahl, E.W. Dijkstra, C.A.R. Hoare (eds.), Structured Programming. Academic Press, London, New York, 1972.

[DodRamAshPar82] W.P. Dodd, P. Ramsey, T.H. Ashford, D.G. Parkyn: *A Prototyping Language for Text Processing Applications.* ACM SEN Special Issue, Vol. 7, No. 5, pp. 50-53, December 1982.

[Dreesbach89] W. Dreesbach: *Die Flucht des Königs.* Deckblatt, Vol. 2, pp. 71-76, February 1989.

[Duncan82] A.G. Duncan: *Prototyping in Ada: A Case Study.* ACM SEN Special Issue, Vol. 7, No. 5, pp. 54-60, December 1982.

[Ehn88] Pelle Ehn: *Work-Oriented Design of Computer Artifacts.* Arbetslivscentrum, Stockholm, 1988.

[Eisen85] M. Eisenstaedt: *Retrospectice Zooming.* In: International Joint Conference on Artificial Intelligence, 1985.

[ElmNava89] R. Elmasri, S. B. Navathe: *Fundamentals of Database Systems.* The Benjamin Cummings, Redwood City, CA, 1989.

[Feather85] M.S. Feather: *A Survey and Classification of some Program Transformation Approaches and Techniques.* USC/Information Sciences Institute, Marina del Rey, CA, 1985.

[Feldman79] S.I. Feldman: *Make – A Program for Maintaining Computer Programs.* Software – Practice and Experience, Vol. 9, No. 4, pp. 225-256, 1979.

[Floyd81] Chr. Floyd: *A Process-Oriented Approach to Software Development.* In: Proceedings of the 6th ACM European Regional Conference on Systems Architecture, pp. 285-294. ACM, 1981.

[Floyd84] Chr. Floyd: *A Systematic Look at Prototyping.* In: R. Budde, K. Kuhlenkamp, L. Mathiassen, H. Züllighoven (eds.),

Approaches to Prototyping, Springer-Verlag, Berlin, Heidelberg, New York, Tokyo, 1984.

[Floyd87] Chr. Floyd: *Outline of a Paradigm Change in Software Engineering.* In: G. Bjerknes, et al. (eds.), Computers and Democracy – A Scandinavian Challenge, Avebury, Aldershot, U.K., 1987

[Floyd89] Chr. Floyd: *Softwareentwicklung als Realitätskonstruktion.* In: W.-M. Lippe (ed.), Proceedings der Fachtagung Software-Entwicklung, Marburg, Juni 1989, pp. 1-20, Springer-Verlag, Berlin, Heidelberg, New York, Tokyo, 1989.

[FloyReisSchm89] Chr. Floyd, F.-M. Reisin, G. Schmidt: *STEPS to Software Development with Users.* In: C. Ghezzi, J.A. McDermid (eds.), ESEC '89, pp. 48-64, Springer-Verlag, Berlin, Heidelberg, New York, Tokyo, 1989.

[FriCor85] A. Friedman, D. Cornford: *Strategies for Meeting User Demands: An International Perspective.* In: Precedings of the Working Conference on Development and Use of Computer-Based Systems and Tools, Aarhus University, Aarhus, Denmark, August 1985.

[FriQuiWer86] K. Friedrichs, G. Quiel, G. Werner: *Sprachen der 4. Generation für wen, für was?* Verlagsgesellschaft R. Müller, Köln, 1986.

[Gilb85] T. Gilb: *Evolutionary Design versus the Waterfall Model.* ACM SEN, Vol. 10, No. 3, pp. 49-61, July 1985.

[GiLiRoSaSoWi82] H. Gill, R. Lindvall, O. Rosin, E. Sandewall, H. Sörensen, O. Wigertz: *Experience from Computer Supported Prototyping for Information Flow in Hospitals.* ACM SEN Special Issue, Vol. 7, No. 5, pp. 67-70, December 1982.

[GOA79] General Accounting Office: *Contracting for Computer Software Development,* General Accounting Office Report FGMSD-80-4, September 1979.

[GogThaWa76] J.A. Goguen, J.W. Thatcher, E.G. Wagner: *An Initial Algebra Approach to the Specification, Correctness and Implementation of Abstract Data Types.* In: R. Yeh (ed.), Current Trends in Programming Methodology, IV, pp. 80-144. Prentice Hall, Englewood Cliffs, NJ, 1978.

[Goldberg84] A. Goldberg: *Smalltalk-80: The Interactive Programming Environment.* Addison-Wesley, Reading, MA, 1984.

[GoldRob83] A. Goldberg, D. Robson: *Smalltalk-80: The Language and Its Implementation.* Addison-Wesley, Reading, MA, 1983.

[Gomaa83] H. Gomaa: *The Impact of Rapid Prototyping on Specifying User Requirements.* ACM SEN, Vol. 8, No. 2, pp. 17-28, April 1983.

[GomSco81] H. Gomaa, D.B.H. Scott: *Prototyping as a Tool in the Specification of User Requirements.* In: Proceedings of the 5th International Conference on Software Engineering, IEEE, San Diego, CA, March 1981.

[Gordon79] M.J.C. Gordon: *The Denotational Description of Programming Languages.* Springer-Verlag, New York, 1979.

[GrycKaut90] G. Gryczan, K. Kautz: *A Comparative Study of Prototyping Tools.* In: Proceedings of the 1990 IEEE International Conference on Computer Systems and Software Engineering, pp. 494-501, IEEE, Tel Aviv, Israel, May 1990.

[HekmatInce86] S. Hekmatpour, D.C. Ince: *Rapid Software Prototyping.* Vol. 3 of Oxford Surveys in Information Technology, pp. 37-76. Oxford University Press, Oxford, 1986.

[HenIng82] J.C. Henderson, R.S. Ingraham: *Prototyping for DSS: A Critical Appraisal.* In: M.J. Ginzberg, W. Reitman, E.A. Stohr (eds.), Decision Support Systems. North-Holland, Amsterdam, New York, 1982.

[Hoare72] C.A.R. Hoare: *Notes on Data Structuring.* In: O.-J. Dahl, E.W. Dijkstra, C.A.R. Hoare (eds.), Structured Programming. Academic Press, London, New York, 1972.

[Hommel80] G. Hommel: *Vergleich verschiedener Spezifikationsverfahren am Beispiel einer Paketverteilungsanlage (Teil 1 und 2).* KfK-PDV 186, Kernforschungszentrum Karlsruhe GmbH, Karlsruhe, August 1980.

[HooHsi82] J.W. Hooper, P. Hsia: *Scenario-Based Prototyping for Requirements Identification.* ACM SEN Special Issue, Vol. 7, No. 5, pp. 88-93, December 1982.

[HorschEtAl85] A. Horsch, B. Möller, H. Partsch, O. Paukner, P. Pepper: *The Munich Project CIP.* Technical Report, Technische Universität München, München, June 1985.

[HouWal87] R.C. Houghten, D.R. Wallace: *Characteristics and Functions of Software Engineering Environments: An Overview.* ACM SEN, Vol. 12, No. 1, January 1987.

[Huenke80] H. Hünke: *Software Engineering Environments.* North-Holland, Amsterdam, New York, 1980.

[IBM71] IBM: *Information Management System IMS/360, Application Description Manual, GH-20-07651.* IBM Corporation, White Plains, NY, 1971.

[IBM78] IBM: *IMS/VS General Information, GH-20-1260.* IBM Corporation, White Plains, NY, 1978.

[IBM81] IBM: *SQL/Data System, Concepts and Facilities.* Technical Report, IBM Corporation, GH 24-5013, January 1981.

[JanSmi85] M.A. Janson, L.D. Smith: *Prototyping for Systems Development: A Critical Appraisal.* MIS Quarterly, Vol. 9, No. 4, pp. 305-316, December 1985.

[JensToni79] R.W.Jensen, C.C. Tonies: *Software Engineering.* Prentice Hall, Englewood Cliffs, NJ, 1979.

[KaHuZi82] U. Kastens, B. Hutt, E. Zimmermann: *GAG - A Practical Compiler Generator.* Springer-Verlag, LNCS-141, Berlin, Heidelberg, New York, Tokyo, 1982.

[KapJou87] S. Kaplan, J.-P. Jouannaud: *Conditional Term Rewriting Systems.* Springer-Verlag, LNCS-308, Berlin, Heidelberg, New York, Tokyo, 1987.

[Kaptelna89] C. Kaptelna: *Entwickeln nach Plan.* Deckblatt, Vol. 2, pp. 79-82, February 1989.

[Kay77] A.C. Kay: *Microelectronics and the Personal Computer.* Scientific American, Vol. 9, 1977.

[Kerola79] P. Kerola: *On the Extension of the PSC Systemeering Model.* In: T. Jaervi, M. Nurminen (eds.), Report of the Scandinavian Research Seminar on Systemeering Models, pp. 50-54, Finnish Data Processing Association, Helsinki, 1979.

[Kerola80] P. Kerola: *On Infological Reserach into the Systemeering Process.* In: Lucas, Land, Lincoln, Supper (eds.), The Information Systems Environment. IFIP, North-Holland, Amsterdam, New York, 1980.

[KerSchaff84] U. Kersten, W. Schaffitzel: *Probleme der Einführung von Datenverarbeitung im industriellen Bereich.* CAE Journal, Vol. 4/5, 1984.

[KieLicSchZue91] A. Kieback, H. Lichter, M. Schneider-Hufschmidt, H. Züllighoven: *Prototyping in industriellen Projekten.* GMD-Studien 184, GMD, St. Augustin, 1991.

[KiKoSiTo79] R. Kimm, W. Koch, W. Simonsmeier, F. Tontsch: *Einführung in Software Engineering.* Walter de Gruyter, Berlin, New York, 1979.

[Kim90] Won Kim: *Object-Oriented Databases: Definition and Research Directions.* IEEE Transactions on Knowledge and Data Engineering, Vol. 2, No. 3, pp. 327-341, September 1990.

[KimLoc89] Won Kim, F.H. Lochovsky (eds.): *Object-Oriented Concepts, Databases, and Applications.* Addison-Wesley, Reading, MA, 1989.

[KnoDis87] G. Knolmayer, G. Disterer: *4GL Vergleich an einem Beispiel aus dem Berichtswesen.* Computer Magazin, Vol. 16, No. 7/8, pp. 41-47, 1987.

[Knuth84] D.E. Knuth: *Literate Programming.* The Computer Journal, Vol. 27, No. 2, pp. 97-111, 1984.

[KraPop88] G.E. Krasner, S.T. Pope: *A Cookbook for Using the Model-View-Controller User Interface Paradigm in Smalltalk80.* Journal of Object-Oriented Programming, Vol. 1, No. 3, pp. 26-48, 1988.

[Kubicek80] H. Kubicek: *Interessenberücksichtigung beim Technikeinsatz im Büro- und Verwaltungsbereich. Grundgedanken und neuere skandinavische Entwicklungen.* Oldenbourg, München, Wien, 1980.

[Kuvaja88] P. Kuvaja: *An experimental Analysis of the Selection and Producitivity of Application Generators.* Research Papers Series A 10. University of Oulu, Oulu, Finland, 1989.

[Lehman81] M.M. Lehman: *The Environment of Program Development and Maintenance.* In: Proceedings of the 6th ACM European Regional Conference on Systems Architecture, pp. 273-284. ACM, 1981.

[Lehman90] M.M. Lehman: *Uncertainty in Computer Application is Certain.* In: Proceedings of the 1990 IEEE International Conference on Computer Systems and Software Engineering, IEEE, Tel Aviv, Israel, May 1990.

[LisZi74] B. Liskov, S.N. Zilles: *Programming with Abstract Data Types.* SIGPLAN Notices, Vol. 9, No. 4, pp. 50-59, 1974.

[Lobell83] P. F. Lobell: *Application Program Generators.* NCC Publications, U.K., 1983.

[LocSchm87] P. C. Lockemann, J. W. Schmidt: *Datenbank-Handbuch.* Springer Verlag, Berlin, Heidelberg, New York, Tokyo, 1987.

[Lunde82] Mats Lundeberg: *The ISAC Approach to Specification of Information Systems and its Application to the Organization of an IFIP Working Conference.* In: T.W. Olle, H.G. Sol, A.A. Verrijn-Stuart (eds.), Information Systems Design Methodologies: A Comparative Review, pp. 173-234, IFIP TC 8, North-Holland, Amsterdam, New York, 1982.

[Martin85] J. Martin: *Fourth-Generation Languages, Volume I, Principles.* Prentice-Hall, Englewood Cliffs, NJ, 1985.

[Martin86] J. Martin: *Fourth-Generation Languages, Volume II, Representative 4GLs.* Prentice Hall, Englewood Cliffs, NJ, 1986.

[MatVar87] H. Maturana, F. Varela: *The Tree of Knowledge.* New Science Library, Boston, 1987.

[MayBeLo84] H.C. Mayr, M. Bever, P.C. Lockemann: *Prototyping Interactive Application Systems.* In: R. Budde, K. Kuhlenkamp, L. Mathiassen, H. Züllighoven (eds.), Approaches to Prototyping, Springer-Verlag, Berlin, Heidelberg, New York, Tokyo, 1984.

[McCarthyEtAl62] J. McCarthy, P.W. Abrahams, D.J. Edwards, T.P. Hart, M.I. Levin: *Lisp 1.5 Programmer's Manual.* The MIT Press, Cambridge, MA, 1962.

[Meyer88] B. Meyer: *Object-Oriented Software Construction.* Prentice Hall, Englewood Cliffs, NJ, 1988.

[Mills71] Harlen Mills: *Top Down Programming in Large Systems.* In: Randall Rustin (ed.), Debugging Techniques in Large Systems, pp. 41-55. Prentice Hall, Englewood Cliffs, NJ, 1971.

[Milner84] R. Milner: *A Proposal for Standard ML.* In: Proceedings of the 1984 ACM Symposium on Lisp and Functional Programming, Austin, TX, 1984.

[Miranda] D. Turner: *Miranda: A Non-Strict Functional Language With Polymorphic Types.* Vol. LNCS 201. Springer-Verlag, Berlin, Heidelberg, New York, Tokyo, 1985.

[Mumford77] Lewis Mumford: *Mythos der Maschine.* Fischer Taschenbuch Verlag, Frankfurt/M., 1977. Originalausgabe: 1964/66.

[MUProlog84] Department of Computer Science: *MU-Prolog Reference Manual.* The University of Melbourne, Melbourne, September 1984.

[Myers89] B. A. Myers: *User-Interface Tools: Introduction and Survery.* IEEE Software, pp. 15-23, January 1989.

[Neumaier86] Herbert Neumaier: *Prototyping, Erfahrungen und Nutzen.* Beiträge des Fachgruppengesprächs der GI-Fachgruppe 4.3.1, Stuttgart, 1986.

[NorDra86] D. A. Norman, S. W. Draper (eds.): *User Centered System Design.* Lawrence Erlbaum Associates, Hillsdale, NJ, 1986.

[Olle78] T. W. Olle: *The Codasyl Approach to Data Base Management.* Wiley and Sons, New York, Chicester, Brisbane, Toronto, Singapore, 1978.

[Paige83] R. Paige: *Transformational Programming: Applications to Algorithms and Systems.* In: Proceedings of the 10th ACM POPL Symposium, pp. 73-86, Austin, TX, 1983.

[PapTho85] T. Chr. Pape, K. Thorensen: *Development of Common Systems by Prototyping.* In: Precedings of the Working Conference on Development and Use of Computer-Based Systems and Tools, Aarhus University, Aarhus, Denmark, August 1985.

[PapTho87] T. Chr. Pape, K. Thorensen: *Development of Common Systems by Prototyping.* In: G. Bjerknes, P. Ehn, M. Kyng (eds.), Computers and Democracy, pp. 251-278. Avebury, Aldershot, U.K., 1987.

[Parnas72] D.L. Parnas: *A Technique for Software Module Specification with Examples.* Communications of the ACM, Vol. 15, No. 5, 1972.

[Parnas85] D.L. Parnas: *Software Aspects of Strategic Defense Systems.* Communications of the ACM, Vol. 28, No. 12, pp. 1326-1335, December 1985.

[PartStei83] H. Partsch, R. Steinbrüggen: *Program Transformation Systems.* Computing Surveys, Vol. 15(3), 1983.

[Pereira86] L.M. Pereira: *Rational Debugging in Logic Programming.* In: E. Shapiro (ed.), International Conference on Logic Programming, 1986.

[PetSiLeCa83] L. Petrone, F. Sirovich, A. Di Leva, G. Capello: *Program Development and Documentation by Step-Wise Transformation: An Interactive Tool.* In: Proceedings of the ICS 1983, Nürnberg, 1983.

[PEWorkshop86] University of Trondheim: *Programming Environment Workshop '86: International Workshop on Advanced Programming Environments.* Trondheim, 1986.

[Robinson65] J.A. Robinson: *A Machine-Oriented Logic Based on the Resolution Principle.* Journal of the ACM, Vol. 12,1, pp. 23-41, 1965.

[Rook86] Paul Rook: *Controlling Software Projects.* Software Engineering Journal, January 1986.

[Rzevski84] G. Rzevski: *Prototypes versus Pilot Systems: Strategies for Evolutionary Information System Development.* In: R. Budde, K. Kuhlenkamp, L. Mathiassen, H. Züllighoven (eds.), Approaches to Prototyping, Springer-Verlag, Berlin, Heidelberg, New York, Tokyo, pp. 356-367, 1984.

[Schmitt83] A. A. Schmitt: *Dialogsysteme.* B. I. Wissenschaftsverlag, Mannheim, Wien, Zürich, 1983.

[Schneider83] H.-J. Schneider: *Lexikon der Informatik und Datenverarbeitung.* Oldenbourg Verlag, München, Wien, 1983.

[Schoder87] Wilfried Schoder: *Die Anwendung von Expertensystemen im Software-Engineering.* In: Proceedings der KI-Konferenz '87: Methoden der Künstlichen Intelligenz im Software Engineering, pp. 11-36, 1987.

[SchStu83] G. Schlageter, W. Stucky: *Datenbanksysteme: Konzepte und Modelle.* 2. neubearb. und erw. Auflage, B. G. Teubner, Stuttgart, BRD, 1983.

[Shakel85] B. Shakel (ed.): *Human-Computer Interaction – Interact '84.* Proceedings of the 2nd IFIP Conference on Human-Computer Interaction, London, 1984. North-Holland, Amsterdam, New York, 1985.

[Shapiro82] E.Y. Shapiro: *Algorithmic Program Debugging.* MIT Press, Cambridge, MA; London, 1982.

[Simonsm88] W. Simonsmeier: *Der CASE-Markt im Aufbruch.* Computer Magazin, Vol. 7-8, 1988.

[Smith82] D.A. Smith: *Rapid Software Prototyping.* Computer Science Dept., University of California, Irvine, CA, May 1982.

[Smoliar82] S.W. Smoliar: *Approaches to Executable Specifications.* ACM SEN Special Issue, Vol. 7, No. 5, pp. 155-159, December 1982.

[SquBraZel82] S.L. Squires, M. Branstad, M. Zelkowitz: *Working Papers from the ACM SIGSOFT Rapid Prototyping Workshop.* ACM SEN Special Issue, Vol. 7, No. 5, December 1982.

[Steele84] G.L. Steele Jr.: *Common Lisp - the Language.* Digital Press, Burlington, MA, 1984.

[SteeleSuss78] G.L. Steele Jr., G.J. Sussmann: *The Revised Report on Scheme - A Dialect of Lisp.* Vol. AI Memo No. 452. Artificial Intelligence Laboratory, MIT, Cambridge, MA, January 1978.

[Strous86] B. Stroustrup: *The C++ Programming Language.* Addison-Wesley, Reading, MA, 1986.

[SwaBal78] W. Swartout, R. Balzer: *On the Inevitable Intertwining of Specification and Implementation.* Communication of the ACM, Vol. 25, No. 7, pp. 438-440, July 1978.

[SymbolicsProlog85] Symbolics Inc., *User's Guide to Symbolics Prolog.* June 1985.

[Utopia85] The UTOPIA Project: *Graffiti 7.* Technical Report, Swedish Center for Working Life, Stockholm, 1985.

[Veljkov90] Mark D. Veljkov: *Managing Multimedia.* Byte, pp. 227-232, August 1990.

[VineRennTjoa82] G. Vinek, P. F. Rennert, M. Tjoa: *Datenmodellierung: Theorie und Praxis.* Physica-Verlag, Würzburg, Wien, 1982.

[WagKnoDis87] H.-P. Wagner, G. Knolmayer, G. Disterer: *Werkzeuge zur Individuellen Datenverarbeitung.* Computer Magazin, Vol. 7/8, 1987.

[Wedekind74] H. Wedekind: *Datenbanksysteme.* B. I. Wissenschaftsverlag, Mannheim, Wien, Zürich, Vol. 1, first edition, 1983.

[Wegner87] P. Wegner: *Dimensions of Object-Based Language Design.* SIGPLAN Notices, Vol. 22, No. 12, pp. 168-182, October 1987.

[WinoFlores86] T. Winograd, F. Flores: *Understanding Computers and Cognition.* Ablex, Norwood, NJ, 1986.

[WirfsWilk89] R. Wirfs-Brock, B. Wilkerson: *Object-Oriented Design: A Responsibility-Driven Approach.* SIGPLAN Notices, Vol. 24, No. 10, 1989. Proceedings of the OOPSLA'89 Conference.

[Zave84] P. Zave: *The Operational versus the Conventional Approach to Software Development.* Communications of the ACM, Vol. 27, No. 2, pp. 104-118, February 1984.

[ZihlEng89] A. Zihlmann, R. Engel: *Mit Bildern entwickeln.* Deckblatt, Vol. 2, pp. 66-67, February 1989.

# Index


4th generation language 81
algebraic language 136
$\alpha-\beta$ test 52
application generators 82
authoring system 82

breadboard 36, 38-39, 47, 68, 166-168

CASE 102, 145-146
chief programmer team 58-59
client-supplier model 73
compilation 140
    extended 140
conceptual schema 104
    example 109
controller 76-77

data definition 108
data definition language 106
data dictionary 108
data file management systems 103
data integrity 107
data manipulation language 106
data model 104
database systems 81, 136-137
    access rights 104, 106-107
    attributes 104
    card-index paradigm 82
    characteristics 108
    complex prototype 120
    concepts 102
    data integrity 107
    database 103
    entities 104
    host language 106
    key attributes 104
    modelling concepts 105
    relation 104
    simple prototype 114
database-oriented development systems 81, 102
    and strategy 128
    and target system 126
    examples 108
    prototyping requirements 123
datalogical modelling 104
declarative language 107
demonstration prototype 167
derivation 141
developers 7-9, 14, 17, 23, 29-30, 32, 35, 38-39, 50-52, 54, 57, 59, 63-64, 68-69, 73, 82, 85, 98-99, 114, 126, 128-129, 137, 144, 146, 148, 151, 156-157, 159, 164-167, 170-171, 173-175, 178-179, 181
development process 15, 139
    documentation 170
dialog sequence 87, 90, 94, 99, 124, 128, 163, 188
    example 117

Eiffel 74, 138
evaluation 11, 30, 51-52, 67, 69, 146, 150
    activities 10, 13-14, 17, 30, 54, 70, 88, 91, 99, 124, 156, 159, 162
    feedback 12, 15, 21-22, 27, 30, 32, 54, 58, 70
    types of 13
evolutionary prototyping 39
evolutionary system development 49-51, 55-56, 59, 67-68, 70-71, 73-74, 146-147, 158, 166, 168, 175-176, 178-182
    examples 51
experimental prototyping 39, 137, 140
exploratory prototyping 38
external schema 104

form definition 91
    form-oriented editor 91-92
form editors 90
form interpreters 91
formal language 17

formal specification 133
formal specifications 29
functional component 74
functional programming 135
functionality 74

hardware trends 40, 60, 130, 167, 180
hierarchical database models 105
horizontal prototyping 39
hypermedia 82, 155, 158, 171, 177

implementation 133
infological modelling 104
information system 10
- description 28
- model 16

inheritance 72
installation 17
interaction 74
interaction type 75
interactive component 74
interactive programming 63
interface design 36, 39-41, 61, 65, 73-75, 80, 87-88, 91, 98-100, 102, 108, 112, 116, 125, 127-128, 176, 179
internal schema 104

life cycle models 24
life cycle plans 24, 26-27, 29-31, 33, 144-146
- problems 7, 28, 32
- V model 19

Lisp 83, 132, 135, 143, 149-150, 158, 168
logic programming 134
logical data independence 103
logical schema 104
- example 110

maintenance 30-31, 50, 160, 178
management 30-31, 35, 39, 178, 181
menu editor 117
menu generators 116
metaprogramming 140
milestone documents 31, 44, 58, 146, 165, 174, 181
ML 83, 135, 140
model 76-77
model-view-controller paradigm 75, 138

network-like database models 105
nonprocedural language 107

object 72
object-oriented design 72
- class 72
- inheritance 72
- objects 72

object-oriented language 137
office system 43
off–the–shelf software 52, 57
order processing system 41

pilot system 37
problem-solving 27
procedural language 107
process model 67
- evolutionary 67

program synthesis 141
programming environment 83, 132
- concept 144
- construction language 147
- construction language requirements 148
- design language 147
- document language 148
- example 152
- languages 147
- process language 147
- process language requirements 148
- project language 148
- tool language 147
- tools 153

programming in the large 125
programming in the small 125
project organization 179
Prolog 83, 132, 134, 137, 142, 149-150, 152-153, 157, 168
prototype 34
- and application system 40

and languages 151
and screen generators 91
and VHLL 132-138, 141
kinds of 35
prototype proper 36
screen maps 94
term 7
prototyping 33
and evolutionary strategies 166
and life cycle plans 161-162, 165, 189
and programming environments 144
documentation 170
examples 41
goals 38
groups involved 173
practice 160
project acquisition 162
requirements analysis 162
screen generators 87
surface-down 163
term 6

query by example 107
query by form 107
query language 137

rapid prototyping 8
rationalistic world-view 27
relational database models 105

screen design 80
example 116
screen generators 80
and target system 97
data dictionary 116
requirements 88
test 90
screen maps 87, 89
delimiters 89
field identifiers 89
follow screen 96
input 89
interpretation 94
output 89
semantic integrity 107
separation of specification and implementation 28, 132
Smalltalk 61, 75, 137-138, 142, 150, 158
software construction 7-8, 11-12, 24, 26, 29, 63, 65, 71
term 17
software development 6, 10-11, 13, 15, 33, 39, 49, 51, 55, 60, 62, 66-67, 74, 80-81, 83, 85, 138, 140, 145, 147, 149, 154, 158, 176
concepts 15, 18
process 34
software development process 51
software engineer 63
software engineering environments 144
software project 32, 50
contract 180
controlling 31, 57
management 24, 26, 58, 181
software quality 26, 62, 87, 128, 178
software reconstruction 65
software specification 17, 133, 138, 141
software trends 60
software version 68, 71
specification 132
storage definition language 106
system development 10
problems 56
system development strategy 67

technical entities 72
technical infrastructure 179
tools and prototypes 84
transactions 108
transformation approach 140
problems 142
derivation 141
extended compilation 140
metaprogramming 140
program synthesis 141

user development 85, 164, 168-169

user groups 17, 46, 54, 62-63
user requirements 61-62
users 7, 9, 14, 16-17, 24, 29-30, 35, 38-39, 51-54, 58, 61-62, 64, 67-69, 72-73, 75, 78, 81-82, 85, 93-94, 99, 124, 130, 146, 150, 162-170, 174-177, 179-182
users involvement 30

validation 14
verification 13
versioning 54
vertical prototype 112
 example 112
vertical prototyping 39
very high level language 131
 algebraic 136
 characterization for 131
 functional 135
 grammar-oriented 136
 logical 134
 main groups 134
 query language 136
 reason for 131
 selection 142
 set-oriented 136
 term 83
view 76-77

waterfall model 24-25, 49-50